Praise for
No Surrender: A World War II Memoir

"*No Surrender* is the most hard-hitting memoir of escape and evasion that I've ever read—definitely not for the fainthearted!"

—Colonel Cole C. Kingseed, *New York Times*
bestselling coauthor of *Beyond Band of Brothers*

"Readers will marvel at the heroics of this nineteen-year-old paratrooper after he floated down on D-Day into Nazi-occupied France. . . . This is a moving portrait of a humble man who was awarded a Bronze Star and named a chevalier of France's Order of the Legion of Honor, going on after the war to become a respected New Jersey politician."

—*Publishers Weekly*

"Sheeran's vivid, personal account of warfare represents an important piece of history. I highly recommend this riveting, action-packed book."

—Marcus Brotherton, author of *We Who Are Alive and Remain*,
A Company of Heroes, and *Shifty's War*

"James J. Sheeran, a resourceful Screaming Eagle, delivers his own thrilling story with powerful emotion in *No Surrender*. His escape from a Nazi POW train, fighting with the French Resistance, the sacrifices of his elite 101st Airborne at Bastogne, it all jumps from the pages in suspenseful detail."

—Forrest Bryant Johnson, author of
Phantom Warrior and *Hour of Redemption*

"Sheeran so seamlessly and descriptively weaves his story that from the first sentence, I couldn't put the book down. I devoured every detail, from his capture on D-Day to his harrowing escape, to the wild twists of fate and colorful characters he encounters as he finds his way back to I Company. Another courageous Screaming Eagle, yet he shows us the war from a completely different angle. An invaluable addition to the books by the brave men and women who fought the greatest war in history."

—Robyn Post coauthor of *Brothers in Battle, Best of Friends*

NO SURRENDER

A WORLD WAR II MEMOIR

JAMES J. SHEERAN

BERKLEY CALIBER, NEW YORK

THE BERKLEY PUBLISHING GROUP
Published by the Penguin Group
Penguin Group (USA) Inc.
375 Hudson Street, New York, New York 10014, USA
Penguin Group (Canada), 90 Eglinton Avenue East, Suite 700, Toronto, Ontario M4P 2Y3, Canada
(a division of Pearson Penguin Canada Inc.)
Penguin Books Ltd., 80 Strand, London WC2R 0RL, England
Penguin Group Ireland, 25 St. Stephen's Green, Dublin 2, Ireland (a division of Penguin Books Ltd.)
Penguin Group (Australia), 250 Camberwell Road, Camberwell, Victoria 3124, Australia
(a division of Pearson Australia Group Pty. Ltd.)
Penguin Books India Pvt. Ltd., 11 Community Centre, Panchsheel Park, New Delhi—110 017, India
Penguin Group (NZ), 67 Apollo Drive, Rosedale, Auckland 0632, New Zealand
(a division of Pearson New Zealand Ltd.)
Penguin Books (South Africa) (Pty.) Ltd., 24 Sturdee Avenue, Rosebank, Johannesburg 2196,
South Africa

Penguin Books Ltd., Registered Offices: 80 Strand, London WC2R 0RL, England

The publisher does not have any control over and does not assume any responsibility for author or third-party websites or their content.

Copyright © 2011 by James J. Sheeran, LLC
Cover image by Alfredo Barraza Jr., United States Army in Europe
Book design by Tiffany Estreicher

PRINTING HISTORY
Berkley Caliber hardcover edition / February 2011
Berkley Caliber trade paperback edition / February 2012

Berkley Caliber trade paperback ISBN: 978-0-425-24538-5

The Library of Congress has catalogued the Berkley Caliber hardcover edition as follows:

Sheeran, James.
    No surrender : a World War II memoir / James Sheeran. — 1st ed.
        p. cm.
    Includes index.
    ISBN 978-0-425-23958-2
    1. Sheeran, James. 2. World War, 1939–1945—Personal narratives, American. 3. World War,
1939–1945—Underground movements—France. 4. World War, 1939–1945—Campaigns—France.
5. United States. Army—Parachute troops—Biography. 6. Prisoners of war—Germany—Biography.
7. Prisoners of war—United States—Biography. 8. World War, 1939–1945—Prisoners and prisons,
German. 9. Escapes—France—History—20th century. I. Title.
    D802.F8S479 2011
    940.54'1273092—dc22
    [B]
    2010027881

PRINTED IN THE UNITED STATES OF AMERICA

10 9 8 7 6 5 4 3 2 1

Penguin is committed to publishing works of quality and integrity.
In that spirit, we are proud to offer this book to our readers;
however, the story, the experiences, and the words are the author's alone.

Preface

When I met Jim Sheeran in the early '80s, he recounted his incredible wartime experiences and told me that he had always wanted to write his wartime memoir.

Jim was dyslexic and as a result he was extremely observant and possessed a keen memory for details of his surroundings. From the moment he jumped out of the C-47 over Sainte-Mère Église, Normandy, France, on D-Day minus 8 (hours), he remembered almost every scene and every event that happened during the ensuing months of his unique war story as told in this memoir. Based on his memories, and with efforts to get others' perspectives through a number of interviews with his buddies from his outfit, particularly with Burnie Rainwater, who took the journey behind the lines with him, he had prepared various vignettes all written in long hand throughout the years. By the time I met Jim, his secretary had already begun typing up his drafts and also begun transcribing his various interviews.

After the war his French-born mother had corresponded with a number of her countrymen who hid him and helped him during the war. Jim had saved all those letters and postcards, which, some forty-nine years later, provided us the basis to begin our reconnection with some 80 percent of those who hid him.

On the fiftieth anniversary of D-Day, we took Burnie back to France with us and met with more than one hundred members of the Maquis who had fought alongside Jim and Burnie in the Argonne Forest during the war. We gathered at their campsite in the forest—*La Fontaine de Ferdinand*—and had a wonderful picnic in the forest. They presented Jimmy (all the French comrades called him Jimmy) with an old aluminum lunch box. Jimmy knew right away that it was his lunch box from the days he had spent in the forest, because it bore the letters *JJS USA*, which he remembered carving on its back—only the box had been pitch-black back then from being used every day over the campfire.

During the next twelve years, we returned every year to verify the facts told in this book with those who had shared parts of Jimmy's adventures.

Finally, Jim spent almost five full years from 1998 to 2003 working on finalizing his book. His daughter Josette Sheeran (Shiner), then a journalist and now the executive director of the World Food Program, had published an article about her father's wartime experience in the *Washington Times* edition commemorating the fiftieth anniversary of D-Day, and subsequently she worked on the book with him whenever she could. He also spent more than a year working with Chris Slevin, a young writer who helped Jimmy organize all the vignettes into the chapters of the book. I know Jim would want to express his special thanks to Chris for the impressive writing skills and enthusiasm that he contributed to the project. Finally, the draft book was further edited by Laurie Rosin, a professional book editor who was also intrigued by Jimmy's story and who was instrumental in getting the book to Scott Miller of Trident Media.

Today, as the book is finally getting published, I am sure Jim is smiling in Heaven. It was truly his lifetime dream and his most fervent wish to bring his incredible life experience to the world to enjoy.

Lena Chang Sheeran, Jimmy's partner in life, love and business
October 2010

CHAPTER 1

I didn't know exactly when zero hour was, but I knew it was getting close. Soon enough we would be strapping on our parachutes, guns, and gear.

General Eisenhower showed up unannounced. Thousands of paratroopers stood around the encampment, more than I had ever seen at once. The general spoke from a microphone, but he didn't need it. Every man remained silent and hung on his words.

General Eisenhower's talk made me feel determined to do the job. I'm pretty sure it did the same for almost everyone there. He mentioned religion, and all the troops seemed to get it. Guys found the right chaplain and attended services that afternoon. Those who had no religion, or thought they had none, decided not to chance it and attended any service they could find. Some went to a couple of different services for extra protection.

I walked off by myself and found a place to pray. I said, "Please,

God, help me make it." Then I felt guilty. What right did I have to ask God for help? I never had prayed when the going was easy.

No way could I sleep after hearing the general, but I went back to the pup tent and tried to rest. Burnie was already there. He lay on his back, staring straight up. In the half-light I could see the whites of his eyes. The confinement bothered him. Burnie Rainwater was a full-blooded Cherokee and liked to move around and sleep under the stars.

I could have made small talk to pass the time, but he could have initiated the conversation, too. The silence spoke for itself. We both wanted to be alone with our thoughts.

The grass floor of the pup tent vibrated from the movement of trucks and men. I was anxious but not afraid. I knew just how to jump and land with my machine gun and where to have it set so I could get the field of fire I wanted.

Most paratroop outfits formed after jump school. Those men decided to be paratroopers after being drafted. My outfit all enlisted as paratroopers. We wanted to be in the 101st Airborne from the beginning, and we had been together from the start, for nearly two years.

Everyone knew his job. Everyone was good at everything, and some were more than good. No one could throw a grenade better than Engelbrecht. No one was faster at getting up a hill and signaling the situation on the other side than Calhoun. No one could slip his chute and land precisely where he wanted better than Neeper.

Everything we'd worked so hard for was about to happen.

Now I rolled onto my side and used my arm as a pillow. My gear was spread out next to me. My rifle lay before me disassembled. I didn't feel like putting it together. Instead I closed my eyes and conjured mental pictures of my home and my family. The images of my mother and father and our house were as detailed as if I were standing in New Jersey at that moment and not killing time in a military camp in southern England.

I was a nineteen-year-old machine gunner, a private first class, and hadn't seen a hell of a lot of life. Not that I didn't want to—I just hadn't found it yet. I'd been laid twice, once in Paducah, Kentucky, right after I completed my five jumps to qualify for paratrooper, and once in Chattanooga, Tennessee. I was scared to death both times. I had seen those army training films about VD, showing guys going blind, with their pecker falling off, enormous balls, and holes in their lips. Those films had me terrified and searching for symptoms for months.

I'd lived through sex. Would I survive what I knew would be one of the greatest invasions of all time?

Our outfit, the 506th Regiment, Company I, Third Battalion, First Platoon of the 101st Airborne Division, would jump eight hours before the main invasion forces hit the beaches. We and the Eighty-second Airborne were to be the first in. I could not think of the invasion on a big scale. I was too small a part of it and much too confused.

Restless, I stood up and stepped outside the tent. For the first time all day, the camp was relatively still. The balmy June air embraced me, and under other circumstances I would have enjoyed sitting in the grass under the late-day sun. My bones had just begun to thaw from the cold and damp English winter. Instead I was eager for nightfall. The darkness would change my restlessness into excitement, give me an edge, and help me concentrate. I'd need all three for the impending jump that would propel me into the great unknown.

Some trucks had moved, and a few men huddled in small groups, talking low. Many of my powerful thoughts and feelings focused on the guys in my company. They had become like family to me during our hard training. We were lucky—Sergeant Al Engelbrecht, our platoon sergeant, was probably the best noncom officer in the service.

We didn't call him Sergeant Engelbrecht. To us he was "Lud"—a plumber from generations of plumbers out of Syracuse, New York. He put himself through the same physical punishment he inflicted on us—running through ditches, slogging through mud, and climbing fences. Most of the time he finished ahead of everyone else. When a man does that, you have no choice but to follow him.

Because of Lud, I felt I had a chance to survive the war.

"Our drop zone is outside Carentan, a small farming village," Lud told us. After chow, he had ordered us to the briefing room. "Proceed south and assemble with the rest of the company and battalions. We'll move out together, fight our way west, capture the bridge across the Douve River on the road connecting Saint-Mère Église and St. Come du Mont, and hold it until the main invasion forces advance. Expect to fight for three days before we can look for some relief from the beaches."

Three days . . .

"The enemy we'll face is the German Sixth Parachute Brigade."

We had heard they were tough, a crack, combat-hardened outfit.

Lud paced in front of us, all six feet, two inches of him—a two-hundred-pound paratrooper. "The Germans will throw everything they can at us, from every tank in the immediate area. But we're not going to let them through. If they retake the bridge, they'll catch our guys on Utah Beach with nowhere to hide. That beach ain't nothing but a narrow strip of swamp and sand with cliffs to block escape."

His intense gaze drilled through us. "Now, does everyone know exactly what to do when you hit the ground?"

Everyone nodded.

"All right. The password is *flash*. The response is *lightning*. Your life may depend on your remembering those two words, so repeat them a few times to yourself."

He pulled out a metal box and handed out toy metal clickers, a little heavier than the crickets that Cracker Jacks used as favors in boxes of caramel corn. "If you hear movement nearby and don't know who it is, get your ass flat on the ground and snap your cricket one time. If a friend hears the click, he'll say 'flash,' and you'll say 'lightning.'"

"What if we don't get no response?" one of the guys asked.

A few men snickered at the soldier's stupidity.

"Hey! Keep it down!" Lud said, then turned to the soldier. "Shout 'It's the enemy!' Any more questions?"

Silence.

"I want each of you to put your rifle together blindfolded, again and again. You're going to land in darkness. Everything has to be working. And I want you to practice the password and response over and over, so nothing—nothing!—will make you forget them."

Lud snapped to attention and shouted, "Captain McKnight! Atten-shun!"

We all jumped up as a big, tough guy with movie-star looks strode into the briefing room.

"At ease." The captain stood with his hands locked behind his back.

Since we were only a few hours from the start of the invasion, I did not expect his appearance to be up to his normal standards. Even so, his tailored jumpsuit lay just right on his football player's frame. The pleats were perfect. A length of camouflage silk wrapped neatly around his neck and tucked into his jump jacket.

His boots were spit shined, and the pearl handle of his Colt .45 revolver gleamed.

Usually I thought his fashion sense was hilarious. Did the U.S. Army really need its own Beau Brummell? Tonight, though, the officer's vanity annoyed me. It meant that McKnight's orderly had wasted precious time buffing the captain's boots instead of resting or writing to his family.

McKnight gave us the standard-issue pep talk. By the time he wound down, I was ready to get going right then and there. The other guys in the room buzzed with excitement. Yeah, let's just get the job done!

When the captain finished, he threw a high-ball salute at us, did an about-face, and smartly walked out.

We broke down to our platoons for more detailed briefings. We asked questions and viewed more maps of different scales, aerial photos, terrain descriptions, and learned more about the big picture and the little picture. Then we were sent to draw our K rations. The Cracker Jack–sized boxes contained a small can of processed eggs, meat, or cheese; crackers; a couple of Hershey bars; foul-tasting lemonade mix; three packs of Lucky Strikes; three wax fuel disks for cooking; some invasion money; and an escape kit with a silk map of France and a small French-English word guide.

I wondered about my mother's home village of Domremy-La-Pucelle. My mom and pop spoke French around the house so my sisters and I could not understand what they were talking about. Now I wished I had learned more French as a kid.

The army also issued us three condoms, just like when we went on leave. I didn't know when the brass thought we might take time out to find a willing girl in the midst of D-Day. I used mine as garters to secure my jump pants around my boots.

We got clips of thirty-caliber rifle shells for our M-1s, grenades, and parachutes. Every soldier's face, from the company jokester to the quiet strongman, turned deadly serious.

Burnie's gear was similar to mine, except he had a machine gun and machine-gun ammo.

We walked in a group back toward the tents. Freddy Hoffman— we called him Huff—held up his clicker. "Has everyone noticed that when we jump, fully armed, into combat after two years of intense training, our lives may depend on a toy cricket?"

"Yeah," Burnie said. "A gizmo probably made in Japan."

On another day, it would have been funny, but now no one laughed. Nor did anyone complain. Instead we drilled, as Lud had ordered, straight through the night. We practiced putting our rifles together with our eyes closed. We worked with deliberation, fitting them into our harness.

A rifle shot ripped through the silence.

"Ya think someone shot himself to get out of the jump?" Huff asked.

"Nah," his friend Murray drawled. He was from Alabama. "Some horse's ass probably shot himself cleaning his rifle."

I wondered if anyone would crack and pull some stunt to get out of the jump. That would be better, I decided, than having the guy on my left or right flank in battle.

I glanced over at Burnie. He was sharpening the blade on his knife. Burnie had been raised in the Carolina forests. He was a good shot with his rifle, but the knife had always been his weapon of choice.

One time some zoot suiters had tried to rob us outside a casino in Paducah, Kentucky, near the Indiana border. Those guys were ready to cut us up and steal our winnings. But Burnie grabbed one guy, pinned him against a car with his own knife, and threatened to cut his balls off if any of the others moved. He meant it, and they knew it. One of them ended up driving us all, at knifepoint, to Evansville, Indiana.

Burnie had a love for America—the dirt, the trees, the wildlife— that was visceral. He saw his mission in this war as a way to defend the land he adored. He wanted to finish the job and get back to the woods.

I grasped the Joan of Arc medallion my mother had given me before I left home. The happy memories of home and family were what I most valued, what I was fighting to preserve.

In a few short hours I would be somewhere in France, fighting to free my mother's homeland from the invaders, just as my father had done one generation before me. Different war, same invaders. I grasped the medallion in my fist and held it over my eyes and prayed I would be the last man in our family to go to war. I'd do my best as a soldier to bring peace to the world, and when I got home to the States, I would try to make a difference then, too.

Outside our tent, voices were picking up again. I opened my eyes to see Burnie sheathing his knife. "We better get going, Jimmy," he said. "It's time."

As we suited up, I could see hundreds of C-47s lined up on the grass, ready to take off at the same time. Each one had colorful characters drawn on it. The C-47 was just a two-propeller airplane with a door on the side, intended for use as a transport vehicle. No armor on the belly. No armor anywhere at all. Inside, two rows of wooden benches stretched out on both sides.

I thought about what was happening and tried to track the moments. I didn't want to let even one instant pass without notice, since I didn't know if I would live out the hour.

I strapped my rifle to my left leg under the parachute harness and secured my razor-sharp trench knife—the bayonet—to my left boot. The pockets of my rifle belt held the ammo clips, and hanging from my belt were my grenades, canteen, compass, first-aid kit, and shovel. We carried over a hundred pounds of hardware.

I stashed my jump knife in the secret pocket of my jump jacket, along with my medallion—Joan of Arc, the patron saint of soldiers. Could she protect me?

"All right, men, let's go!" Lud waved us forward to a C-47 called *Ugly Duckling*. It would take us over the English Channel, and from six hundred feet over the Normandy peninsula, we would jump one by one into the darkness.

About thirty paratroopers comprised our "stick." I was number eighteen. Behind me was Lud, and next to me sat Huff. I looked at each man and wondered what he was thinking. We didn't know what we were going into, but we knew it would be awful.

Sweat ran down every soldier's face, from the captain to the lowest private. Some guys were throwing up. Over the engine's drone I could hear them hacking and heaving. Other men were praying, their hands clenched. Some just sat there quietly, staring.

Cal sat in a trance-like state. He had gotten married in the service and spoke often of great plans for the future with his beautiful wife.

Captain McKnight caught me studying him. He gave me the thumbs-up. I returned the gesture, then leaned over and checked my reserve chute. For years I had burned with the desire to be on this plane and in this fight.

I looked at Huff, a skinny guy with a big Adam's apple. When it moved around a lot, I knew he wasn't doing too well. "Ya scared, Huff?"

"Yeah, Jimmy. Scared stiff. Me and everyone else." He nodded toward the other guys.

I looked at one of my closest buddies, Johnny Simpson, the Philosopher. I had gotten to know Simpson more than most of the other guys. In the beginning he was my assistant machine gunner. He dreamt about battles and being in the middle of conflict. Battle thrilled him in ways I had not witnessed with anyone else—even our officers. He talked about seeing both sides and believing your cause is right until you triumph over the other.

Was Simpson thinking about this experience in terms of Greek mythology and grand epics? Was this to be a struggle worthy of the tales he loved to read? What was he looking for? Glory? He'd had a rough childhood. What was he fighting to get back to?

And Lud, what was going on in his mind? I looked over to see he was vomiting into his mask. Maybe his throwing up made other guys feel okay about doing the same.

Suddenly the buzzer sounded. Christ, time to stand up. One minute to go. Could I do this?

"Hook up!" McKnight shouted.

"Hook up, men!" Lud echoed.

We were all standing and grasping the man next to us. My knees had never been so weak.

"How are you doing, Neeper?" I asked.

"This will be a snap, Jim. See you on the ground."

The C-47 lurched. Flak hitting the ship sounded like rain pounding a tin roof.

"Go!" McKnight shouted. "Go! Go! Go!"

One man after another stepped out into the black sky and disappeared. Then it was my turn.

I jumped.

CHAPTER 2

Tracers from machine-gun cross fire and red and green flak burst all around me. The Germans had known we were coming. We had been sold out.

My chute banged opened, and shrapnel tore through the silk. I had to get to the ground, or I'd be shot. All I could think was "God bless me."

I looked for an opening to land, but all I saw was trees and anti-parachute spikes set up to deflate our chutes and impale us. No one had even mentioned spikes during training, and I had no idea how to deal with them. I was on my own. I felt for my medallion inside my collar and held it tight.

I wanted to drop my rope but knew I would get lost in the trees in front of me. Somehow I had to get over them. I remembered a new technique guys had started to do in training: They climbed up the chute to keep from getting caught in trees. I reached for my two front risers and climbed up them like a monkey. A tree brushed my backside, and a moment later I landed with a splash, ankle-deep in water.

I heard German soldiers shouting from behind a hedgerow only twenty feet away. I was hidden by reeds, but I feared the enemy must have seen me land. Breathing hard, I lay back in the water, assembled my rifle, put in a clip of ammunition, and set it on my chest while I reached into my pocket and pulled out a grenade. I put that on my chest, too, and then slid my hand into my boot for my trench knife. I sliced my risers and straps as silently as possible, but my breathing sounded very loud to me. I slipped out of my chute, tucked the grenade back in my pocket, and peered through the reeds at the hedgerow. What could I do? Germans surrounded me.

My orders were to go west until I reached the army's assembly point. I took out my compass and crept farther into the swamp until I came to a ditch where the water was up to my hips. The reeds concealed me as I continued westward.

I heard noise ahead of me but did not see anyone. I reached for my trench knife; my rifle would have brought the enemy on the run. The sound neared until it was only a few feet away. I brought my knife to the ready and, trembling, whispered, "Flash."

"Lightning." Freddy Hoffman emerged from the reeds.

We were both shaking with cold and fear.

"What'll we do, Huff?" I knew other guys from our outfit had to be nearby. Where were they?

"I don't know, Jim. The Germans have a tight line." He pointed toward the west.

"Then we better try to knock out some machine guns." We had six hand grenades between us.

"Okay, Jim." He added matter-of-factly, "War is hell."

When we saw a burst of machine-gun fire, we moved toward the action, to the edge of the hedgerow. We were only about fifteen feet from the gunners, so we had to make good on the job, or it would be our last.

We each lobbed a grenade and then ducked for the blast. The guns were silenced, so we crouched and ran farther down the hedge to a cluster of enemy soldiers—too many for us to take out with two more grenades. Getting them all at one time was the only way we could survive. I didn't like the idea of using up all six grenades so quickly.

Huff and I moved on toward another burst of machine-gun fire. We tossed two more grenades, then all hell broke loose. They were after us. We ran back to the ditch and hid for the rest of the night, up to our hips in cold water.

The dawn threw light on the enemy beyond the reeds and hedges. Their numbers increased as the daylight grew. Huff and I hardly moved. Our grenades had been submerged all night, and I didn't know if they would detonate. My muscles cramped from my standing so long in unimaginably cold water. We stood still for two more hours after sunrise.

I wondered where Burnie Rainwater might be. We had not landed far from each other. He had a tripod and machine gun, while my rifle was soaked and jammed with mud. Under the present conditions, I couldn't even clean it. Not even an M-1, the army's most serviceable rifle, would be useful at that point.

One thing was obvious: Huff and I couldn't stay where we were. We were failing fast. My stomach, legs, and feet were so cramped from the horrible night in the ice-cold water, I could barely move. I tried to walk, but my legs felt like two pieces of waterlogged wood. Only a few muscles in my body could function.

Slowly, slowly, we crept from the reeds and water. It was a mistake. Half the German Army seemed to converge on us.

"Quick, Huff! Tear your maps and shove your rifle into the mud! Get rid of your ammo!"

"Sie halten!" a guttural voice ordered behind me.

I had no idea what that meant. A command for our execution?

We had reached the edge of the swamp when my legs collapsed. As I pitched forward, a rifle shot sang over my head. Death seemed inevitable. I stood, expecting to meet a hail of hot pellets. The Germans held their fire and motioned us to put our hands behind our heads. I'll never know how I managed to obey—my arms felt as heavy as cement. I managed to clasp my fingers and hold on with all the strength I had left.

I felt intense guilt about surrendering. I had let my outfit down. I wanted to be in the fight with them. Could I have done something different that would have turned out better? I never stopped asking myself that question.

I stood opposite the German soldiers and was surprised that except for our uniforms, we looked the same. I had seen many newsreels and built up many strange notions about the enemy wearing monocles and sneers. Huff and I were fortunate to have been captured by the enemy's Sixth Parachute Brigade. They, too, were combat soldiers, and combat soldiers tended to understand each other a little better than other soldiers. They lived the same life we lived and knew they might pay the same price if they shot us point-blank.

The sergeant looked me right in the eyes. I sensed his understanding the physical pain we were in. "Put your hands down," he told me in English.

It felt wonderful.

"Empty your pockets."

I removed three soaked Hershey bars, which the sergeant quickly took and split with his men. He also offered me a piece, but I refused. I knew I would not be able to keep it down.

Next I took out two packs of soaked Lucky Strikes. The sergeant told me to put them back in my pocket, but I dropped them on the ground. Why add weight to an already heavy burden? The sergeant apparently noticed my chagrin, for he reached into his pocket and placed one of those horrible German cigarettes in my mouth. What should have tasted like a foul combination of corn silk and sawdust tasted to me like a rich tobacco blend.

I removed three emergency heating units. The pinkish wax Sterno disks were about the size of a silver dollar and about a quarter-inch thick. Once ignited, they would burn for five to seven minutes, long enough to heat our field rations. The Germans took off the paper wrapper and studied the disk. An oafish-looking character popped the Sterno in his mouth. He had apparently established his stupidity among his comrades. Otherwise I would have been among the honored dead of Normandy when he angrily spat out the fuel disk.

The Germans didn't even bother to examine my soaked K rations. When my captors saw no ammunition, they allowed me to put the rations back in my pocket. I was tempted to throw them away, but because I didn't know what would be in store for me, I held on to them.

I sneaked a look at Huff. His eyes were wide with fear, but the Germans' behavior toward my friend appeared very professional. The officer facing Freddy spoke clearly and handled him gently, considering the circumstances.

The sergeant took my razor-sharp trench knife from my shoe. As he examined the glistening silver blade, his expression indicated a newfound respect for the Allies. He muttered something, then ordered me to place my hands above my head again.

A lieutenant strode over, shouting a command to the sergeant.

The tone of his voice caused me to question my initial idea about the Germans' sense of decency. The lieutenant acted tough. He ordered us and three German soldiers to follow him to the edge of the swamp. At another quick command, his three soldiers vaulted over the hedgerow. They reappeared, dragging a wounded American soldier by his arms. The poor guy was groaning, and his face was covered in sweat and tears. They dumped him at the lieutenant's feet.

The soldier raised his head and looked meek, pitiful before the lieutenant. My heart sank as I recognized him from training—one of the Brown twins, from Alaska. He looked over at Huff and me, and his face brightened, then dimmed, realizing we were captives.

The lieutenant motioned him to stand. As he struggled to comply, I saw a gaping hole in his hip. He collapsed to his hands and knees and then lay facedown on the ground.

The lieutenant's eyes were obsidians, and his expression hardened as he shouted a quick order. One of his soldiers stepped back, cocked his Smizer submachine gun, aimed it at Brown, and pulled the trigger. The blast slammed into Brown and kicked him back almost two feet.

I squeezed my eyes shut and burst into tears. I couldn't help it. Witnessing Brown's murder crystallized my understanding of what we were fighting for and how real and earnest this war was. My fists balled in frustration. I wished I had thrown those last two grenades. More than anything, I wanted to get back into battle. I would do whatever I could to make sure that happened.

Brown was the first man I had seen murdered in cold blood. We all knew he was in terrible pain and wasn't going to survive. Still, I could not be cavalier with someone else's life.

The lieutenant looked at us and said something to the other soldiers. What was he saying? I didn't know a word of German. I was trying hard to be sharp, but I was so hungry and defeated, I couldn't concentrate. My imagination carried me off, and his words sounded like *Ve are going to enjoy killing those boys, too, ja?*

He motioned us to walk ahead of him. I thought each step would be my last, but we moved past German equipment and soldiers and found ourselves in a small village. Maybe the lieutenant wanted an audience to witness our execution. Three German soldiers approached and saluted the lieutenant. After a few words, this trio marched us farther into the village. The change of personnel had been routine, but I interpreted everything as being ominous.

An old French lady walked out of her farmhouse and stood by the roadside. She began to weep. She was already mourning for me as I walked past her. I visualized my own funeral, in a foreign land, with old men and women crying for me and my buddies, while my own mother and father were notified by telegram.

At the outskirts of the village, the escort led us into a small, fortified dugout. Not another American was in sight. I guessed that our location had a strategic advantage for the Germans but not for us.

A surly German officer awaited us.

"We're going to get the works," I whispered to Huff.

"The works?" the officer asked in perfect English. He looked alarmed. "What are they?"

I didn't answer.

He told us to put our arms down and to take a seat. He offered us both an American cigarette. I smoked mine to the end. I sat back and stretched, starting to feel a weight removed.

"Sit up and pay attention," he said gruffly, then bombarded us with questions.

So the cigarettes were a bribe. That epiphany made the aftertaste bitter. He wanted us to talk, but Huff and I refused. The Geneva

Convention stipulated that soldiers were required to give only their name, rank, and serial number. The 101st Airborne patch was on our shoulders—no mystery there.

After a half hour, our interrogator called in three soldiers who took us to a small field where about twenty other Americans were under guard. They all stood up and asked what had happened to us. One of the prisoners was my friend Burnie Rainwater. He looked at my soggy uniform and blue lips, then shook his head.

"Jimmy, take off your clothes and hang 'em on a tree."

I took his advice, and the result was like walking into a warm house. I felt better with each layer I removed, and as I sat down next to Burnie under the warm sun, I was almost comfortable.

"When I first saw you, I thought you and Huff were both seriously wounded," he said.

"I guess we were in really bad shape," I admitted. I looked at my clothes and watched a soft breeze lift them gently. They would be dry in time for sunset, when I would want to put them on again.

We talked among ourselves as darkness surrounded us. We all wanted to know as much as we could about the other soldiers and officers in our units.

"What did you see?"

"Did Johnny Simpson make it?" I asked, praying for the well-being of my friend.

No one had seen Johnny or heard of his fate.

"Did you see anyone else?"

"Colonel Wolverton got hung up in a tree and was shot dead before he could cut himself out of his harness."

"Whitty's static line was attached to the airplane. He was hit by shrapnel just as he jumped. He was killed as he hit the ground with an unopened chute."

I told the others about Brown.

We each recalled the jump the same way, but that was ancient history already.

We all believed we were going to win the war. It was just going to be tougher than we had thought.

CHAPTER 3

My jacket had dried in the sun, and as I shrugged it on, I felt something poke me in the chest. I froze, incredulous. My jump knife was in the secret pocket, concealed within the seam just below the collar. It was about four inches long and had a spring-loaded switchblade. If the Germans ever found it . . . I stopped that thought. I had no intention of letting that happen.

We were in extremely dangerous territory, with American shells landing near us. The enemy rounded us up and marched us to another field, putting us more directly in harm's way, so one of our own bombs could take us out. These bombs could bring about the Nazis' defeat, so I never wished that the attack would end for my own sake. We all ran for a trench and huddled in it.

At last the shelling stopped. We stayed in the trench. A German soldier came to sit down next to me. I moved to make room for him. He had intelligent-looking eyes, finely chiseled features, and small, neat ears. He carried himself like a gentleman. I glanced at his uniform. He was a sergeant.

"Ve liff true dat one," he said, and glanced up at the sky. "Maybe ve be lucky and liff true da var." He took a small, creased photograph out of his pocket and showed it to me. *"Dies ist meine Ehefrau Ute."*

A lovely young woman smiled at me from the picture—a good match for the young sergeant. "She's beautiful," I said, and meant it.

He told me they'd been married only a few months and were expecting a baby. His love for this woman underscored every word. He reminded me of Neeper, who never missed an opportunity to show off a picture of his beautiful wife. I wondered how Neeper had done on the beach and where he was at that moment.

The sergeant asked me questions about America, then shared more about his own background. He was a paratrooper who had served in Crete, Italy, and Russia. He told me how many jumps he had made. He made a moue and said, "I don't like dis assignment. Much more I would prefer somet'ing else for my country."

"I heard you paratroopers got pretty chewed up in Crete," I told him. "I wouldn't have liked it much, either."

He pointed at the patch on my shoulder. "You jump. You like?"

"Yeah, I do," I answered. "Partly because I feel it's my duty."

We talked quite a bit about the war and what was happening on both the western and eastern fronts. We reached a level of comfort where I felt I could challenge him a little. "Why are the Germans fighting?" I asked. "Why are you in this war?"

He shrugged eloquently. "I don't know. I vonder, too, alvays. Ve Germans don't dislike Americans." He paused to look at Ute's photo, then tucked it back in his pocket. "You? Vhy you fight?"

I thought the answer was obvious, but I told him anyway. "We're fighting against Hitler and the evil he's spread! Why are you fighting for him?"

His wide-set eyes registered surprise. "I am *not* fighting for Hitler. I fight for Ute! I vant to return home to *Meine Ehefrau und Baby.*" He pointed a finger at my chest. "*Und Sie?* Are you fighting for Roosevelt?"

I could not even answer him. How could this man have distanced himself so completely from Hitler's atrocities? Could he really believe he was not supporting Hitler's inhumanity? I thought about how impersonal war had to be; otherwise soldiers would go mad, some of them.

"Vhy you come here to fight, so far from vere you liff?"

"We couldn't stay home and do nothing," I explained. "If Germany beat England and Russia, then German soldiers would show up in my own backyard. America couldn't let that happen."

A commanding officer appeared, and the sergeant assumed a more formal attitude toward me, ordering me to join the other prisoners. As he walked away, I thought about how different the world would be if we could all just talk to the enemy about the simple things—our loved ones, our hopes for the future, the sort of world we wanted for our babies. The sort of world my parents had wanted for me . . .

I was the son of Lucie Munier Sheeran, who came from the French village of Domremy-La-Pucelle, and John Sheeran, a first-generation American who had grown up in New Jersey. They met when Pop was stationed in France during the first world war.

I grew up in Passaic, New Jersey. My sister Frances was a year older than I, and Jacqueline was five years younger. Melva, the baby, was ten years younger.

Now I heard all hell breaking loose at the end of the ditch where

I was lying. I craned my neck to see wounded German soldiers coming in. They seemed full of fear. Beyond them were at least twenty Americans. When I recognized Captain McKnight and Major Horowitz, I walked toward them. On the way I spotted a fellow with a slender frame and straight blond hair. Johnny Simpson—one of my best pals.

"Johnny!" I shouted, and ran to him.

He looked as happy to see me as I was to see him. We could not have been more different, but I found him intriguing, and we had always gotten along. He was an intellectual. He played chess, sometimes with himself. Usually his hand was wrapped around a book. In my whole life I had read *The Adventures of Tom Sawyer*, *A Tree Grows in Brooklyn*, and *Man Without a Country*, and only because my father forced me to do it. Johnny never cared about that. He consistently asked for my opinion and was interested to know what I would do in a certain situation.

Johnny wasn't like the other guys, either. When they got a pass in England, most would go to pubs near the base or to London to look for girls. Johnny spent his time researching the history of the region. He visited English castles and ancient churches.

"What happened to you?" I asked.

"I had the choice of becoming a prisoner or dying without taking a Nazi down with me," he said. "Simple decision."

A German soldier yelled at us to join a column he had formed, and Johnny and I marched side by side toward a road jammed with German soldiers and horse-drawn artillery heading toward the front. The Americans stayed in the center of the road, with the German guards flanking us. I lost track of Huff and Burnie, but I knew they would do okay.

The land on both sides of the road sloped down into fields pocked by enormous bomb craters. As we walked, we heard screams behind us. We had moved no more than a few yards when the horrible sound of artillery shells sent me diving for the ground. I flattened myself in the dirt and tried to protect my head from whatever came next. A frightening *crack* slammed my eardrums. A large shell hit less than twenty feet away, and the enormous explosion caused the ground to buck under me, to send me flying into the air. When I crashed down onto the road, I felt as though my body had split in half.

Suddenly all was quiet except for the muffled cries of the wounded. I did not move for a moment, then climbed carefully to my feet. Ahead, a few men lay sprawled in a ditch. I didn't know if the explosion had tossed them there or if they'd managed to position themselves before the attack.

I turned around. Two men directly behind me had lost their legs. I and a couple other guys ran over to them. One was unconscious, but the other was hollering, "Mama! Mama!"

I was shocked to hear that, but I might have done the same thing. I watched a couple of GIs take out their syrette of morphine and give the injured an injection. Nothing more could be done for them. We had to get the hell out of there in case the bombing started again.

I wanted to find Johnny. I looked around for him in the confusion and called his name. When I saw him running up to me, I was happy he was okay. But his eyes looked strange.

"I lost my hand," he said.

I thought he was joking. I looked down. His wrist was torn away except for a few shreds of skin. His hand was barely attached, and blood poured from the gaping wound.

"Jesus, Johnny!" My head was spinning as I tried to remember first-aid training. "Are you in pain?"

"Can't feel anything."

We both knew that the numbness was temporary. Before long he would be in terrific pain.

I took a syrette of morphine from my kit and, trembling, shot it into John's upper arm. I poured sulfanilamide powder on the wound to guard against infection and then applied a tourniquet. He was losing an enormous amount of blood despite my efforts to stanch it. I had to get him to a doctor, or he'd die.

We walked about a half a mile with artillery attacks all around us. The Germans moved along the side of the road, keeping to the ditches and training their rifles on us, although they seemed more concerned about their own survival than about guarding us prisoners.

With each whistle we dived into a ditch with our captors. While we waited for the explosion and then for the fallout to stop, I released Johnny's tourniquet, to make sure his arm wouldn't get gangrene from lack of circulation.

His pain had become unbearable. I knew he wouldn't have left me, and I didn't intend to leave him.

I peered up at the sky, which was stained with smoke. Before long, night would fall. Darkness would loosen the Germans' control over us, and when that happened, I'd escape with Johnny. I spotted an opening in the field where we could hide until the action went elsewhere. Until then, I had to do something to help my friend.

I ran over to a German officer. "Water?" I asked, and when he shrugged, I pointed at his canteen and pantomimed why I needed the water.

He nodded his understanding and handed over his canteen. It gave off the strong smell of liquor, maybe cognac. I battled with myself. Giving alcohol to Johnny would thin his blood—not a smart maneuver, considering. But overriding that concern was wanting to relieve his pain. I held the canteen to my friend's lips, and he gulped thirstily, then gagged.

He needed more morphine. I had to get Johnny to an aid station.

I returned the canteen to its owner. He thanked me for returning it, and I thanked him for lending it—a strange moment of mutual respect that maybe only soldiers in combat can know.

I got back to Johnny's side, and he was sobbing, begging for morphine. I opened his first-aid kit and gave him another shot. I released the tourniquet again, knowing we'd have to move out soon. The blood flowed like a fountain.

The morphine, the liquor, and the loss of blood caused Johnny to lapse into semiconsciousness. I couldn't let him pass out. I couldn't leave him.

"Come on," I urged. "We have to move out."

I helped him to his feet. He draped his good arm around my shoulder, and I half carried him across the ravaged landscape, up and down bomb craters that were, some of them, eight or ten feet deep. I was weakening. The physical burden of carrying him became almost impossible.

Finally we reached Carentan. The entire town was in flames, and the bombed-out craters were too much for Johnny. He had completely lost his sense of balance. I didn't have the strength to move him much farther.

I looked toward the head of the column. The Germans were moving us across a half dozen more large craters, to the outskirts of Carentan. I carried Johnny to a German officer and showed the man Johnny's hand. "Doctor?" I asked.

The soldier pointed to a cottage about a quarter mile away. *"Sie werden einen Doktor in das unterbringt finden."*

I needed about a half hour to carry my friend to the German aid station. I tried to keep him alive—and myself distracted from the impossibility of what I was trying to do.

"Hey, Johnny, remember when the surgeon general came from London, and we had to get ready for a 'short arms' inspection, and you had to piss? So you asked me to make up your bunk, too, while you took a leak?" I started to laugh at the memory, but tears ran down my cheeks at the same time.

"So the surgeon general told us all to strip, skin it back, and squeeze forward. If he found a discharge, he'd think you had VD. He'd send you to the hospital, then the brig. Remember, Johnny?"

Each of us had obeyed, and everyone came up clean—until the general got to Johnny. Out came the telltale droplets.

"I can still see how the general's eyes bugged out of his skull. I knew it was only piss, but I couldn't resist shouting, 'Simpson's got it! Simpson's got the clap!' Jesus, Johnny, everyone cracked up laughing, even the doctor!"

I was laughing now, but I was sobbing, too. "Your face went scarlet. You were the most embarrassed guy in the world! Shit, we've had some good times! And when your arm is taken care of and you're feeling better, we'll have more. I swear it, Johnny."

I dragged him through the cottage door. Two soldiers wearing bloodstained aprons came forward and took him from my arms. I noticed a pot stove. Were they going to cauterize Johnny's wound on hot metal? Without anesthesia? The horror must have shown on my face, for a third man pointed me toward the door. *"Sie werden jetzt verlassen müssen,"* he said, waving me out.

I stayed just outside the door. I couldn't leave till I knew what was happening to my friend. My screams joined his as the Germans chopped off Johnny's hand and then tossed it into the stove.

I felt limp, bereft. I had no friend to look after or to look after me. I leaned against the door, too sad to move.

"Sie! Kommen Sie hier!"

I looked up to see a German officer waving at me to fall in with a dozen other prisoners. He marched us to a large house not far from the aid station. I was relieved not to be carrying Johnny, but my exhaustion could not be measured.

The officer sent us, one by one, into the house. When my turn came, I was met by an officer who told me to sit down and remove my boots. As I unlaced the sturdy boots, I looked around. This large home was a German command post.

I pulled off my boots and socks, and four soldiers came in after me and were quickly relieved of their boots, too. I expected a cursory examination to result in our getting ointment for blisters, but instead the officer ordered us to leave.

I didn't understand what was going on. The Germans had our parachute boots. How were we supposed to march in bare feet?

I was still without an answer when I saw Johnny being put on a truck with other wounded soldiers. Dirty gauze formed a ball around his lower arm. He looked so weak, he could hardly stand, but the wounded were jammed together so tightly on the truck, they could not sit down.

The Germans were not letting us move freely, so I shouted to Johnny and waved my arms overhead, but he neither heard nor saw me. I could only watch from a distance as the truck pulled away, taking Johnny to his fate and leaving me to mine.

CHAPTER 4

I first heard about Hitler's war when I was fifteen years old. My family had moved from an apartment in Passaic to a single-family home on Collamore Terrace in West Orange, New Jersey. Passaic and West Orange were only about fifteen miles apart, so we didn't feel far removed from our roots or extended family. Still, the white colonial was quite a step up for us.

Every Saturday my buddies and I walked to the neighborhood movie theater. We'd watch a great adventure flick, which lasted about forty minutes. At the most exciting moment, just as the hero was about to fall off a cliff or be trapped by the villain in a dark alley, the movie would end. "Come back next week and find out what happens to our hero," a voice behind the screen intoned. We would eagerly await the next installment of the serial.

Following the main feature, we watched Pathé Newsreels, produced in Britain, showing Hitler saluting his goose-stepping troops as they paraded before him. A map of Europe appeared on the screen,

with arrows indicating the Nazis' advance and clips of women crying into their aprons. To my friends, the place looked impossibly far
away. To me, Europe was close to home, since Mom and Pop had
met in France.

I studied Hitler's angry face and harsh gestures on the movie
screen. Saturday afternoon after Saturday afternoon, my friends and
I watched this monster trying to gobble up the world. I felt repulsed
and mesmerized. How many of us in the theater, I wondered, would
ever see this evil man up close?

I sneaked a look at the familiar faces around me. The flickering
light of the screen revealed expressions I had never seen before. Fear.
Bewilderment. Disillusionment. I was stunned by the immensity
of the threat Hitler posed. We all were. The German Army looked
powerful enough to invade America and do to us what it had already
done to France and Poland.

My stomach ached because I knew I would end up in that epic
struggle.

The months fell away, and my friends and I could feel Hitler's
threat like a hot, rancid breath on the backs of our necks We went
to the movie house on Saturdays just to watch the newsreels. The
cliffhangers of the serials seemed trivial by comparison. I studied the
war photographs in *Life* magazine, and the images ran through my
mind when I lay in bed.

After the attack on Pearl Harbor, I felt electricity sparking in the
air at my high school. The principal called the entire student body
into the auditorium, where President Roosevelt's radio speech was
broadcast over the loudspeakers. His announcement shot into my
gut like a rocket: The United States was at war, and we all must be
on one team.

All the junior and senior boys gathered outside school. Everybody—I mean *everybody*—talked about enlisting. I would be graduating in June 1942. I looked at my friends and made my own announcement: In six months, I would join the military.

I taped a map of the world to a wall in my bedroom and tracked the Germans' advance by sticking pins into the occupied areas of Europe. As graduation neared, I marked West Point, Fort Bragg, Fort Dix, and Fort Benning.

Week after week I said goodbye to guys a year or two older than I who were reporting for duty. I knew them. I had played football against them, hung out with them, was friends with their younger brothers. The whole country seemed to be part of the war effort. I waited impatiently for my turn.

But after graduation every branch of the military rejected me because I was color-blind. I tried to improve my vision by eating carrots, but that did not help.

I was the odd man out, and my girlfriend's mother needled me about it.

"So are you going into the service yet, Jimmy?" she asked sweetly, opening the screen door for me one day when I came to visit Lee. "Have you found an outfit that'll have you?"

I struggled to mind my manners. Mrs. Geikie knew full well how diligently I was trying to enlist. Didn't she think I was a good prospect for her daughter's future? Or was it because her husband was British and my pop was Irish?

Lee came up behind her mother. "Come on in, Jimmy! Calvin is here! You can say hi."

Calvin Scott was a gawky older guy who was sweet on Lee. He was just out of boot camp, and the army had sent him home for a brief visit before shipping him out for Europe.

Cal jumped up from the couch. He barely filled out his uniform, but I had no uniform at all. "Hey, Jim," he said, and offered a hand with a weak grip.

"Hi, Cal." I shook his hand, doing all the work.

"Doesn't he look sharp in those dress blues?" Lee asked.

"Very," I agreed. Her being impressed made me feel lousy.

We all sat down. Calvin planted his elbows on his knees and leaned forward. "Tough luck, you being rejected," he said insincerely. "Tell me: Can you see I'm wearing blues?" He flicked a glance at Lee. I wanted to strangle him.

"News travels fast," I said. "Doesn't it, Lee?"

Cal shrugged. "I heard from my aunt Daisy," he said, letting Lee off the hook. "But she didn't tell me what you're up to. How are you keeping busy while we're saving the world?"

"I'm an electrician at the federal shipyard in Kearny," I said.

More accurately, I was an electrician's helper, hired at a quarter an hour. I had to fight for the job. Shortly after I started, the union went on strike, and I went out with them. The strike was in its second week with no end in sight.

"But the union's on strike," Lee offered unhelpfully.

Cal looked at me, his eyebrows raised in question.

I felt ridiculous. "I got another job as a machinist, working the graveyard shift at the Crucible Steel Mill." The mill was also in Kearny. That job, making 9.2 shells for the British, paid thirty-five cents an hour. I wondered how people could get by on that. How many hours would I have to work at a dime an hour extra to make up for the pay lost during the strike? I was just a kid out of school, but I realized then how hard life had to be for blue-collar workers trying to support a family.

I had to make a better life for myself. I wanted to be a good provider for Lee and eventually our children. She would expect that, and so would her parents and mine. I'd make sure Lee never regretted sticking with me instead of favoring Calvin. First, I had to get out of my dead-end, low-paying job. I had no idea how that would happen, but I knew if I kept my eyes and ears open, an answer would present itself.

My family had one car (most families had none), and Pop let me drive to work each night. On the way home on the morning of August 25—my mother's birthday—I noticed a large advertisement across from the post office. The sandwich-billboard showed a paratrooper gripping the risers of his parachute. *JUMP INTO THE FIGHT!* it exhorted.

Holy shit! I thought. This is it! I swerved to the curb, then jammed on the brakes of Pop's car. I turned off the ignition and dashed into the recruitment office. "I'm ready to jump! I'm ready to jump!" I shouted, breathless.

The officer laughed heartily. "Can you wait till we get you up in the air first?" he asked, and pointed me to a chair in front of his gray metal desk.

I sat down hard. "Will you take me without color tests?"

"Don't worry about that, young man," the officer said. "We want you as badly as you seem to want us."

He explained that the paratroopers division was new to the army, and the 101st Airborne needed to be populated. "I'll give you the yarn test," he said. "Follow me."

I walked with him over to a counter against the back wall. "Will this take long? I have to get the car home by eight-thirty so my pop can drive to work."

"We have plenty of time," the officer said, and pulled out a little basket with short pieces of yarn in it. "Pick out a yellow one," he ordered.

The strands looked identical to me. I held my breath and chose one.

"Great! Now pick out a red one."

I had no idea if he was bullshitting when he praised me for selecting the red snippet.

After a few more, he looked me in the eyes. "We're going to take you. Just pass the physical." He paused. "How old are you?"

"Seventeen, sir."

"Be sure to get your parents' written permission."

I was so excited, I forgot about Pop needing the car. I drove straight to the recruiting station on Church Street on Manhattan's Lower East Side. It was a fifteen-mile trip. I expected to walk right in and complete the process, but by the time I found the end of the line of would-be recruits, I was three blocks from the office. Everyone standing in the queue looked like me—eager to be a part of the cause and impatient to pass his medical exam.

We spent the time with lively conversation and off-color jokes, and the line moved quickly. We talked about how basic training was supposed to be the toughest and most exhausting experience any of us would ever go through. The guys around me seemed equal to the challenge physically and mentally.

"We'll learn as we go," a tall, big-boned fellow said confidently.

"Hell, I bet a lot of the officers are learning as they go along," a wiry kid chewing on a toothpick said.

Once we were inside the station, the orderlies had us line up bare-assed. As each fellow reached the head of the line, the orderly shouted to him, "You! Go to the doctor, turn around, bend over, and spread your cheeks!"

A freckle-faced guy in line ahead of me bent over on command, grabbed the cheeks of his face, and pulled them as far apart as he could. The whole place roared with laughter, including the recruiters. He was the first sad sack I met in the service, and I knew he would not be the last.

I felt like a sad sack myself after I took my physical and, while waiting for the outcome, remembered I still had Pop's car. I tried to get a recruiting officer to speed things up. Fortunately the results were ready, and I got a thumbs-up. I was elated. Pop's transportation problems could not tarnish my mood. I figured he would have found another way to work.

I ran to the car. Finally I was a part of the war effort! My life was on track! I would have a uniform and look sharp in it. Lee and her parents would hold me in high regard.

All I needed was my parents' signature. I would have a much better chance of getting Mom's permission if Pop was there when I asked. How would I convince them I was mature enough to serve my country, when I hadn't even gotten a birthday present for my mother?

Flying down the road to East Orange, I set my inner compass for Muir's Department Store. I had just been paid twenty-eight bucks for a week's work, with overtime. Maybe a really nice gift would earn some other guy his mother's permission to join the army, but I doubted my mom could be swayed. I decided to try anyway.

"Happy Birthday!" I hollered, bursting through the front door.

My beautiful mother came out of the kitchen, and her eyes fell on the big white box with a red ribbon, grasped in both my hands. Muir's had had a sale on pastel-blue coats with a fur collar—the sort of garment Mom had always wanted but would never buy for herself. I bought it and still had three bucks left to burn a hole in my pocket.

"What you do, Jeemmee?" she asked in her lovely, soft French accent.

"It's a surprise, Mom—a big one. I'll tell you when Pop gets home." I quickly handed Mom the present along with a big hug and kiss.

She knew something was up. She called Pop at the office and talked to him in French. I had no idea what she was saying.

I picked Pop up at the office that afternoon. I was bursting to tell him on the ride home. As soon as we walked in our front door, I popped it: "I joined the paratroopers! I've already passed the physical, and all I need is your permission! You have to sign it for me, please! I just can't stand not being in the fight!"

Silence.

Pop looked pale and stared at Mom. She was unsteady, quivering as if she was going to be sick. And then she started to weep. I had never seen her act so unhappy, so *hurt*, when something good happened to me.

"What's wrong?" I asked. "You know how hard I've been trying to get into the service." I looked from one to the other. "You know I've been itching to join the fight."

Mom and Pop spoke feverishly in French. The more they talked, the harder she cried and the lousier I felt. I adored my mother and couldn't bear to watch her cry.

"I know you're worried because it's the paratroopers," I said, "but I'll be getting fifty extra bucks a month just for jumping."

She would not look at me.

"Please. Please let me join up."

I took her hand and led her to a chair in the living room, then hunkered down beside her, never letting go of her hand. "Being a paratrooper will keep me safe," I explained with all the wisdom of adolescence. "Paratrooper units fight on their own, so I'll know everyone alongside me. I won't have to worry about the guy on my right or left not being there when I need him. Every paratrooper has to prove his courage by jumping before even seeing combat."

Her gaze settled on me. She was still shivering, and tears streamed down her cheeks. And yet she managed a magnificent smile with all the comforting warmth of a mother's unconditional love. "Okay, Jeemmee. You go. I just hope you know how to open a parachute."

We both stood, and I hugged her until she broke away from me and walked out of the room, wiping tears from her face.

Pop gave me a hug. He was crying, too. "Jim, I want you to sit down with your mother, alone, and ask her to tell you about her life in France."

"But she never talks about—"

My mother returned, holding something in her hand. "Keep thees with you wherever you go," she told me, "and St. Joan weell take care of you."

She pressed into my palm the bronze Joan of Arc medallion that my mom's parents had given to her. About the size of a silver dollar, it showed St. Joan astride her horse, and across the top were the words *Avant Le Bataille*.

"Before the battle," my mother whispered, translating for me, then curled my fingers around it, closing my hand into a fist.

"Mom . . ." There were no words. This was her most precious possession. I could feel the heat of it, the heat of whatever had happened to her and her family in France, the heat of history and pain, searing my palm.

She nodded once, then left the room quickly.

I looked at Pop.

"I know she never talks about it, Jimmy, but I want you to try to draw it out of her. You must understand what upsets her so much. You must hear about France."

CHAPTER 5

═══════

W e walked in bare feet through most of the night. My feet were a mass of blood and small cuts, but the Germans had no concern for our well-being. When I thought I had found the outer reaches of my misery, the bombing started again, forcing us to hobble toward what little protection might be found in a ditch or crater. Shrapnel sliced into my right wrist, and the cut was painful.

My stomach was empty, my wrist throbbing. Walking through the darkness, I had no idea if we had walked for one hour or five. I was heartsick. I thought they would march us to Germany and that each one of us would die along the way. What else could the future hold except more misery and then death?

I forced myself to think of Johnny, which reminded me to be grateful and saved me from utter despondency. I turned my thoughts to home, my old friends, and Lee. I worked to create as vivid a picture as possible of my life in New Jersey, but reality crashed in on me, and with it came the pain and hopelessness.

I looked at the sky. Ahead, the horizon was beginning to lighten with the dawn. We followed a rough dirt lane until we arrived at a big French home with a large courtyard and barn. German soldiers in the black uniforms of the Gestapo were everywhere. I recognized them from the newsreels back home. They were the feared and hated secret police of Hitler's army.

German soldiers called us five at a time into the courtyard and made us take our helmets off, place them on the ground, inverted, at our feet, then empty our wallets and jewelry into them. My wallet held pictures of my family and Lee, and my only jewelry was a wristband from Lee. I'd hate to lose any of it. The worst, though, was losing my St. Joan medallion, which had meant so much to my mother and me.

Then the Germans ordered us to strip. I really began to sweat then, worrying about my jump knife concealed in the secret pocket of my jacket. My clothes were in a single heap, but no one inspected my jacket. I was amazed. We were told to dress, then the soldiers marched us to the barn. My helmet and its contents stayed behind. I should have known better than to think the Gestapo might return my personal belongings or, for that matter, do anything decent.

We climbed a ladder inside the barn to the hayloft, and the rungs dug into my bloodied feet. We were allowed to sleep. I collapsed into the hay, and within a minute I was dead to the world.

"*Wachen Sie auf! Stehen Sie auf! Jetzt!*"

I awoke to the shock of a German soldier kicking the soles of my tender feet. I screamed from the pain, and he kicked me again.

Time for us to move out. As I climbed down the ladder, I dreaded the thought of where and how far we would trek. We lined up in the courtyard and waited while our captors counted us and argued among themselves. Another thirty prisoners added to our group brought our number to sixty. Many of the men had bare feet with dried blood and scabs.

A truck roared up, and we piled into the open back, packed so tightly against the railing, we couldn't move. The vehicle, one of three in a small convoy, pulled out onto a rough, narrow, dusty road with deep drainage ditches on both sides. Every time the truck made the slightest turn or hit the smallest bump, the group shifted, and someone stomped on my feet.

Occasionally we passed patches of woods jammed with German troops and equipment. I felt empathy for those poor bastards who no doubt had to push forward in darkness toward the front lines. Their route took them through a clear and frightening display of Allied air superiority: The ruins of what had been columns of German supply trucks, tanks, and other military equipment lay smoldering along the roadside. Death was everywhere—charred crisp and black.

Our contingent, unmarked in any way as prisoners, was an easy target for our fighter planes. Keenly aware that our own planes would strafe us, we talked about what we would do when it happened. Our only hope was to wave at the pilot and pray that he would grasp that we were prisoners. And if our signal failed? No one talked about that, although surely it weighed heavily on every man.

We came to a halt after a few miles and were ordered out of the truck. I looked at the men who had ridden in the other vehicles and found Huff and Burnie among them. I couldn't join them, but I was very happy to see they were alive.

"*Wer spricht Deutsch?*" an officer asked, walking back and forth as we lined up. "*Wer spricht Deutsch?*"

I gasped as Maury Goldberg took a step forward. "*Ich*

spreche deutschen ziemlich Brunnen," he said, and was given the job of interpreter.

I was in agony, wondering how Goldberg could have been so foolhardy as to single himself out. I could not have been alone in my fear for his safety. The German officer spoke to him for about five minutes, and I watched them closely. Nothing about Goldberg suggested he was Jewish—except his name. His family was of German descent, and he appeared as much an Aryan as the officer. He did not seem at all worried about his decision. Time would tell if he had been clever or stupid.

Goldberg walked over to us. "Ol' Fritzy there says we should stay in the trucks if we're strafed. The guards will go for the ditches and will shoot any of us who jump out. Stay in the trucks."

The Germans had thought of everything, I thought as we piled back into the truck. We were almost to the outskirts of St. Lo when I saw four American P-38 fighter planes in the distance. I knew what was in store for us. These boys had caused all the damage we passed on the road. Tension and terror overwhelmed me, for within minutes, those planes with their fifty-caliber machine-gun bullets and rockets would swoop down on us.

The Germans hunkered low in the roadside ditches as the planes sped down. The bullets pounded the truck while we prayed to God for protection. Men cried out all around me, and one vaulted over the tailgate, trying to escape. He would have been better off to let the American fighter planes finish the job instead of giving the Germans the pleasure of shooting him point-blank.

The bombers made a single pass at us. The attack lasted only a few seconds, but they were among the most horrible of my life. That anyone in the truck was still alive was miraculous. Seven officers and ten enlisted men were dead—men who had stood beside me moments before, listening to Goldberg, had been reduced to gore. Ten others were seriously wounded. I had never seen worse carnage. Knowing so many Germans had died in the assault gave me no comfort. My stomach heaved until I was puking bile.

I worked my way over toward Burnie and Huff as we collected dog tags and buried as many of our soldiers as we could. The Germans stole the boots from the dead and kept them. Many of us were still barefoot.

Two of the three trucks were out of commission. We propped up the wounded in the remaining truck or lay them down beside it. Then, ragged, beaten, hungry, and exhausted but still more alive than dead, we began our march to our destination.

After a short distance I could see a town set high on a hill that rose in the midst of flatland. St. Lo looked close but proved to be a long way off—particularly for those of us without shoes. As we approached the town, moving up the hill on bloody feet, we could see it had been transformed into a fortress with tunnels, air-raid shelters, and bunkers. Most of us knew that the Allies, intending to expand their territory from Normandy, had planned to clobber St. Lo to remove a prime, fortified obstacle.

Our bombers had already reduced some of St. Lo's threat. Destruction was everywhere. The hillside was strewn with rubble—toilets, sinks, and furniture. In the town just five or six buildings were still standing.

A Catholic cathedral stood defiantly on the hilltop. I was astonished that it had escaped damage in the midst of all the carnage. About five hundred feet from the cathedral, on a small plateau of land at the top of the hill, I saw what had to be our destination: a prison compound surrounded by a high fence.

German soldiers suddenly appeared one by one. They stared at us impassively, then returned to their work. At the very top of the hill, we could see for miles in three directions. Looking back whence we had come, I saw our red footprints stretching down the hill and onto the road. Only the tough and the lucky had made it there.

My family never taught me how to be tough. I didn't need to defend myself in the neighborhood. The kids I knew just figured out how to survive on their own at an early age.

When the time came for me to start kindergarten, Pop explained, "You'll go through an Italian neighborhood when you walk to school, and you'll probably have to fight some of the kids living there. If you want to, you can avoid that neighborhood by walking a couple of blocks out of your way. Then you won't have any problem."

"What should I do?" I asked him.

"You'll have to make that decision yourself," he answered. "You'll either walk around it or go through it, have your fight, and get it over with."

I remembered the anguish of making that decision as I stood at the point of no return on the edge of the neighborhood. I decided to walk through it.

Sure enough I got into a fight, and I fought every day for the first week of school, while I proved I could take a licking and land a few punches myself. From that point on, I never had a problem.

The Germans were the bullies now. I had taken my last licking from the enemy, I decided. From now on, I'd be delivering the blows.

CHAPTER 6

We had all been guessing at what a German POW camp would be like. As we approached the prison at St. Lo, some of the guys perked up. Their pace quickened from their heightened expectations.

"Maybe it'll be as decent as what we have for our prisoners."

"Might have a post exchange."

"If it does, I'm getting a carton of cigarettes, a couple sandwiches, and a DO NOT DISTURB sign."

"Think there's a game room?"

"We'll find out soon enough."

The guys sobered as we passed two concentric walls of barbed wire. The outer layer was high and neatly strung. The inner was very thick and tangled and impassable.

Inside the prison compound was one small barn sitting in the midst of barren ground. As verdant as France was, not a blade of grass, bush, or tree survived inside the fence. One by one, we filed in. I was filled with dread.

The guard seemed much kinder than the guards who had marched us to this moment. He looked down at my throbbing feet, shook his head in disgust, and gave me an encouraging pat on the back as I walked by him.

As I was about to enter the camp, I glimpsed a cluster of tiny wild strawberries growing on a stake. Nothing in the world could have looked better to me. I picked as many as I could find, until the guard saw what I was doing. I gulped down a handful and stuffed another handful into my pocket before he shoved me back in line. I shared the strawberries with the men next to me as the gate slammed behind us.

The Germans lined us up.

"Dolmetscher!" an officer called out, and Goldberg moved forward.

A couple of officers spoke to him for several minutes. He stood with his blond head tilted, listening intently, nodding his under-standing, saying a few words in response or asking for clarification.

Meanwhile we sat in the dirt and tried to relax.

"Anyone got an extra fag?" a fella asked.

We searched through our pockets, looking for cigarettes. If only I had saved the wet tobacco I'd thrown away when I was first taken prisoner. I'd discarded two packs of Lucky Strikes, which would have been enough to keep me and a few guys satisfied for days under these conditions.

Goldberg came back to face us. He had our undivided attention. "We'll be here for at least a week. They said the food situation is pretty bad."

One of the guys got pissed off, and we all told him to shut up.

"They want us to turn in our names and home addresses so the Germans can announce a roster over the radio and say that we're safe and sound."

"And hungry, the bastards," the same man grumbled.

"The Germans will probably be able to say a personal message to our folks if we tell them where we're from . . ." Goldberg's voice trailed off, and he shrugged uncertainly.

"Sounds like a good deal to me," one man drawled. "My kin'll be worried sick. Iffen they hear Ah'm okay, it'll do 'em a whole world o' good."

A strong voice came from one of the soldiers who had kept to himself for the trip. His tone left no room for discussion. "No one— not one man—gives his name or his parents' address, or he'll answer to me."

I could not imagine standing at a microphone, talking to my parents, with a German pressing a gun in my back. The very thought made me tremble. I didn't want the Germans to film how I looked, my feet blistered and bloody, and the wound on my wrist sore and red.

I knew my thoughts were shared by every other guy in the bunch. No one wanted his parents to be aware of these conditions. The propaganda tactics might have been effective early on, but they had worn off fast.

I looked at my wrist. I was pretty sure the wound had turned septic, and before long blood poisoning would set me on fire and send me into delirium.

"We're going to bunk in the barn," Goldberg said. "They want us to line up single file."

We filed in one by one. The stench of rotten hay and filthy animals nearly drove us back outside.

"Jesus, this is worse than a zoo," Huff said.

"An old zoo," someone added. "Where the cages are never cleaned."

I passed into the barn and tried to ignore the odor. We'd get used to it sooner or later.

"Cliquot!" ("Cliquot the Eskimo," as the guys in boot camp used to call me, I guess because I had very dark hair and slightly slanted eyes.)

I turned to see my friend Ralph Kent. "Holy shit! When the hell did you get here?"

"Just yesterday, Jimmy. I am glad to see you!"

He was a paratrooper with the Eighty-second Airborne. I pointed at the stripes on his jacket. "How did a fuckup like you become a sergeant?"

"Shit"—Ralph laughed—"this isn't my jacket. When my sarge was hit, I took his jacket off so I could treat his wound. He didn't make it, and by then it looked like we were going to be captured. I put the jacket on, figuring I might get better treatment as an officer."

"How's that working out for you, Sergeant?"

Ralph looked around and snorted in derision. "Not so good."

Being with Ralph immediately lifted my spirits. Even Burnie and Huff and the other guys around us looked cheered by our reunion and my friend's affability.

"Come on, Jim, let's find a place to sack in," he said.

We found a place under the tin roof. We wouldn't have much room to move around, but we'd stay dry in case of rain. Ralph pulled out a cigarette, lit it, and then held it out to me for a drag. "I don't have many left, but you can share with me till we run out," he said.

He also gave me half a Hershey bar, and from that moment we were brothers. We made things easier for each other and shared our most private thoughts, which I sorely needed. For the first time I took in the stark reality that we were confined, trapped.

We talked a lot about home and girlfriends, football and the old gang. Eventually we discussed freedom and how we might escape.

"My dad was a soldier in World War I," I said. "I try to imagine how he would handle this situation."

"He and the other Passaic guys were as tough as nails," Ralph said. "Like Tommy Mooney . . ."

"Pop would be holding his head high and figuring out ways for him and the boys to escape."

My dad was the charismatic leader of his gang. I tried to follow his example, but in my mind I couldn't get the gang past the barbed wire. Our situation was so dire, I doubted I would ever find humor in anything again. Ralph must have realized how blue I felt. Why else would he have asked if I remembered Gus Kelsh?

The mere mention made me laugh. "Oh, yeah. He lived down the street from us."

Ralph's smile was wide. "He was a friend of my pop's. The first time I heard your name was from Gus."

I felt like I was sitting in a confessional. "Gus had an apple orchard in his yard. I used to steal his apples, and he'd open fire on me with a salt-and-pepper gun as I hauled ass out of his yard."

"Knowing Gus, I doubt he was seriously taking aim at you," Ralph said, "but he was sure pissed about losing those apples."

I sighed. "I never thought I'd get shot at again, after that."

We lapsed into silence. I looked down at my wrist. The wound looked less angry, and the pain had lessened. Maybe I wouldn't die of blood poisoning, after all.

The other fellows had already settled down, lying on the damp floor of the barn, packed together for body heat. Ralph and I joined them.

The first night in St. Lo was quiet. The Germans didn't bother us for hours, and there was little if any action in the air. I dreamt of home and my family and girlfriend. I could have been in the most

51

comfortable bed in the tallest hotel and not have enjoyed it more than those few hours in that hay. I must have dreamed of everything beautiful the world had to offer—the war was worlds away . . . all was forgotten—for I awoke smiling.

––––––––––––

Early in the morning, Goldberg walked in and told us there was no possibility of our eating that day. We hadn't expected much food, but we guessed we'd get something. It had been a long time since we had eaten anything substantial.

Something was different about Goldberg. His voice quivered a bit as he made his announcement, a sharp contrast to the assertive manner he had been showing as our interpreter.

We passed the day waiting for information, for shoes. Nothing materialized. Everyone seemed to be taking our capture in stride. We sat and talked. We tried to think of a way out. Ralph and I sat in a small circle with some other fellows and talked about home. Goldberg came to join the conversation, and we all quickly made room for him to sit down.

I could see something was still bothering him. He seemed distant.

"Maury, you're in the group but not really here," I said gently. "What's up?"

He licked his lips and cleared his throat before answering. "I am scared stiff about being a Jew," he admitted, and his amber eyes swept around the circle. "The Germans"—he cleared his throat again— "made accusations about my religion and pushed me around this morning."

We all tried to figure out an answer to Goldberg's problem, but he was completely at the mercy of our rough, merciless captors.

"They wanted to know if I was circumcised," he said quietly.

"Hey, lots of guys who aren't Jews get circumcised," Huff said.

"Anyone here circumcised?" Goldberg asked, and we all shifted our weight uncomfortably. No one answered. He cleared his throat again.

"Even so," Huff insisted, "it doesn't prove you're a Jew. It just proves we aren't."

"You've got to stay strong," I said. "You're acting real sure of yourself, and that's good."

"They need you to be the interpreter," Burnie said. "That's more important to them now than anything else."

We had to agree with that logic and did our best to allay Goldberg's fears. The Cherokee rarely spoke, so I knew how much Goldberg's plight was bothering him.

I went back to my corner and lay down while Ralph stayed with the others. I closed my eyes and remembered a Jewish kid—the only Jewish kid—who lived in the neighborhood. Everybody used to talk about "the Jew," and some said it was his fault Christ had died. I didn't understand completely how the ungainly, skinny kid could have been responsible for a crime of that magnitude, but the more the gang talked about this kid, the madder I got at him. I decided I was going to have to beat him up.

The next morning I waited outside his house until he came out to go to school. When we had gone around the corner, I beat the living crap out of him. I went to school; he never got there that day.

When I came home, my mother told me that a constable wearing a silver badge had come to the house and accused me of beating up his grandson. She said she didn't know what he was talking about. Then she brought out my father's badge, for being the deputy mayor of Passaic. It was gold. She showed it to the constable. For the constable, that gold badge settled the issue.

I had completely forgotten about that incident until listening to Goldberg dredged it up. I'm glad it came back to me. It deserved to be thought about again, from my adult's point of view. Seeing Goldberg's fear and recalling my own mindless prejudice distilled the war to an immediate, highly personal level. More than ever I committed myself to escaping and fighting the Germans. This was my war now.

––––––––––

The sun went down. Night blanketed the room, and I listened to the deep, even breathing of the other men. My feet ached so much, I couldn't pass into the dream world. I lay on my thin layer of hay over the concrete floor and focused on getting out of the camp. A long road awaited me . . . I hoped.

My family had most likely received the army's telegram listing me as missing in action. I was determined to make sure my family knew I was alive. It would be the happiest message any mother could receive.

Finally I dozed off, only to be awakened by a terrific blast that sounded like it came from right next to me. Directly overhead was the roar of what seemed like a thousand aircraft. I could do nothing but hope that if a bomb landed close by, someone else would take the shrapnel. I'm sure every man in the barn had the same selfish thought.

The first few minutes of the attack taught us that if a bomb whistled, it would land nearby. At that terrifying sound, we all huddled closer to each other, clenched our teeth, and tightened our asses.

For an hour the bombs came down like rain, one after another, so many of them, so close to us, that the shrapnel tore through the barn. The bitter taste of sulfur burned my mouth and throat. The assault was bigger than anything any of us had ever known.

And yet not one bomb was a direct hit.

Not a single man was lost.

The thunder of the planes receded. All was silent but for the muffled sobs of some of the men. The man next to me shook as he cried. I prayed no one had lost his mind from the stress.

In a few minutes, we started whispering, assuring one another we were okay. The experience had been so intense, it left us too weak and weary for nervous laughter or little jokes to relieve the strain. Soon the mumbling dissolved into silence, and we dropped off to sleep.

A blast at dawn sent us running outside. American P-47s, sent to take out the buildings left standing by the heavy bombers, had little to accomplish. The hilltop cathedral, the prison camp, and a few old buildings were only partially standing.

Our only chance of surviving the spot bombing was to let the pilots know we were prisoners. We waved our arms, handkerchiefs, underwear, and anything else we thought could be seen from ten thousand feet. We never knew if the crew recognized us, but bombers never came near the camp again.

After the bombers left, our adrenaline subsided and our thoughts turned to food. This was our fourth day without eating, and my stomach felt like a hard knot. I was not hungry anymore, but I was concerned about my thirst. We were all very dry; my eyes and hair itched.

A few guys asked Goldberg to speak with the German commander about the food situation. Maury didn't want to do it, but he knew we depended upon him. Watching him walk off in search of the commander, I admired his courage.

Before long he returned. The news was not good; the food situation for that day was "nearly impossible," the Germans had told him. We all sat down and relaxed, wanting to conserve our strength.

Not having shoes bothered me. My feet were not going to heal until they were protected. I didn't want to ask Maury to be my mouthpiece, so I took it upon myself to visit the commander's office.

I knocked on the door. Someone hollered in German, and I presumed it was permission for me to enter. I walked in, and the commander said something to me. I figured he was asking me what I wanted. I lifted my foot and showed him the bottom of it. I didn't have to say anything else. I knew he understood what I meant.

He called in a guard—the one who had patted me on the back when we entered the camp. The commander said a few words to him and gestured to me to get out of his office.

A half hour later, the kindly German entered our bunk area, carrying a pair of old French shoes that had been worn beyond repair. They did not fit, but I motioned to the German that I would keep them. The man wore an apologetic expression.

To my surprise he reached into his pocket, took out a piece of bread, and handed it to me. No lavish banquet had ever looked as tantalizing as that piece of stale bread. Next he handed me a cigarette.

He left me there, in my glory. I took one bite of bread and chewed it for so long, it seemed to turn back into dough.

I was just about to take another bite when Huff, Burnie, and Goldberg walked in.

I might have been completely self-centered during the bombing, but I couldn't be selfish with the food that I held in my hand. We three enjoyed a couple of good mouthfuls of food, glorious food, and I managed to save a bite for Ralph.

Then came dessert—the cigarette. First, though, I went to get Ralph. We sat in a circle, I lit the fag, and we took turns puffing on it.

We sucked on it so fast, the ash became superheated, and the tobacco got soggy. But if we hadn't smoked it fast, some of the tobacco would have gone up in smoke between drags. We took it down to about a quarter inch, then knocked the ash off the end and hoarded the stub. Five stubs combined would equal one full-sized cigarette.

My friends went back into the barn while I stayed outside. Wired after the feast, I decided to figure out how to fix the shoes. Making certain no one was watching, I took my jump knife from its secret pocket and slashed the right side of the right shoe and then tried to put it on. It still didn't fit, so I sliced open the left side. Now the sides fit fairly well, but my toes were cramped.

I studied the shoe, then made a bold move: I cut open the front of the shoe. Now only the heel was tight. I made a slit right down the middle of the heel. The alterations were a success. My foot was secure and protected, and the French shoes felt like a pair of expensive oxfords.

I slipped my knife back into its pocket, then I glanced around. The courtyard was empty except for the kindly German noncom, busy performing some menial chore. I thought about escape. I assumed we would be leaving St. Lo soon because the Allies had ruined the place. The Germans would not waste the time to search for me when they were about to move.

I looked around. I could easily run the couple hundred yards to the tall grass and hide until the Allies arrived and took possession of St. Lo. It seemed like the perfect opportunity. I tensed, ready to sprint.

"Don't do it! The timing's not right!" my instincts warned. Or was it fear speaking?

"But what if I don't get another chance?" I agonized. "What if I do the wrong thing?" It could kill me.

CHAPTER 7

"The Germans are moving us out," Goldberg told us.

We gathered around him, hoping for details he probably did not have. We were a ragged, hungry bunch. Those of us with beards looked older than our age, and the others looked too young to be POWs. We'd been in St. Lo for five days—five days with very little to eat. If we had to march any distance, we would probably lose some men along the way.

"Where are they taking us?"

"Alençon, just outside Paris," Goldberg said. "We'll walk today, rest tonight, and God willing, be there tomorrow morning." He paused and looked at us before adding, "They have a mission for us. It's a dangerous one."

The guards counted us off and put us into ragged marching columns. Our bodies and legs were supported only by our will to survive. The lucky guys, mostly officers, got jump boots. A few soldiers wore Dutch wooden clogs, while the majority wore an odd collection of old, too-small French army shoes. The other prisoners had adopted my idea for slicing open the sides and removing the toe of the footwear. Fortunately the Germans didn't think to ask how the alterations could have been made without the use of a sharp blade. Neeper and a few other fellows remained barefooted because their feet were simply too large for any available French shoes.

Repeated bombings had carved craters into our route and strewn debris along the way. As we passed the ruins of buildings and houses, my heart filled with pity for those who had called those places home. Their lives had been decimated, and their treasured belongings exploded into a thousand shards.

Finally the Germans allowed us to rest briefly. Our guard yelled at us constantly, especially when the occasional American bomber showed us its wings and then quickly disappeared. German bombers made frequent flyovers.

At first our guard's shouting made me jumpy, but soon I became used to it. I sat down and noticed a small country ham among the debris at the roadside. I scoop it up and stuck it inside my shirt. Knowing I had the food made me even hungrier. As my body heat surrounded the ham, its aroma intensified, torturing me. I knew I had to be patient. I made some others aware of our good luck, and another soldier grinned and opened his shirt just long enough for me to see a can of beans he had found in the rubble. Getting into the spirit of things, the men snatched up handfuls of grass whenever they were able, with which we would make soup.

The next morning we arrived at our destination, a French monastery. The Germans took us into a large room with concrete floors and stone walls. The monastery had a forced-hot-air heating system that was not working, but a vent proved to be an excellent hiding place for the ham and can of beans.

Now the guard's yelling worked to our advantage; as long as he was hollering, we knew exactly where he was and when he was about to enter our room. Had he seen us with the food, no doubt he would have shot us.

That night we prisoners had ourselves a meal to remember. I considered the probability it would be the last real food we would eat for weeks. We took the ham from the vent, stood in a circle around the meat, and unceremoniously pulled it apart with our fingers. We all shared it—there were a lot of us, and by now most of us were friends—and after we sucked the ham clean, someone stuck the bone back up into the vent. Later, we put that bone in with the liquid from the beans and some grass, and heated it up with one of the wax fernos the German soldiers didn't take and enjoyed some soup.

We were fortunate to have found the food. The Germans didn't feed us for two days. On the third day, the Germans gave us permission to eat a horse that had been strafed. Some guys did, but I decided to take my chances that something more appetizing would present itself. On the fourth day, our captors brought us grass soup and peppermint tea, which settled my stomach but was not enough nourishment to keep us going. We were debilitated and getting skinnier by the day. I doubted my own ability to march any distance.

I was so weak, in fact, that when a truck pulled up to the monastery on June 13 and we were ordered to climb into the back, I couldn't do it without help. None of the men could.

Goldberg repeated that we were heading toward Paris. As we were loading, a bomber flew overhead, and the Germans, enraged, shouted at the planes and cursed the Americans. One Nazi even knocked down a few of us prisoners with the butt of his rifle.

"There has to be an airplane hangar cut into those cliffs," Ralph guessed, and we squinted at the steep mountains surrounding the area.

"The Allies and the Axis must use them," another fellow said. "The cliffs are natural hideouts for planes."

If so, that would explain how the aircraft could "dust" the ground with bombs and then suddenly disappear under the cliffs.

As the truck transported us to Alençon, we watched many trains moving east and west along the horizon. The extremely large Alençon train station was a major factor in the Germans' effort to keep supplies and troops moving to the front lines.

Would our dangerous mission involve the station? I wondered, but I couldn't imagine in what way. Whatever we would be required to do, I and the others deeply resented working to help the enemy. The alternative—being shot dead on the spot—was worse. As the days passed, though, I began to view my death as inevitable . . . unless I took action to change my future. I refused to sacrifice my life as a result of passivity. The Germans didn't care if I lived or died. Only I did. I had to be the one to make sure I lived.

I began to think more and more seriously about escape. It gnawed at me even more than hunger. When our forced labor was solitary or when we were working together but not allowed to talk, all I could think about was escape. I was obsessed with the thought, and most likely the other guys were thinking about it, too. If I was going to die no matter what I did, then I was going to die making a mad dash toward freedom.

"Ralph Kent!"

I turned to see Goldberg standing next to a German officer who was pointing at Ralph. The Nazi's eyes made a line toward me, and he pointed.

"Jim Sheeran!" Goldberg called out.

Manny Furtado was next.

Goldberg waved us over from where we had been rebuilding a bridge all day. The sun was beginning to set, and I was bone tired. The officer directed us to a truck, and soon we found ourselves in a temporary barracks set up along the road to Alençon. Inside the enclosure was a long lean-to with a corrugated tin roof on posts. A big kettle filled with grass soup bubbled away just outside the barracks. About twenty Americans sat around. No one spoke, and the tension was thick in the air.

I didn't know what we were about to do, but I was glad Ralph and I were still traveling together. We went up to a few of the men, introduced ourselves, and asked what was going on.

"Lemme see y'all's hands," one soldier drawled.

Ralph, Manny, and I held out our hands.

"They look awright to me," the Southerner said, and nodded his approval. "Steady Eddie."

"We doin' brain surgery?" Manny asked, smirking.

"Jest about raht," the soldier drawled, then elaborated.

Our job was to dig up unexploded American bombs that lay about three-quarters buried in the ground. For some reason I could not fathom, the Southerner seemed to relish making the explanation. "Now, these here bombs have a fuse that was s'posed t' go *boom* when they hit the ground." He shrugged, an odd smile on his face. "But fer some reason, they's still in one piece, waitin' on us."

We had no way of knowing when the bomb we were disarming might blow. Knowing each moment could be my last, I prayed and held my breath as Ralph and I dug completely around the base of an unexploded bomb and fastened a large howitzer to it. Then a German tank disarmed the shell. Extracting one bomb could take a few minutes to over a half hour, but however long it took, it felt like an eternity and I was completely spent afterward.

When we had miraculously survived the disarming of one bomb, the Germans moved us along to the next. Before starting the process, I'd look at the bomb and pray it would not be the one to blow me to smithereens. Ralph and I worked together all the time we were in Alençon. We worked well with each other and knew that if a bomb were to detonate, fate and not the other person's clumsiness or stupidity would have caused it to blow.

The nature of our assignment won us no favors among the younger German officers, who relished giving orders and demanding labor. A couple of the older guards clearly hated seeing what we had been ordered to do. The pair even looked out for Ralph and me. One guard slipped Ralph a piece of bread for us to share. When he knew we would be discreet, he repeated the kindness.

On our third day of work, Ralph and I noticed an overturned, derailed boxcar. Inside the open door was what looked to me like . . .

"Hey, Ralph! You think that's a keg of wine?"

We sneaked down the track, the debris shielding us from the guards' eyes. Soon we were lying on our backs, pouring red wine down our throats. The party ended when one of the old guards shot at us with his rifle. He didn't hit us—I don't think that was his intention—but, Christ, we scrambled out of there and hustled back to work. I felt the heat of his glare as we started digging out the bombs again.

At the end of the day we dragged ourselves back to the prison camp. Never had I been more hungry or exhausted.

A rumor spread that the Germans had found a cow that had been strafed and killed near the railroad tracks. We were fed a little beef stock that night. Because I knew where, when, and how the cow had died, I was willing to eat from it.

After our fourth day in Alençon, we were herded onto buses and trucks for the long ride to a Paris prison. Our restrictions were the same if the truck came under attack: stay put or be shot by the German guards.

This compound was the first permanent prisoner-of-war enclosure I had seen. The steel-mesh fence must have been ten feet high. I could hear the sound of prisoners marching and officers barking orders. Just inside, a group of long-term prisoners, black Africans and French Senegalese, were laboring under the gun. I knew their reputation as strong, tough, and fearless horse soldiers.

They were tall, yes, and big boned and strong, but walking past them, I could see they were undernourished. And yet without hesitation, they threw their Red Cross provisions over the fence to us. They knew we had been living in starvation. What would we have done had the situation been reversed? I wondered. I believed we would have done the same. Some Americans in my group were prejudiced, but I think they overcame their bias after seeing the French Senegalese.

The Germans classified us according to race and sent us into the prison through an entrance that segregated the Senegalese from us. Our side of the prison seemed larger than the black prisoners'. Our sturdy building with its parquet wood floors and high ceilings must have been a gymnasium, with an elevated section at one end, which could accommodate spectators or be used as a stage. Ralph and I staked out that higher area as a place to settle in.

This prison was an upgrade from the conditions at the monastery, but we were uncomfortably shoulder-to-shoulder in a milling mass of prisoners.

We sat down. "I wonder why we're here," Ralph said, looking around. "Weird place."

"That's why," a stranger said, and pointed. "You've finally been discovered."

We followed the trajectory of his hand to see German soldiers hauling in cameras and lights.

"*Achtung!*" someone shouted, and most of the prisoners climbed to their feet and turned their attention to a knot of German officers striding in.

Ralph and I and a few others remained seated. I had just sat down, and General Eisenhower and my parents were about the only people who could have inspired me to jump up at that moment.

German soldiers hustled through the prisoners and poked their weapons at our legs and demanded we rise. Their threats of punishment—solitary confinement without food—had little impact on me. They weren't feeding me anyway.

The officer in charge was a sharply dressed man. He was as handsome as a movie star, which is probably what he was. The cameras rolling, he delivered a scripted speech that told us where we were. We were expected to behave and obey orders, he continued. We would not be there long and would be fed soon, but not that night. The cameramen took wide, sweeping shots of the gymnasium, probably for propaganda purposes. I did not know if the lenses were capable of recording close-ups of our faces.

When that segment was concluded, we watched as German soldiers constructed a wooden platform about six feet high. Once it was secure, more news cameras and lights were handed up to the workmen.

Eventually we tried to sleep, but we were jammed together with barely enough room to lie down.

In the morning I was more than ready for water and food, but none was forthcoming. Nor did we get an order to report to work. We just sat around, watching the men adjusting the cameras and wondering what would happen next.

The answer came soon enough. Someone brought in a ladder for the platform, and lights for the camera blinked on as a high-ranking German took the stage and demanded our attention. Some complied immediately. Others of us slowly stood, looking unimpressed and bored.

Through an interpreter, he ordered us to sit down and remain seated because food was on its way. A half dozen soldiers came in, dragging two large garbage cans to the center of the gym. They lifted the metal lids and then quickly exited.

"That's your food!" the interpreter hollered. "Go get it!"

The cameras rolled, capturing the mob scene, American men acting like animals as they dug into the cans. Ralph and I stood on the fringe, watching the chaos. Nothing could have been more horrible. Whoever managed to fight his way to the food and plunge his hands in a pail got fed. Those who couldn't get to a pail went hungry. Survival of the fittest.

Ralph and I were so far from the rapidly disappearing food, we did not even try to enter the fray. Fights broke out under the harsh glare of the camera lights. Food spilled, and men dived to the floor after it and were trampled.

"That is one sad sight," Ralph said to me.

I felt no sadness, only rage.

Someone tapped me on the shoulder. "Would you like to give a message to your family?"

I turned to see a German officer and an interpreter.

I nodded, though I was skeptical my family would ever see it. The opportunity would distract me from my anger, I figured, and get me out of the gym for a few minutes.

The officer and interpreter escorted me to a nicely furnished office and pointed me to a comfortable chair. Some of the Germans sat at desks, smoking cigarettes or drinking from flasks. After I waited for a while, a beautiful woman with long blond hair and a gentle smile sat down beside me.

"Would you like a cigarette?" she asked in almost perfect English, and held out a pack.

"Sure," I said, and helped myself. I intended to try to learn as much from her as I could, then bring it back to the others.

"My name is Sally." She lit my cigarette and locked her seductive gaze on my eyes as she invited me to face the camera and say my name. I did that. I heard the camera's soft *whirr*.

"Good. Would you like to tell your family you miss them?"

I paused, considering how the Germans could use that bit of film against the army. Before I answered, Sally continued, "Give them whatever message you wish, so they'll know you're alive and being treated well."

I understood this was as obvious a propaganda move as using starvation to strip the soldiers of their dignity, then filming them as they battled for food. I faced the camera and said my name, rank, and serial number.

She signaled the cameraman, and he stopped filming. "Don't you want to send a message?" she asked me. "Won't your parents feel comforted by the sound of your voice? We want to help you. Just say you are being treated fairly and fed well and that the German people are misunderstood by Americans. All right?"

I nodded, and the camera rolled. "I am James Sheeran, and—"

Sally's lips became a thin, white line. She stood up abruptly and pointed to the door. *"Erhalten Sie ihn aus hier!"*

The guard nodded and roughly shoved me back to the gymnasium, where I found Ralph. The room had a sullen, dark feel in the air, and it stank.

"Christ! What's that smell?" I asked, looking around.

"Self-recrimination," he said, his eyebrows raised.

Goldberg appeared from the crowd. "How'd it go with Sally?"

"How did you know—?"

"Axis Sally is famous," Goldberg said. "You're not the first GI to meet her."

I learned that the Germans would broadcast Sally's sultry voice in combat areas, using loudspeakers, to break American soldiers' morale.

"Why aren't you fellows home with your wife or girlfriend?" she would ask. "What is she doing tonight? Who is she out with? Maybe she is cheating on you. You should go home and be with her. Why would you want to die here, so far from home, when your family needs you? You have a life to live! Surrender and end the war now. You can't win!"

"So what'd you say?" Ralph asked.

I told my friends what had happened, and they both looked reassured. I was relieved, too, that I had followed my gut feelings.

Other prisoners who had been interviewed gravitated toward us to compare our experiences with Sally. They all said they had done the same thing; they offered only their name, rank, and serial number. I was proud that we all held up under that pressure and temptation, still committed to supporting our involvement in the war.

Goldberg's blue eyes took in the scene before us. "I just wish we knew how the war is going. That's the toughest thing for me. Having absolutely no idea what's going on."

"We sat under some pretty heavy bombing in St. Lo," Ralph pointed out. "The Allies aren't sitting on their butt, that's for sure."

"We'll defeat the Germans," I said. "That's all we have to know." I had never felt more confident about anything. "The details are just—"

"—details," Goldberg finished for me, and slapped me on the back.

Never once did I, or any of the captured men I spoke with, doubt that we would succeed. We didn't even worry about how we would reunite with the Allied forces. The Nazis would realize they had no choice but to surrender, and our boys would find us.

———

Our certainty took a severe blow the next morning when—after no food or water—we learned we would be shipped to a permanent POW camp. This was the nadir. Our spirit all but broke in half. We were all hungry and sick. We felt ashamed that we had been captured by the enemy and fearful that we would not have the strength to survive whatever would happen next.

We endured a long, bumpy ride in the back of an open-top truck. As we neared Paris, other trucks loaded with American POWs converged, all heading toward the proud and beautiful Arc de Triomphe. My mother and father had lived and worked in this neighborhood after they were married, following the World War I Armistice, so images of the Arc de Triomphe had always held pleasant connotations for me. Now it was to be the setting for a parade featuring five hundred of the first Allied prisoners of war.

The Paris boulevard was lined with collaborators and the wives of German officers, and movie cameras along the way were aimed at the downtrodden Americans. We were to be filmed for propaganda. The choice of location served a triple purpose: to embarrass the French, to boost the spirits of the German people, and to give the impression that the French supported the Axis powers.

My mind raced. "*Do* the French favor the Germans?" I wondered, then scolded myself for letting that thought enter my head. I decided my hunger and exhaustion and the stress had messed up my ability to think rationally.

The cameras rolled. Well-dressed, elite German soldiers marched briskly down the boulevard, their rifles in the ready position. They looked strong and healthy and gave the impression that they had this war under control. They certainly had complete control over us.

I was among the first guys, in the front of the march. I looked around, wondering what I should do. What *could* I do? I vowed I would stand tall, hold my head high, and try to show strength during this propaganda display. I wanted to present the image of a confident and cocky American, and I'm sure the other prisoners felt the same. I kept asking myself, "What can I do to make them realize I am not afraid?"

But by then, looking anything but hopeless and deflated was almost impossible. I was dirty, weak, and emaciated. My world had been blown into small pieces. It was the lowest moment of my life.

I steered my thoughts to my sergeant, Lud Engelbrecht. Of everyone I had met in the army, he alone might have been able to appear defiant in the face of the screaming Germans. He was never far from my thoughts. I often tried to guess what he might do in every situation I faced. What came to me at that moment was when he and I snuck out of Camp Shanks on the Hudson in New York, just two days before our outfit left for England. We hitched a ride to my home in New Jersey, and I introduced Lud to my family. Right away my dad liked this tough kid from Syracuse. I think meeting him, seeing the great person he was, helped my parents feel better about my going overseas.

Thinking about my family, about how I might be standing in the exact place where my parents had stood years before, helped me connect to the core of my being, the love of my family and their love for me. That was where my real strength lay. These streets had been here before the Nazi invasion and would be here after they were defeated. I was hungry now, yes, but that was just a temporary condition. I would eat again, to my fill. I stood there as a prisoner, but in my heart, I knew I would be a free man again. All those conditions were transient. What was real and enduring and ageless and infinite was my family's love.

Suddenly I felt Mom and Pop beside me, to my left and right, holding me up. I felt Mom's family behind me, the ones I had never known, on whose soil I walked. Their hands braced the small of my back and between my shoulder blades, moving me forward. In my mind's eye, the Sheerans were straight ahead, beckoning to me. "You can do it, Jimmy!" they called out, smiling. "We know ya can!" Their voices in my ears drowned out everything else and allowed me to walk with my head up and to look proud and unafraid.

I stared directly into the eyes of the German officers and their wives and collaborators. I smiled as we began to march.

"Look around ya, Jimmy!" I heard Lud say. "See what's really going on. Don't let 'em fool ya."

The spectators moved with us. There weren't thousands in the streets; it was just a small crowd assembled by the Germans to heap scorn upon the prisoners for the newsreel cameras. Looking beyond the detractors, I saw the *real* French citizens sitting and standing on a high wall about a hundred yards away. They waved their arms overhead, pumped their fists in the air, and flashed us the V for Victory. Seeing those French patriots galvanized me.

I continued to march in the very front with as confident a smile as I could muster. As I neared the newsreel operators along with a concentrated group of detractors, I spotted a young woman in her mid-twenties, looking at me and nodding as a cameraman spoke to her and pointed in my direction.

I knew she was going to spit in my face.

An opportunity was presenting itself to me, and I knew exactly what to do. As I approached, gathering my own saliva, she separated herself from the crowd and ran toward me. The cameraman was on the move, too, staying behind her. I tensed, ready, as she did exactly as I had suspected: She spat in my face. I sprayed her good.

A soldier burst from the crowd, shouting in German. As we marched past the bank of cameras again, another soldier gripped the muzzle of his rifle like a baseball bat and took a swing. He hit me across the middle of my back and knocked me to the ground. I went down hard.

I heard the crowd cheering and laughing. Tears sprung to my eyes, but I refused to look beaten. I refused to show pain or injury or fear. I forced myself to stand and even smile. I walked on and turned to look at the French people standing on the wall. Their enthusiasm reminded me of my football days. I had just scored a touchdown.

CHAPTER 8

Once the newsreel filming was complete, the guards marched our column down a blacktop driveway that dead-ended at a red-brick structure. It looked like an institution, and the sun glinted on the upper half of its many double-hung windows. Each window was open, and SS troops—identifiable by the black uniform—crowded in the lower half, watching us. I felt the burden of their ominous gaze.

"Gestapo headquarters," Burnie Rainwater muttered from behind me.

We were herded into a courtyard where the guards shoved us against the building. Spit rained down on us from the troops in the windows, but that did not matter; I refused to feel insulted. Considering the evil acts for which the SS was known, I waited for them to pick us off with bullets, shooting fish in a barrel, for a summer afternoon's amusement. Fortunately we were not confined for long in that area.

In that small space I found my buddy Hal Christiansen, who had been with me since training camp. We had quite a reunion. He had been captured shortly after I had been and taken to various temporary camps. Huff was there, too. He had been trucked into Paris the day before, with Captain McKnight. I introduced him to Ralph. He already knew Burnie.

I glanced over at the captain. The last time I had seen the once-dapper officer was shortly before my pal Johnny Simpson had lost his hand. McKnight looked awful. I wondered how it must be for an officer to be held captive.

Hal and I didn't have much time to catch up. The guards marched us to La Gare du Nord, a Paris train station. During the truck ride to Paris and now during our movement inside the city, evidence everywhere indicated the extent of the bombing.

The guards brought us to concrete train platforms. Everyone was anxious for us to get moving somewhere. The German soldiers were jumpy, and their edginess frightened us, but we had nowhere to go. We stood on a platform with about forty old French boxcars on the tracks behind us, hemming us in. When Pop had recounted his tales of World War I, he spoke of the French boxcars that transported troops and supplies throughout France. Half the size of those in the U.S., they were called "forty and eight" cars because they were only large enough to hold forty men or eight horses.

"The French railroad tracks were much narrower than the norm," Pop had explained, "to give them an advantage over the Germans. The Germans' trains couldn't use the French tracks to transport troops and supplies." He laughed and shook his head. "It was a real big nuisance to the enemy."

On the platform Goldberg again served as interpreter. "Count off into groups of fifty," he called out, "to facilitate the boarding of the boxcars."

Ralph and I stuck pretty close to each other in hopes of getting into the same group. He and I had hidden our friendship from the Germans, who would have separated us immediately as potential conspirators. Other than the two older guards who had watched us dig around the unexploded bombs, few men—including the other prisoners—knew we had a strong bond.

As the counting hit the forties and approached us, I started to worry about our sticking together. He and I had been together since St. Lo, and the thought of separation devastated me. He had not only provided true and steady friendship but a strong link to home, family, and friends.

"Forty-eight," said Burnie Rainwater.

"Forty-nine," said Captain McKnight.

"Fifty," I murmured.

"One," said Ralph.

I felt numb as Ralph went with his group to line up opposite a boxcar. I flashed him a wan smile and a thumbs-up. He grinned and good-naturedly gave me the finger.

Goldberg hollered at us to stand in formation while the Germans completed arrangements to ship us out to Germany, so I moved to stand closer to my group. After a short while, nearly all of us sat down on the cold concrete platform. Our display of defiance and unity made me feel a little better, but the relief was fleeting; our small expressions of free will were meaningless because, whether we stood or sat, we were still prisoners.

I tried another trick: Making a connection to my family had raised my spirits at the Arc de Triomphe, so I did it again. Pop could have traveled in the very boxcar I was to enter. They certainly looked World War I vintage. As the idea settled over me, I felt better for a moment.

Each car had wooden sliding doors and one window, a foot square, laced with barbed wire. When we loaded up, I would study whatever covered the window on the inside. This scrutiny was not unusual for me; I had trained myself in childhood to focus on details. Even then it was a survival technique because I had difficulty reading. To compensate, I paid close attention to everything that transpired in the classroom. I kept up with my class by recalling in detail what I had seen and heard in class lessons and discussions.

I smiled to myself, thinking of the window. No matter what precautions the Germans had taken, the aperture was just large enough for a man to squeeze through it and escape. Even better, the window was located at the back of the boxcar, within easy reach of a sturdy vertical bar affixed to the exterior. Any man who wedged his head and shoulders through the opening could grab the bar that was only eighteen inches away, pull himself out, and then swing onto the platform between the cars. From there he could jump off the train.

I quickly looked away, not wanting anyone to notice my interest.

Goldberg served as the interpreter for the entire trainload of prisoners. Accompanied by six German soldiers, he walked along the platform from group to group and confirmed we were going to a permanent POW camp in Germany. The trip would take three days and two nights. "Men will die on those cars," I thought. Many of the soldiers were sick or wounded. Guys in my group had wounds that had not healed. My feet were scarred, and a shrapnel wound left my back aching, but nothing I'd die from. The ones who were much worse, whose skin was pasty white, were goners.

"Each group of fifty men has two German soldiers assigned to guard them," he continued grimly. "They'll take turns riding on the roof of each boxcar. If you try to escape, they will shoot you. For every man who tries to escape or manages to escape, the Germans will kill ten of us for not preventing it.

"They're going to give us something to eat when we board. It'll have to last the trip. We won't be getting any more."

"What about water?"

"We'll be given a drink of water, too, and we'll stop for water each day—if we cooperate," Goldberg said, flicking a glance at the Germans. He didn't believe it, either.

Then Goldberg made eye contact with me. I had never seen such misery in any man's face. This ordeal had turned him into an old man. I believed that if I got back home, I would be able to go forward with my life and be, at my core, pretty much the same person I had been when I shipped out. After looking into the depths of Goldberg's eyes that moment and seeing straight through to his heart, I knew he was changed forever. Even if his body managed to survive, the light in his soul had gone out.

We were each given a two-inch length of hard sausage and a piece of bread crawling with maggots.

"Does anybody have any extra maggots?" someone joked.

"Hey! It ain't fair!" another complained. "He got more maggots than me."

But no man gave away his share. We picked off the maggots and inhaled the bread.

More than bread, we needed water. Hunger became less noticeable the longer I went without food, but my thirst only increased exponentially, and the taste of water—even dirty water—was better than nothing and satisfied me for hours. Our stomachs had been so empty we seldom needed to take a leak or crap. Ironic: We were finally being fed but wouldn't have a place to shit for three days.

Everyone noticed that there were no Red Cross markings on this train, nor any indications that it was carrying POWs. We had been trained to look for them. "Hey, Interpreter," someone with a British accent called out, "what happens if the train is strafed by Allied fighters or dive bombers? Will they let us out to find protection?"

A German soldier appeared to understand the question, and he screamed, *"Nein! Sie werden verschlossen innerhalb des geschlossenen Güterwagens bleiben, zu den Sie zugeteilt sind!"*

"No," Goldberg translated. "We stay locked in the car we are assigned to."

This was frightening to all of us. We were well aware of the Allied superiority in the air. Our aircraft targeted everything German that moved. The British were famous for their nighttime strafing, and the French Resistance had made a great contribution by sabotaging German trains and equipment. If our planes attacked us, we would just have to stand there and take it, as we had done in the trucks. Some would be killed. Others would live to see the inside of a German POW camp. Who would be considered the lucky ones?

The guards climbed to the roof of the boxcar, and we were ordered to board. I took a few deep breaths of fresh air. None of us had washed since before we jumped on June 5. By my reckoning it was approximately June 28. Once we were locked inside with the stench, we would have trouble breathing. I looked at the window to see half-inch boards nailed across it—no air from there. I noticed a crack in the floorboards and put my jump jacket on it and lay down. Finding a crack was important to me. The air from the crack might save my life.

The sliding door slammed shut with a solid *thud*, leaving us in darkness. The locking bolt slid into place, and the train rolled out of the station.

In the gloom I could not make out who was around me or how close or far they were. For all that I could see, they could have been yards from where I sat or only inches away. I knew Huff and Christiansen, McKnight and Rainwater were in my boxcar, but even that made no difference.

More than three weeks had passed since D-Day. I had experienced a range of emotions, some of them the darkest I had ever known. Before the war, I had felt fear but never the terror of recent days. I had been angry, but rage shook me now. I had been lonely, but the utter desolation isolating me now defied description. Never had I let myself fall into despair . . . until now.

At that moment dread filled me. I had signed up to fight for other people's freedom, only to lose my own. My last chance at freedom vanished with the slamming of the heavy boxcar door. Every moment took me closer to Germany, more inextricably into the clutches of the enemy. The only path my future could take was defined by the railroad tracks. Options and opportunities no longer existed. The end was at hand, already written.

The rhythm and rocking of the boxcar lulled me into a sort of listlessness. I felt no anxiety or nervousness, no sorrow or regret. I was beyond emotion. I felt gone.

Light from the crack in the floorboard awoke me. I lay quietly, aware of the changing rhythm of the train. Many times it stopped and started, stopped and started, and then finally it jerked to a halt. I heard the bolts thrown back on the boxcars. I felt disoriented. Could we be—? No, three days could not have passed yet—unless I had lost consciousness.

Our door slid open, and sunlight stung my eyes, but the fresh air felt as warm and sweet as an embrace. Outside, green and yellow were enmeshed in a blur that could not be a POW camp.

We were allowed to climb out. We remained in our groups as the Germans performed a head count: *ein, zwei, drei . . . achtundvierzig, neunundvierzig, fünfzig.*

No food, but some water—a reward. As we drank, a train loaded with heavy military equipment passed by on a parallel track, heading toward the front line, toward our buddies.

I looked for Ralph, and he and I drifted close enough to speak quietly. We speculated that we were among the first prisoners of war transported by train to Germany . . . worried about being strafed while locked in a box . . . taking small comfort that at least the Germans would get hit, too.

"Zurück hinein! Jeder! Jetzt!" the guards ordered, gesturing with their weapons at the train. Ralph and I quickly asked around if anyone would switch so he and I could ride together. No one wanted to chance it, and I couldn't blame them.

One of our guards climbed to the roof of the boxcar and ordered us, in German, to count off again while he kept his rifle on us. The bravado seemed unnecessary. We were broken men.

I approached another guard and pointed at the back of my wrist. He showed me his watch. Four-forty. About another four hours of dangerous daylight, I thought.

"You have an appointment?" Burnie Rainwater asked.

I felt fortunate that he and I had ended up in the same pack. The Indian was a good soldier. When he served as my assistant gunner, I learned that no one had better instincts than he.

Like me, he spoke proudly about his father, a World War I veteran like Pop. While my dad settled down, Burnie's father, a farmer, couldn't extinguish his newfound taste for adventure. He kept the family on the move, and Burnie and his siblings never stayed long in any school. Whatever they learned they picked up on the quick.

A German standing in front of the sliding door helped me climb into the boxcar. He turned his face from the stench. I wish I could have gotten away from it, too.

I claimed my spot on the floor, and when darkness fell, I used my jump knife to dig away at the thin fracture and increase the airflow. I could not risk altering it very much, for more light coming in the next morning would attract notice. I rolled up my jump jacket, lay my head on it, and thought about my parents, who had met on a train . . .

Pop had entered the service along with seven of his closest friends from Passaic. All were Irish-Americans except Joe Weigle, whose family was French-Alsatian. They arrived in France in 1918. Pop quickly rose to the rank of corporal, and several of his Passaic pals were assigned to his detail. They viewed his fluency in the French language as a means of meeting beautiful local girls.

All were eager to serve. Tough Tommy Mooney always enjoyed a fight, so a bloody war held great potential for a swell time. A dangerous mission outside the Argonne Forest corrected any notion that the war would be fun, and it won them a short leave in an army camp where soldiers could rest and relax. Their transportation was a local train with frequent stops that lasted ten to fifteen minutes, so passengers could get on and off at each station.

At that time the trains carried both civilians and soldiers, who could be combatants on the battlefield. For example, a German soldier might sit quite contentedly alongside a French one. World War I was so different from World War II and, indeed, so was the world then from now.

When Pop and his nine men boarded the train, he noticed my

mother sitting next to a window. He knew from that first moment the raven-haired beauty, dressed all in black, would be his wife, and he was determined to make a favorable impression on her before any of his buddies could enter the competition.

"Regarde! La plus belle fille de toute la France est ici!" he said in perfect French. Then he blew my mother a kiss.

My mother blushed shyly, and Pop thought he had accomplished his goal. In the next instant, though, he realized she was not traveling alone. Entering the small circle of his tunnel vision was the beauty's chaperone—an older woman not at all pleased by my father's bold behavior. She instructed the lovely girl to ignore him.

This fed Pop's determination to do everything in his power to make a long-lasting impression. At the first station stop, he and his loyal men hurried out to the platform, assembled in parade formation under his beloved's window, and performed precision drills for ten minutes while he barked out the commands. Then with a blazing smile, he looked up at the beauty's window, only to see the chaperone's profile. The woman had changed seats with her charge.

At each stop, Pop ordered his men off the train and onto the platform. He searched to make eye contact with my mother, whom he saw peeking around her chaperone's bulk to look through the window. He snapped off a sharp salute after each command, and at the end of the performance, he blew her a kiss. Pop repeated this routine at each stop, and he grew more and more enthusiastic as his men, perspiring profusely, paraded back and forth under her window.

When Pop and his men departed the train at Chateau Thierry, he ordered them to stand at attention and salute his future bride as the train continued on toward Paris. She waved goodbye as the train pulled away from the station . . .

The smell of urine on the dark, dank POW train brought me back to reality. The stale air was dense with the smell of fifty bodies. I had stopped twisting my knife into the thick wood floorboards because I had made no more than a half-inch gash since our last stop. My lack of progress mocked me, told me I wasn't thinking straight. I wrapped my arms tightly around my body, wondering if I might suffocate.

"Sick old horses on our way to the slaughterhouse," someone said into my ear.

I peered up into the darkness.

Burnie, kneeling above me, shook my arms loose from the grip I had around my torso. His black eyes burned like coals in the darkness.

"Jimmy, do you want to try to escape?" he asked.

"What?"

"I have to get out of here and away from these bastards!" he said. "Do you want to try it with me?"

"You bet your ass I do." I tried to sit up but couldn't.

Burnie clutched my arm and helped me, while he hunkered down. "I do not know what chance we have—"

"We've got no chance if we let the Germans decide for us."

"—and the risks are great."

"We have nothing to lose."

"And those we leave behind?" he said.

No doubt the Germans would make good on their threat to kill ten POWs for each man who tried to escape. Twenty men would pay with their life for our freedom. Thinking of it made me sick. I cared deeply about my friends' fate, but ultimately I was responsible only for myself and to the government of the United States of America. I had joined the army to fight the Germans, and I sure as hell wasn't going to be able to do that locked in a boxcar barreling east down the tracks.

"Anyone who wants to join us can," I said. "Any man who stays behind understands the risk."

Burnie and I felt our way along the wall, searching for some weak spot in the construction. As we made our way around, we told the others of our plan and invited them to join us. Whoever wanted to go should move to stand near the window, which we learned was the only possible way to escape. I was grateful to have studied the boxcar in such great detail at the train station and when we stopped for water. We would need to remove the boards covering the opening, then deal with the heavy barbed wire on the outside. Our only tools were my jump knife and our fingers.

"I think my jump knife is strong enough to clip the wire," I told Burnie.

"What about the guards?" he whispered.

"The darkness will hide us."

"The others will try to stop us," he said.

I nodded. Leaving other men behind, putting their lives in jeopardy, was a heavy burden. Again we debated our decision, but our resolve was strong. We had to try an escape. Excitement replaced despair. Only six inches separated us from freedom. Getting through the window would be hard work, but once the way was open, we could leap to the platform and from the train and be free. *Free!*

I knew without any doubt that some benevolent power watched over me, guiding me toward the right decisions and actions. I believed my mother had invoked Joan of Arc and won her divine protection for me when she had given me permission to enlist. Mom had been clutching her treasured medallion of St. Joan, and maybe because it had been on my mother's birthday, the saints had been predisposed to granting her a wish.

Three other American prisoners agreed to go with us. Neither

Burnie nor I knew those soldiers. I waited for Huff and Christiansen to join us, but they never came over. I felt a special responsibility to them because we had been together since training camp. We were good and genuine friends. I wove through the press of bodies to find them. They were sitting together, and I squatted next to them, wriggling down between two men who smelled septic.

"Come on, guys!" I pleaded. "At least give it a try!"

Huff shook his head. "I understand what you're trying to do, but Hal and I want to take our chances staying with the car."

"Hal?" I said, looking at him.

He shook his head.

"Why?"

He looked at me with pained eyes. "I—I don't think you have a chance of making it," he said. "I wish you and Burnie would reconsider and stay with us here."

"We've been on the move for two full days and two nights," Huff said. "My guess is that we're out of France and somewhere deep into Germany. Even if you get off the train—"

"We'll head for Switzerland. From there we'll try to get back to our troops."

Huff looked at me with resignation. "There's no talking you out of it, is there?"

I shook my head. "Any chance of talking you into it?"

Huff grinned. "Naw." He took my hand. "But, Jesus, Jimmy, God bless you for your courage. I'll pray for you."

I found my way back to Burnie and the three others. He looked up at me expectantly, and I shook my head. I was disappointed, but I couldn't dwell on it. We had to plan our escape. I hoped these new guys could be counted on to act smart.

"If any of us is shot as we jump," one of them said, "no one has any obligation to help. We're on our own. Agreed?" His eyes bored into us.

We all nodded.

"No one feels guilty about leaving someone behind to die," another guy said. "If we turn back to help one guy, we're putting everyone else at risk."

"That's right," Burnie agreed.

Putting everyone else at risk reminded me of the German's threat to kill ten for every one man who tried to escape. We were five. That meant fifty would be shot because of us. The boxcar held fifty. We had just condemned the entire group to death.

As Burnie and I went to work loosening the boards on the window, I felt McKnight's eyes on my back. The boards fit tightly together, but at the ends was just enough room to get my fingertips in and begin to pry the wood loose. We worked so hard on the first board, our fingers bled. The other three on our team helped us yank off the first board, and then prying off the rest was relatively simple. With each one came a blast of fresh air. If only for that, our efforts were of value.

Next, the barbed wire.

"Uh, pardon . . ."

I looked behind me to see a British paratrooper.

"Terribly sorry I can't join you. Have a wife and two little ones at home, you see, and my first duty is to them." He cleared his throat. "I, uh, think my best bet is to go on to the camp in Germany. But I'd like you to have this."

He handed me a government-issued escape kit. "Might come in handy, my good man."

I saw a small hacksaw blade. I looked up and grinned at him. "Hey, thanks!" I pulled out a soft cloth. "What—?"

"Map of France, on white silk," he said. "Quite the thing."

"I don't know what to say!" I told him. "This is a huge help, really boosts our chances!" I pumped his hand. "I wish you good luck and, um, a happy reunion with your family."

I respected his thoughtfulness and conviction that he was choosing the right path for himself. His hope was so strong, I believed everything would work out for him. But my journey would be different.

I went to find Hoffman and Christiansen and showed them the hacksaw. "Change your mind?"

"Good luck, Jimmy," they said, and remained seated.

"Good luck to you, too," I said. We shook hands, then I pulled them into a three-way hug.

I went back toward the window to find McKnight talking to Burnie. As soon as he noticed me, the officer turned on me. "Private Sheeran, your duty is to obey orders, and I am ordering you to stay put on this train."

"I am obeying orders, sir," I said in a respectful tone as I passed Burnie the hacksaw. "My duty is to return to my outfit, and this is the best way I can do that, sir."

"I am responsible for all the men in the boxcar." He seethed. "Your scheme endangers every last one of them!"

"Sir, you and every other man in this car are welcome to join us when we escape," I replied. "Anyone who chooses to remain behind has, I believe, made the decision well aware of that risk."

While McKnight and I were conversing, Burnie had gone back to the barbed wire. He sawed in one area while one of the other men used my jump knife in another. Soon the barbed wire was cut, and Burnie did his best to push it aside. I laid my jacket along the window ledge to protect us from the sharp ends. The three strangers were small-boned men, and they went through first, as smooth as otters, and disappeared into the night. Burnie waited with me, so we would land near each other. As soon as he vanished through the window, I turned and saluted McKnight. "Goodbye, sir. God bless you and the men under your command."

With tears in my eyes I flashed the V for Victory to Hal, Huff, and the Brit who had eased our way with his selflessness. Then I turned, and all the strength in the world filled my arms, shoulders, and legs. I felt like a human cannonball as freedom called my name.

I was bigger and broader than the others, and my shoulders tried to hold me back, but nothing could stop me now. I would have chewed off one of my arms to fit through that opening. I scraped through, swung out, and snatched my jump jacket off the barbed wire.

I reached for the vertical bar. The train was a fast fucker, flashing down the track at about thirty miles per hour. I got a good grip on the metal bar, took a deep breath, and swung my legs toward the platform between the cars.

CHAPTER 9

Eight hands grabbed me and pulled me to the platform. I gained my balance and joined the others. I felt safer than I had in a long time. The feeling was electric. We grinned maniacally at one another for a moment, then got back to business. We men had precious little strength to hold on to the rocking, bucking platform, and the German soldiers would be ready to blow our brains out. We had to jump soon.

I had no idea where we were, and the train was rushing us toward captivity at thirty miles per hour. I peered out at the darkness. I could just make out the embankment along the track. It looked about five feet high. Along the edge of the tracks was a bed of large blue stones, and white posts standing about a hundred feet apart probably secured fencing.

If I looked out rather than down, the train did not seem to be moving as fast. I did not hesitate. Within moments of hitting the coupling platform, I threw myself into the void, as if I were jumping with a parachute.

The impact felt like taking a hard hit in a football game. I landed on the blue stones and knew I had cut up my knees, but I didn't think I had broken any bones. I heard the next man hit the ground, then the next and the next. Then I heard shots.

I leapt to my feet and was on the move. The soldier who had been shot wrapped himself around a post. He had to be conscious to hold on like that. Despite our pact we all crouched down and ran to him. The train kept moving; the *bump, bump, bump* of the wheels on the tracks kept time with my racing heartbeat.

"Go!" he yelled at us. "You can't wait! You have to go!"

We tried to move him, but his lower extremities would not move. "Go! Please!"

He was right. We had no medical supplies to help him, and carrying him would be a death sentence for the rest of us. We carried him to the side of the tracks, said a prayer for him, and took off down the track until the train was a good distance away. As I ran, I wished I had learned the name of that brave man we left behind. I would have called his parents and let them know how their son died in pursuit of freedom under extremely difficult conditions.

Out of breath, we paused to consider what to do next.

"You think we're in France or in Germany?" one fellow asked.

"Germany," Burnie said.

"I think so, too," I said. "We were told the trip would take three days and two nights, and this is the second night."

No one contradicted us.

"Think another train's behind ours? That'll be coming along soon?" the other asked.

We had no way of knowing. Our only certainty was that we had to move quickly.

"I vote for following the track back to Paris," suggested a soldier we didn't know.

I thought that was a crazy idea, but I was struck by his wanting to vote on a strategy. Land of the Free. "What do you think, Burnie?"

"Switzerland," he said.

I nodded, seeing the logic in that. Whether we were in eastern France or western Germany, Switzerland would still be to the south. We would have a chance to get back to the allied troops from that neutral country.

We didn't waste time trying to talk the others into following our plan; four men traveling together would attract more attention than a pair. We would all be safer by splitting up. We said goodbye and good luck and parted ways.

The small moon helped us establish a direction. We took off on a route perpendicular to the east-west tracks. Burnie and I did not speak. We just ran, as quickly and as quietly as possible, ten yards from each other, through open fields. We did not need to discuss avoiding wooded areas; if any German troops were in the area, they would bivouac in the woods.

I was greatly comforted by Burnie's presence. I had known him a long time and trusted him. Between the two of us, we had everything we needed to get where we wanted to go . . . except fluency in French. My thoughts returned to my parents. Maybe through some miracle a long-dormant gene would suddenly allow the language to flow from my lips when I needed it. A smile eased my tension as I thought about my parents. My mother's recollection of seeing my father for the first time on the train to Paris always triggered much hilarity in the Sheeran household . . .

According to Mom, she was attracted to Pop's liveliness and openness as much as he was overcome by her beauty. While his brashness startled her chaperone, Madame Blondeau, my mother was totally enthralled that the spirited young officer could speak French without an American accent.

As Pop had suspected, Madame Adele Blondeau immediately changed seats with Mom to hide her from "that fresh American." While he barked out commands for close-order drills under the train's window, my mother was greatly amused.

"Ignore him, Lucie!" Madame Blondeau insisted. "What makes him think he can act like a general?"

Lucie Munier, however, had always been a willful girl, and she chose to ignore her chaperone's instructions. "The heck with that!" she thought. "We will probably never see each other again." Aloud she said, "I don't know that soldier's name or where he is stationed, but he seems very nice, and he has made me laugh for the first time in days."

That was significant, for my mother was in the midst of enduring the saddest days of her young life, just after her parents . . .

A cough nearby interrupted my reverie. I crouched down, signaled to Burnie, and made my way over to him. I told him what I had heard.

His white blocky teeth shone in the darkness. "Don't worry, Jim," he said matter-of-factly. "I heard it, too. That was a cow. They sound just like humans when they cough."

"You're shitting me."

"No. It's true."

At that moment I comprehended more accurately how well my Cherokee buddy from North Carolina and I complemented and needed each other to survive. "Thanks, Burnie." I thumped him on the back.

He nodded, and we started to run again, moving thirty feet apart.

We ran all night, thinking we were in a flat, open field between wooded areas. It was dark, and a light drizzle refreshed me. I tilted my head back to collect more water on my filthy face as I ran. I stuck out my tongue and wet my mouth. I scrubbed at my scalp without breaking stride.

The light rain intensified nature's fragrances, and even though I couldn't see the green, growing lushness around me, I could smell its vibrant aliveness, and after so much sickness and death, it brought tears to my eyes.

Maybe *that* was the dormant gene in my city-boy's blood, a deep and intense connection with nature from my mother, who had been born and raised on a farm. Her love of the land was rooted in many generations of Munier farmers who grew crops and raised horses and caught fish in the Meuse River. The ancestral land was partly in Domremy and partly in the village of Greux. Every year her father plowed the profits from his harvest back into his land, and eventually he had one of the largest farms in the region.

My mother's favorite time of year was the grape harvest, when all the village children would gather at the Muniers' farm, climb barefoot into huge vats—as many as ten children could fit into a single vat—and stomp on the grapes. A party atmosphere prevailed. Some years the harvest was so abundant, the festivities—and the work— would go on for a week, after which her father made the wine.

He stored bottles of wine and vinegar in the farmhouse cellar, along with bushels of potatoes and other root vegetables and rounds of aging cheese. Upstairs in the huge fireplace, the family hung sausages and hams, and in the attic, the Muniers dehydrated apples in the dry heat.

In the orchards and groves, the family picked whatever fruits they wanted. Mom's favorite was a small, yellow plum, which she called a *mirabelle*. It grew only on grassy hilltops around Domremy, and for only a few weeks in July. "It had the most sweet flavor in all the world," she would say with great nostalgia. "You could taste its sweetness for days."

At daybreak, Burnie and I crested a hill that overlooked a small village of approximately thirty modest, L-shaped dwellings. We cautiously made our way down the hill, moving quickly from behind the trunk of one full, lush tree to another until we came to a large bush at the settlement's edge. We crawled under the bush and waited for some indication of our whereabouts. We didn't know if we were in France or Germany but, for safety's sake, assumed we were in Germany.

I took a good look at Burnie in the breaking sunlight. He had a nasty gash on his head, and blood mixed with sweat and filth caked his closely shorn scalp. My legs were cut up, but I was more worried about him. Only the will to survive and a miracle could have superseded our debilitation caused by the starvation and injuries we had suffered.

The closest house was large and gray, and nearby was its barn whose double doors were open, allowing us to see all the way through it.

Burnie and I patiently watched the house and waited for some sign of life. Suddenly a goose flew out of the barn, and a little boy, maybe four years old, was in pursuit.

"Vous êtes une terreur sainte!" a girl yelled, and as we watched, a young redhead wearing a blue dress covered by a white apron burst from the barn and ran after him.

I grinned. "Burnie, I think we're in luck—and in France. She just called that kid a holy terror."

"I thought you didn't speak French."

I laughed. "About the only two words I know are *holy terror*. It's what my mom and my aunt Jeanne called me when I was being bad."

The girl continued to scold her charge and shooed him into the house.

"That barn looks good, Jimmy," Burnie said. "Two doors. Two ways out." He rubbed his chin, thinking. "Should we make a run for it?"

"Yeah. We need to look at our injuries." We were both in pretty bad shape. Distancing ourselves from the train tracks earned us the luxury of sitting without worrying about capture ... at least for a little while. From the protection of the barn we could decide what to do next.

We dashed inside the building. A loft stretched the full length of the interior, and at its center was a large mound of hay. "Brother," Burnie said, "I believe that hay is calling my name—"

"—and singing a lullaby."

We scrambled up into the loft and dug into the center of the mound, where no Germans would find us.

"Nothing smells better than fresh-cut hay," Burnie said. "My dad had me working in the barn when I was only—"

"Ah ah-ah-*choo!*"

Within thirty seconds, I was coughing, sneezing, hacking, and wheezing. Hot, sticky tears streamed from my burning eyes. My throat and nose were congested with phlegm. "Ah-*choo!*"

"Shut up, Jimmy! Someone'll hear you!"

I sneezed, rapid-fire, into the silk map I dug from my pocket. "They wah-wah-wah—*Ah-choo! Ah-choo! Wesh-choo!*—hear us." I gasped. The map was soaking wet.

"C'mon," Burnie said, casting a sad glance at the soft hay before we climbed down from the loft. "We'll find a better place."

As I descended I noticed a huge beehive, almost taller than I, in the perfect shape of a pear. Food. "Burnie," I whispered, and pointed at the hive.

He looked at the beehive and nodded to me.

"You're an Indian, Burnie. How do we get that honey?"

"I don't know how *we* get it," he said, "but I'm not getting near that thing."

"I have to eat," I said. "Since we're in France, I think we can go to the back door and ask that girl for help."

Burnie's shrug said, *Lead the way.*

I decided to tell her we were hungry, sick, and injured . . . as if she wouldn't be able to tell just by looking at us. I could almost taste the bread she would offer, with marmalade. Or a chunk of sausage. And cheese. My hand was poised to knock on the door when I saw the huge red swastika scratched into the wood. We immediately ran back to the barn.

"Someone must have scratched the swastika as a warning," I whispered to Burnie.

"Whoever lives there must be a German sympathizer."

"What'll we do?"

We had to resolve this situation immediately. Just beyond the village, an open field stretched into the distance.

"Should we run?"

"No," I said. "I don't have the energy." I glanced back at the house. Three people in the second-floor window looked back at me: two men—one of them armed with a rifle—and a woman.

"Burnie," I whispered, "don't look now, but I think we're in trouble."

"Just stay calm," he said. I followed his gaze and saw a man walking toward us with long, sure strides. Burnie and I were about to have our first encounter since jumping from the train. A wave of nausea threatened to take me down.

The man stopped a few feet away, then lobbed a piece of bread toward us and waited.

"Merci!" I said, and ripped the bread in half to share with Burnie. *"Merci beaucoup!"*

I stuffed the bread in my mouth and tried to talk around it, but the Frenchman motioned me to silence. *"Vous mangez,"* he said kindly. *"J'attendrai."*

Fresh bread. Bread without maggots. Bread without mold. I swallowed, then patted my stomach and thanked him again. While I explained as best I could our situation, a second man approached us. He directed us to follow him. The two Frenchmen escorted us into the house to the right of the gray home, then led us down to a wine cellar. *"Ceci est notre cellier,"* he told us, and gestured toward a small wooden table and four chairs.

Burnie and I sat down, and the men poured us each a small glass of red wine.

The men spoke little English, but I understood them well enough through their gestures and from having listened to my parents speaking French. The men wanted to know our destination and goals. I answered that we wanted to get to the Swiss border and were hopeful the French Underground might help us accomplish that. I also requested French civilian clothes and a doctor.

The men said nothing. Their expressions told us nothing. They got up and went upstairs.

A short while later, a woman with sharp features and a pointy chin came downstairs carrying two plates with eggs and a hunk of bread. The French cook eggs differently than Americans, and when I looked at my plate, I saw a one-egg omelet that could have been prepared by my mother.

I was so hungry, I wolfed down the food and then licked the plate clean. Starvation had shrunk my stomach, and soon I felt horribly sick. The same thing happened to Burnie.

We sat. We waited. We slept.

We had the time to wash ourselves, and the woman who had served us the omelets now brought down a bowl of water, a bar of soap, and some rags, then left us to our ablutions. I helped Burnie clean his head wound and tried to conceal the extent of my concern. I dropped my trousers and examined my knees. I had cut them up pretty good on the rail bed rocks.

"You do not have attractive knees," Burnie said with a straight face.

"When I was a kid," I told him, "my next-door neighbor, Mr. Rollander, caught me stealing lilacs from his yard. He chased after me, but I outran him, no problem. Then I tripped and fell in a pile of broken glass and hurt my knees really badly."

"That's what the scars are from?" Burnie asked.

"Yeah." I shook my head. "But I kept stealing lilacs and kept running. The Rollanders never caught me again."

"When we get back home," Burnie said, "please do not live next door to me."

Humor kept us going in those tense hours in the cellar. We did not know if the men intended to help or betray Burnie and me. By hiding us, they endangered themselves and other villagers who weren't even aware of our presence. By turning us over to the Germans, they would win favor with the invaders. Which would they choose?

The French were not indifferent to the Germans. A huge resistance movement had sprung up, comprised of individual groups serving many valuable purposes. The Maquis was an aggressive, armed guerrilla army. Another group provided the Allies with information about German troop whereabouts, movements, equipment, and numbers. The French Underground, much like the Underground Railroad in American history, hid fugitives and moved them out of harm's way in a network of homes, caves, and encampments in the forest. When one of our hosts had referred to the cellar as a *caverne*, or cave, I'd felt a flush of hope.

Offsetting my optimism was the swastika on the neighbor's door. The German military was characteristically brutal when it suspected collusion with the Resistance. As with the soldiers' threat to kill ten prisoners on the train for every one escapee, the Germans would execute members of the local populace to retaliate for an act of sabotage. Sometimes the victims were guilty only of being handy when the Germans were looking for people to kill.

In some instances, death was the easy way out. The SS and Gestapo thought nothing of torturing their suspects, torturing the children of their suspects, and sending the daughters away to military brothels.

So which would it be? We had no choice but to sit and wait and hope for the best.

CHAPTER 10

Early the next morning we heard men's voices and the sound of heavy footfalls moving across the floor above us. Soon the wait would be over, and Burnie and I would know what fate held in store for us.

Five strangers came down the stairs. Two sat with us at the wooden table. The others stood along the walls, arms folded across their chest. Their eyes never left us. The youngest appeared about fifteen—a wiry kid with eyes that issued a dare and oversized fists to make good on it. I liked him right away. One looked around Pop's age—he joined us at the table. The other three were probably in their twenties.

"What do you need?" he asked in English, and slid his identification across the table to me.

His name was Abel. Perfect. He turned out to be a chief in that region's Underground. His companion at the table was an Underground partisan.

"French clothing. A musette bag to stuff our uniforms and dog tags into."

"A weapon," Burnie said.

"I have my jump knife," I said, "but Burnie doesn't have anything to protect himself."

"You need a doctor," Abel said to Burnie, pointing at his head.

Burnie's hand went to his wound, and he touched it gently with his fingertips. "Jimmy does, too. His knees are shredded."

"I try to get you one, but I make no promise."

"We'll be grateful for anything you can do," I said.

"Where exactly are we?" Burnie asked.

"Apparently you are in God's hands." Abel grinned and shook his head in wonder. "Had you not noticed the swastika on the *Bürger-meister*'s door, you would have met a German sympathizer in charge of feeding their military with local produce."

He paused and let that sink in. "You are also in France, close to the Belgian border." His expression turned grim. "Many of our sons and brothers were soldiers captured by the Germans at the Maginot Line." He nearly spat the word *German*. "We will help you in the same way we pray someone is helping them now."

He was referring to a line of concrete fortifications, tank obstacles, machine-gun posts, and other defenses France constructed along its borders with Germany and Italy after World War I. The French believed the fortification would give them time to mobilize their army in the event of attack and compensate for their relatively small standing army.

It hadn't worked. The Germans put a decoy force opposite the Line while a second force cut through Belgium, the Netherlands, and the Argonne Forest north of the main French defenses. By avoiding the Maginot Line, the invaders had penetrated well into France in less than a week.

Abel stood and motioned us to rise. *"Levez-vous, s'il vous plait."*

When we did, he measured us with his eyes, then left with the others.

Down the stairs came our hostess, who had apparently been waiting for Abel's thumbs-up before introducing herself. Madame Lombard proved to be cheerful and chatty, occupying our attention until Abel returned with a doctor, musette bags, and French clothing, including tams, which provided more scalp coverage than a beret. That was a crucial choice; Burnie and I both had the short "butch" haircut of all American troops.

"You stay one more day," Abel said. "Someone will come for you. Wait for him."

I felt relieved a French companion would start us in the right direction and give us much-needed confidence to be out in the daylight.

"The first day of the journey may be the most difficult. You will have to cross a bridge to go over a canal. A German soldier checks all French identity cards at the bridge."

Abel must have read the question in my eyes, for he said, "We do not have the ability here to get you a forged card. Maybe farther along on your journey you will meet someone who can help you with that." He shrugged.

"What should we do?" I asked. I tried to seem calm, but my mind was already working on a strategy to sneak across the canal that night.

"We will lure the German guard away from his post long enough for you to cross over. Tomorrow your escort will come with a smart idea."

The doctor had cleaned out my cut knees and packed them with an herbal poultice. They were feeling less painful and swollen already.

"When you go out and begin your trek," Abel instructed, "do not act as if you are a fugitive. Walk naturally, relaxed, and only in the daylight. Avoid the woods. If you see Germans, just keep walking. Ignore them. Try not to speak at all to anyone."

The doctor, now disinfecting Burnie's gash, spoke quickly to Abel, who translated. "Never write down the names or addresses of people who assist you."

Again we thanked Abel and the doctor. Expressing the extent of our gratitude would be impossible, and we all knew it.

After they left, we stayed in the cellar and pulled on our secondhand clothes. Burnie and I had never seen each other in civilian garb. We were taller than most of the French, and the pants were way too short. We tried not to laugh at each other, but when Madame Lombard came down the stairs and saw us standing there, she let out a whoop, which got us going. We needed the release a good laugh afforded.

I asked Madame for a pencil or pen and a piece of paper so I could write a letter to my family. The odds of our surviving were slim, and I needed to let my family know I tried my best to be a credit to them and to America. I wanted to say that I refused to die as a prisoner and had escaped and was trying to get back to my unit. Most important, I wanted to tell them how much I loved them and how often thoughts of them had brought me through the most difficult moments.

Madame Lombard found a pencil after much searching, and the only one she could produce had such hard lead, my strokes were very light and difficult to see. When I finished my letter, I experienced a great relief—my family would not be disappointed in me because I had been taken prisoner.

Madame took the letter and held it to her heart, covering it with both hands. "I know how important," she said solemnly. "I promise to send away as very soon as France is free."

Switzerland was a long distance from the village, and we were eager to start the journey. The morning seemed interminable. Finally the teenager who had accompanied Abel on the first visit arrived in the afternoon. He pulled out a map, spread it across the table, and showed us we were in the Sedan section of France, at the northeastern corner of the country, near the borders with Germany, Belgium, and Luxembourg and very close to the Maginot Line. I took out the silk map the soldier on the POW train had given me, and we compared the two, to make sure Burnie and I could keep our bearings.

We gathered our belongings into the musette bags, slung the straps across our torsos, and bade Madame an affectionate *au revoir*.

I thought the teenager would be our escort, but I was in for a surprise. He told us our guides were in the yard, waiting for us. Outside were a young boy and girl, about eight and ten years old. They, too, lived in the village. Abel had thought of everything: the boy's hair was almost black like Burnie's and straight. The girl's coloring was a good match for my own. The boy took Burnie's hand, and the girl grasped mine, and off we went, looking more like young fathers on a stroll with their children than American GIs behind enemy lines.

Sometimes the children skipped ahead and brought us back an interesting pebble or a leaf. They sang songs. They giggled at who-knew-what. We traversed acres of rolling fields. I breathed deeply of the pure air and lifted my face to the warmth of the sun. Burnie was in his heaven, the out-of-doors.

Late in the afternoon we came to a steep decline with loose soil. The little boy picked up a walking stick for Burnie and me. *"Vous faites attention,"* he warned.

"We're accustomed to being careful," I replied.

We came to a house that the boy and girl seemed to know quite well. Without knocking, they opened the front door, and seated at a table were three older boys and a girl and their mother, who was about the same age as my own mother.

"Je suis Madame Petitpois," she said, rising. *"Vous êtes les bienvenus chez moi."*

"Thank you for having us, Madame," I replied, having recognized the word *maison,* house.

She was an attractive woman who had obviously been a great beauty. In heavily accented English, she introduced us to her children seated around the table. Her daughter, Odette, looked years beyond her age of sixteen, and she had inherited her mother's lovely features. "My boys and Odette will get you across the bridge."

As if that were a cue, Odette and two of her brothers got ready for the walk. Madame served us food and tea, and the little ones who had brought us there sat at the table and watched us eat.

"Once you are across the bridge," Madame said, "go to the village of Vandy. The priest is expecting you."

We went down a road that ran along the canal. Eventually the road turned into a path from which we could see farmhouses, a red barn, and then the guardhouse. I was able to discern the outline of one soldier holding a rifle. Others may have been out of my line of vision. Beyond the guardhouse, down an incline to the water, was the bridge.

"Sit there," Pierre said, pointing to the ledge of the canal. "Hang your feet over the canal and relax."

We four took off our shoes and did as Pierre instructed, leaning back on our elbows and watching the breeze play in the trees across the water. After a time, Odette and brother Charles left us. I watched them walk up the slope and approach the guardhouse.

In about a half hour, Charles returned alone. "You can go now," he said. "Odette is in the woods with the guard."

Pierre and Charles walked across the bridge with us. Charles pointed to a large hill in the distance. "That is the gendarmes' training camp. Avoid it. They are German collaborators."

"You will have to skirt that area by avoiding the roads," Pierre said. "Probably you have been told not to leave the roads. This is your only exception to that rule."

"Remember Vandy," Charles said. "Your next destination is Vandy. The priest's church has been blown nearly to bits by a bomb, but you'll find him inside or somewhere nearby."

They hugged us, kissed our cheeks, and wished us *bon chance.*

We embraced our friends, asked them to thank Odette, and left. We were on our own.

Within the hour we passed a pair of German soldiers. Their proximity frightened me, but apparently nothing about our appearance or demeanor drew attention, and we were not challenged. We walked on, and I felt more confident.

Needing to make contact with the priest before dark, we rested only about five minutes every hour or two. We came to another canal and the remnants of a bridge that had been blown up. The only way across the water was through it, and we got soaked. When we climbed up the bank, we could see Vandy ahead, and the badly charred steeple of the Catholic church. We headed for it.

"I'd like to find some farm tools to carry," Burnie said, "as part of our getup."

The area seemed populated by more German soldiers than French citizens, and although we tried to walk normally, the survival instinct added some speed to my gait. We came upon a discarded hoe and a shovel near a bomb crater outside Vandy, and Burnie and I each took one. The destruction worsened as we neared the blackened steeple, and when we came upon the remnants of the church, a tall mound of rubble sat like a giant molehill where the sanctuary had been.

I took a long look up at the steeple. I whispered, "This church must have been so beautiful, on the side of the mountain."

"It's a terrible shame," Burnie agreed quietly.

We walked around to the back of the property and found a flower garden and, just beyond, a school and a small shelter that probably had been a caretaker's shed. The sunlit yellows, reds, and greens were vibrant against the gray and black of the charred rubble.

I had thought the priest would be expecting us, but he did not seem to be around. Burnie and I used our farm tools to work in the garden and appear occupied. After a while a woman walked out of the church rectory and came toward us. Uh-oh.

"Vous les hommes, venez avec moi," she said, and walked back toward the building.

You men. *Avec* means "with." We're supposed to go with her. Burnie was watching me. I swung my head toward the rectory, and we fell into step.

She spoke to the priest while we waited, looking at the floor.

"Oui, on leur a dit de venir ici. S'il vous plait, demandez à Josette de venir aussi," the priest told her.

The woman left immediately, and the priest smiled wanly at us. He was sweating profusely, and I had the feeling he would be hugely relieved once we were on our way out of his district.

"There is much intensity in the village," the priest told us warily,

110

as if we were to blame. "You know that the gendarmes are with the Germans, right? We have to be even more careful."

We waited.

"No priests are celebrating mass while the Germans are in our country," he said in disgust. "We give the sacraments, of course, but we'll say small masses for just a few people. There are no congregations." He threw up his hands. "Who are we punishing with that policy? That's what I'd like to know!"

The woman returned alone, spoke briefly to the priest, and then left.

"Josette will be along as soon as she can. You'll stay with her and her husband because she speaks English." He cleared his throat. "Well, come along. We'll find you something to eat while we're waiting."

The priest quick-stepped to the rectory kitchen and sat us down. He made himself scarce as the cook served Burnie and me the most delicious soup I had ever tasted—thick lentil and mushroom. She smiled indulgently and put cheese and bread on the table, and we ate it all.

"I beg your pardon!" a young woman said as she came through the kitchen door. "We had guests for afternoon tea, and I couldn't get rid of them!"

I looked up to see Kindness personified, with a babe in arms, at the head of the table. Her husband stood at her elbow. She handed the baby to him, then reached out to grasp Burnie's and my hands. "I'm Josette Boucher, and this is my husband, Jean. And *this*," she said proudly, "is the magnificent Francis."

We shook hands all around.

"Come along," Josette said. "We'll get you all set up at our house."

A quick goodbye to the cook—the priest never reappeared—and we were ensconced in the Bouchers' modest residence.

"I saw you in the garden and suspected you were not French,"

111

Josette confided, "but I did not mention you to our guests because I wasn't sure of their loyalties. As soon as they left, we came to collect you. I hope you didn't wait too long for me."

"We were fine," Burnie said.

"We appreciate your—"

"Not at all," Josette said. "I teach English, so being able to converse with a native speaker is a wonderful opportunity. Jean teaches, too, sports and general education."

"How old is Francis?" I asked, peeking at the baby while Jean poured local wine.

"He's one. You'll be staying in his room."

"Oh, I hate to inconvenience—"

"The Germans are likely to go into the adults' room first in a raid, so if the worst happens, sleeping in Francis's room will give you time to run." Josette smiled. "Besides, I promise he won't mind."

Burnie and I would have preferred sleeping in the little caretaker's shed, but Jean and Josette would not hear of it.

"Sleep in the child's room. It is all right," she said in a tone that told me our objections were approaching the outer boundaries of etiquette.

After drinking a couple glasses of wine, I told them that my mother was from Domremy.

"The home of Jeanne d'Arc!" Jean said, and sang songs from the region, like *"Il Pleut, Il Pleut Bergère."* I remembered my mom singing that song on rainy days, and I sang along with him. Burnie pressed his hands over his ears and rolled his eyes at my singing ability.

The evening with the Bouchers was as heartwarming as any I could have desired. To have gone so quickly from imprisonment aboard a boxcar bound for hell to an evening of wine and music with the loving family . . . from starvation and exhaustion to a full belly and a few days of sleep . . . from festering infections to healing scabs . . . was wonderful but disorienting.

As I lay in little Francis's bedroom and tried to get my mental, physical, and emotional bearings, I felt a mixture of excitement and overwhelming anxiety. The courage and trust exhibited by Mesdames Lombard and Petitpois, the five Petitpois children, Abel and his cohorts, the village priest, and Jean and Josette were gifts I knew I would never forget. I could not imagine a stronger demonstration of French support for the American troops.

My thoughts flicked to Odette Petitpois, only a girl yet willing to sacrifice herself, body and soul, so Burnie and I could traverse a bridge. The thought brought tears to my eyes, of gratitude and profound sadness.

As kind as everyone had been, Burnie and I were passed like hot potatoes from one person to the next. I could never really be sure who was our friend versus who was pretending to be our friend. Anyone we met could hand us over to the Germans for a reward.

But Burnie and I had no options. If we wanted to stay alive, we had to have faith. We had to believe that people were truly trying to help us without a thought to personal gain at our expense.

The next day, a man from the Underground presented himself at the Boucher house. The network was so secretive, I wasn't sure Jean and Josette expected him, thought we would be leaving so soon, or knew where we'd be going next.

"Our destination is Ville sur Tourbe," he said after we started out, "a village quite a distance away. We'll stop overnight at a farmer's house, to break up the journey."

"We are in your hands," Burnie said.

This man had a loose-jointed, rolling gait, and I enjoyed walking with him. He never seemed to tire, and whether we went uphill or down, it made no difference to his rhythm, breath, or posture.

We passed through several villages on our trek, each one identified by a sign at its village limits. In spite of the time we spent walking with this gentleman, he never told us his name.

At dusk we arrived at the farmhouse, obviously the residence of a rich man and his wife. Their large family of ten welcomed us warmly, and our guide bade us goodbye.

The couple's manner was more dignified and formal than their countrymen whom we had met, but they were in no way cold or stilted. Brenne and his wife, Cilla, were very kind and treated us as if we were their sons. Both confided in us separately that they had lost their boy in the war.

"We will be celebrating Bastille Day on July 14," Brenne said. "We always mark the festivities with a big feast, and this year will be no different. My family and I would be honored if you would be at our party."

Cilla seconded the invitation.

Brenne moved between Burnie and me, took hold of our elbows, and said with great emotion, "You are the first Americans we have ever welcomed into our village."

We did not need much convincing. Burnie and I were thrilled with the idea of a feast. The farmer's wife, daughters, and daughters-in-law were in the midst of cooking a big dinner—about seven courses in all—and we joined in its preparation. I felt comforted to see a family prepare the many specialties my mother always made for holidays. Cilla's kitchen was like a ticket home.

Burnie and I ate and drank our way through the evening, and we truly enjoyed ourselves. The family's furniture was old and grand, and the entire house was very tidy. All twelve of us sat around a magnificent mahogany table and enjoyed hors d'oeuvres, a fish course, a meat course, a course with fowl, and then an array of desserts. Burnie and I hadn't eaten that much food in a very long time, and the richness and sheer amount were more than our stomachs could digest. After each course we both had to jump from our chairs and go outside to vomit. But we didn't miss a course.

After dessert we sipped calvados and cognac and sang American songs, in particular the old World War I songs. Burnie had heard me sing at the Bouchers' house, so he knew the standard I set for talent was pretty low. This made him comfortable enough to join in. My Cherokee friend could not sing worth a whistle, either, but we belted out "Mademoiselle from Armentieres" and "Over There," among others. How well we sang did not seem to matter to our host family. They just wanted to hear those songs, and they truly loved every moment of it.

At dusk, which was about ten o'clock, the party ended. A young man named Joseph Lubian came from Ville sur Tourbe to bring us to his house. Burnie and I regretfully said farewell to Brenne, Cilla, and their family.

"We've had a slight change of plans," Joseph explained as we set out. "The Germans recently searched through my house, so I have found you accommodations elsewhere in the village."

I felt uneasy. Should we be heading toward a village where the Germans were conducting searches? If Joseph was under suspicion, should he have been selected as our escort? This snafu introduced another concern: Even if I believed that everyone helping us had our best interest at heart, that still didn't mean their decision-making ability was faultless. If a good person made a bad choice in regard to our travels, the consequences could be fatal.

I kept my concerns to myself and hoped for the best as Joseph took us to the home of Madeleine Camus and her mother.

As soon as we arrived at Madeleine's house, her mother objected to her daughter's involvement with us. Madame Camus was visibly nervous when Joseph made the introductions, and her agitation continued to grow. Joseph cast an apologetic glance at us and at Madeleine, then beat a hasty retreat.

"If these men really are Americans, Maman, then we must help them," Madeleine said, and turned on the radio. She twisted the knob and found American music on the BBC channel.

"Hey, listen to that!" I said to Burnie. "Sinatra!" I looked at Madeleine. "Frank Sinatra is from my home state of New Jersey!"

"Please don't change the channel," Burnie requested.

"You see, Maman?" Madeleine said. "Only an American would react that way to the music."

Madame Camus grudgingly agreed.

"Now let's show our hospitality by giving our guests something to eat. All right?"

Looking extremely put upon, Madame disappeared into the kitchen.

Now that her mother was taken care of, Madeleine showed us a dazzling smile and led us into the living room. A rectangular table in the center of the room was piled with fabric pieces and sewing paraphernalia—a sight I had seen many times in our family's dining room.

"This is my friend Jeanine," she said as a woman walked in from what I guessed was a bedroom.

Madeleine was a beautiful woman, a few years older than Burnie and me, but Jeanine was gorgeous, with raven hair. She was wearing a very stylish black dress missing one sleeve and needing to be hemmed.

116

"Jeanine is a model," Madeleine said, and asked us to make ourselves comfortable.

"My mother was a model," I told them. "In Paris."

"C'est vrai?" Jeanine asked.

"Yes. After my parents married, they moved to Paris for a while, and Mom had worked as a model while Pop built houses." Although I didn't say so, Pop never liked the arrangement. Mom's assignments sent her to nightclubs to show off the outfits. She never cared much for the job, either. She just needed something to do while they were in Paris.

"I design women's fashions and make the dresses to fit Jeanine—"

"Who has an outstanding figure," I thought.

"—then we ride our bicycles into Bar-le-Duc to model the clothes and sell them. That is how we make our living."

"You must be very successful," I said. "You are so sunny and beautiful, I can't imagine anyone saying no to you. Can you, Burnie?"

My friend was in a daze. He just smiled stupidly and shook his head.

Jeanine and Madeleine owned the room. I could tell they were completely independent women who lived by their own rules—the sort of larger-than-life women my mother missed after moving to America, where wives rarely worked outside the home or pursued their own dreams. Jeanine and Madeleine were her people; they could have been her sisters.

"My mother would have loved to meet you," I said sincerely.

"What does your mother do?" Jeanine asked.

"American women pretty much raise their children and make sure the household runs smoothly while the husband works," I explained, then added, "When she was very young, she sewed an outfit—complete with a fashionable hat—that was so exquisite, my

117

grandmother had to confirm to all admirers that it really had been created by her very talented daughter."

Madame Camus came in, carrying a tray with bread slices spread with a mixture of black olives mashed with herbs and oil. She offered the snacks to Burnie and me, then sat down at the edge of a chair in the corner of the room.

"Our guest's mother is French, Maman," Madeleine said.

"Tell us more about her," Jeanine said. "I'm sure you miss her very much."

I nodded. "But being with you makes me feel like I'm with her. It's nice." I cleared my throat, trying to decide what to say. Then I remembered one of my favorite stories—one that would balance the image they might have of her being a boring housewife.

"Mom was raised on a farm, so the family was well fed, but they could not afford luxuries. She always looked fashionable because of her sewing skills, but she needed money for material. Once, she made a beautifully embroidered white dress and needed a picture hat to complete the outfit. But where would she get the money?"

"What did she do?" Madeleine asked, her eyes sparkling.

"She came up with a scheme. She told her friend Robert, who was visiting from Paris, that they were going fishing on the Meuse River. 'Where's your pole?' he asked. She told him she didn't need one. 'What's in that bag?' he asked. 'You'll see. Don't worry. I'll do all the work.' My mother was going to use her brothers' method of fishing."

I sneaked a glance at Madame. I could see she was wrapped up in the story. "At the river, Mom took a stick of dynamite from her bag, lit it, and threw it into the water near the bank. *Boom!* A huge explosion brought dozens of dead fish to the surface."

"Oh, Maman!" Madeleine said, laughing. "Did you hear that?"

"Hmmph!"

"My mother was amazed by her success. She had enough fish to sell to everyone in the village, and she had brought in enough money to make her picture hat. *But . . .*" I paused for effect. "The next day a member of the gendarmerie came to the farmhouse and asked about the dynamite and fish. *'Moi?'* she asked. *'Oui, vous!'* the policeman said. 'You must never do that again!'" I spread my fingers, palms up. "Sorry. I don't know how to say that in French."

"*'Vous ne devez plus jamais faire cela!'*" Madame Camus piped up.

We all looked at her, surprised. "Merci, Madame," I said, inclining my head.

"What did your grandfather do?" Burnie asked. "Mine would have had her head for dishonoring the spirits of the fish."

"Clash of the cultures," I told my friend. "Mom's father was proud of her inventiveness, but he told her to be more careful. He didn't like her messing with dynamite or with the law."

We spent the next little while affably enough, then Madame herself showed us to our room.

"Wake up! Quick! The Germans!"

Burnie and I jumped out of the featherbed. I was fully awake, and my heart was pounding.

"Soldiers are searching the village!" Madeleine hissed. "They are coming near the house. You must hide!"

Madeleine and her mother shoved us toward the back of the tiny house, into a little crawl space. "Do not move. Do not breathe!" Madame warned.

"I'll come for you when all is clear," Madeleine said.

"Where are you going?" I asked.

"Nowhere. Maman and I will go on with our work as usual."

We stayed curled up in the crawl space for what seemed like a long time, and in reality it probably was several hours. When Madeleine gave us permission to come out, tension etched her face.

"The Maquis has destroyed a length of rail tracks, so no eastbound trains can leave Paris. The Germans believe the Maquis in this village are responsible." She took a deep breath. "The Germans have surrounded the town. No one can leave."

Burnie and I looked at each other.

"I knew this was a mistake!" Madame said, and started to weep.

"We don't want to put you in any danger," Burnie said.

"We'll leave as soon as we're able," I told them. "Burnie and I will try to figure something out."

The door opened, and Joseph walked in, scaring us all half to death.

"You don't knock?" Madame said angrily.

He shrugged. "I didn't want to scare you." He looked at us. "Word has spread that two Americans are hiding somewhere in the village. I've put word out to the others that we have to move you along as soon as possible."

"Have you heard anything in return?" I asked.

"They said for you to stay put for a few more days." He made a rude sound in his throat.

I wanted to cut free from Madeleine's house before suspicion grew even more, but we had nowhere to go.

CHAPTER 11

Although Joseph told us to stay put for a few days, a priest came to Madeleine's house later that same day and told us we had to leave because "Too many people are talking about two Americans in the village."

Burnie and I were in a quandary. We wanted to get on the road, but we did not want to fall into the clutches of the enemy. What to do? The priest had no suggestions except to say it was in God's hands.

A solution presented itself soon enough. Madeleine suspected that one of her neighbors, whom she identified as Augustin, was with the Maquis. They were not on intimate enough terms to have discussed his involvement, and his admitting it to her could be considered risky. Nonetheless, Madeleine did not know what else to do but invite him to her house to meet us, and we concurred.

He accepted within the hour. This was all too much for Madame, who had taken to her bed with a sick headache.

Augustin was a big, broad-shouldered fellow with pale skin and hair like straw. He seemed self-conscious about his size, for his posture was so stooped, he almost folded in on himself. He shuffled in, nodding hello, his hands clasped before his chest, like a priest. I had no idea what a member of the armed Resistance would look like, exactly, but this bloodless fellow was not it.

"Augustin," Madeleine said, "this request may seem a little odd, and please forgive me for being, um, bold, but I hoped you might be able to help my guests here."

He glanced at us with ice-blue eyes, then looked at her and waited.

"I would like them to, um, join the Maquis in the Argonne Forest?" She reddened. "They are trained soldiers and could engage in guerrilla warfare with the Maquis?"

Now he reddened, a deep flush starting in his neck and traveling over his jaw. Augustin cleared his throat. For what seemed like a long time he did not speak. He just sat and rubbed the raw knuckles of his right hand with his left thumb. Then he cleared his throat again, and his eyes locked on Burnie's, then mine. They burned with an intense heat I never would have suspected possible, considering his demeanor only moments before. He seemed to inflate, to fill with the force of life.

"Vous êtes les Américains." It was not a question.

I looked at Madeleine, and she nodded.

"Yes," I said. *"Oui."*

"Mon Dieu, ceci est un miracle!"

"Pourquoi?" Madeleine asked.

"Parce que nous avons des fusils américains et britanniques, ainsi que d'autres équipements que nous ne savons pas utiliser."

Madeleine gasped.

"What?" Burnie and I asked at the same time.

Augustin turned to us and said in deeply accented, halting English, "The Maquis need help. From America and English we have the weapons and more we do not know how we use."

We four sat in stunned silence for a moment.

Burnie said, "Not such a miracle. That's why we were brought here and not to some other village." He shrugged.

"Monsieur Rainwater!" Madeleine scolded. "After what you and Monsieur Sheeran have suffered, your being *alive* at this moment is a miracle!"

I reached to pat Burnie on the back. "My friend stands corrected." I looked at Augustin. "Can you arrange for us to talk to your commander in the forest? We'd like to help."

"I talk at him," Augustin said. "I come here . . . *dans la matinèe.*"

"After the movie?" Burnie asked.

Madeleine laughed. "No, in the morning."

The commotion in the village intensified. Madame Camus wanted us to leave for the forest immediately after sunset, and Burnie and I were more than willing to comply. Madeleine learned, however, that the Germans were standing guard there.

Resigned to having us with her and her mother for one more night, Madeleine asked for help rearranging the furniture to make entering the house difficult.

"If the Germans knew you were here," Madame said, watching, "they would burn down my house with us inside."

We eagerly awaited Augustin's return in the morning, but he disappointed us.

"If Germans are roaming the forest," Burnie pointed out, "the Maquis members will make themselves scarce. Augustin may not have been able to locate his commander."

"*C'est vrai,*" Madeleine agreed. "And Augustin could not come back here to let us know that, because he would not want to attract attention."

We sat. We waited.

I felt so awful for Madame and Mademoiselle Camus, I would have been happy to leave under the cover of darkness and take my chances.

"You can't just leave," Madeleine said. "The Maquis need you. How would you find each other if you left us?"

Her point was well taken, so for the next four days and nights, Burnie and I hid in Madeleine's house.

At last several men of the Maquis came to interrogate us. Augustin was not among them. While Madeleine and her mother made themselves scarce, the guerrillas questioned us thoroughly about our duties as paratroopers and our training.

"The Maquis can check your background to confirm your claims to be American soldiers," the leader warned, then watched us closely for a reaction.

"That's all right with me," I said.

"I have access to Britain's radio frequency," he added.

"That must come in handy," Burnie told him.

A heavy silence fell on the room. My friend and I sat quietly, patiently, calmly, maintaining eye contact with the Frenchmen. Minutes passed. For the first time in my days-long stay in that house, I noticed the ticking of a table clock.

The leader stood, his shoulders back, chin up. "I invite you to join the Resistance forces."

A chill went up my spine. "I am most honored, monsieur." This was a very special group of tough, courageous men.

Each man in the circle grasped our arms, then pulled us into a rough embrace and thumped us on the back.

"You will teach us how to use the weapons," the leader said, "and we will teach you how to dress." He pointed at our ill-fitting, short pants.

We shared a good laugh.

"You will know us and we will know you only by an assumed name," he continued. "You will live off the land and be dedicated to assisting in the cause of freedom in any way possible. Agreed?"

We nodded.

"*Bon.* Then gather your belongings. You're coming with us."

The Maquis interrogators faded into the night just as two Frenchmen around my age arrived at Madeleine's back door. In the Camus kitchen they blindfolded us with bandages. Wherever we were going, they didn't want us to know how to get there. They took our elbows and guided us outside.

It had been a tense few days. Our farewells with Madeleine and Madame Camus did not come too soon for any of us.

"The forest is eight to ten kilometers away," said the fellow with the better command of English. "I know you are nervous, but do not worry. You will be fine." He tapped me on the shoulder. "You will ride on my bicycle."

"But I can't—"

"The handlebars."

Off we went.

Balanced precariously on the handles of his bicycle, I was sweating and feeling faint. My head pounded. I had a full-blown panic attack. I felt disoriented and vulnerable. All the while I was thinking, "What the hell is going on? Where are they taking us?"

If they were delivering us to the Germans, there would be no escape, no going home. I had to trust these people with my life. I was completely in their hands. I reminded myself that they were risking their lives for me.

I sensed a profound darkness surrounding us. Certainly the time was well past the curfew imposed by the Germans.

The cyclists conversed quietly in French, and several times I understood a word or two. I attempted to join the discussion, but they ignored me. We were speeding along at a pretty good clip when suddenly I felt a jolt and felt myself hurling through the air. I rolled into a shallow ditch. I heard Burnie go down, too. I could not move; one fellow was holding me down.

While we lay in the ditch, my driver pulled the bandages off my eyes. We all remained very still, holding our breath. I felt the vibration in the ground before I heard the rumble. Headlights illuminated the trees above us, and a convoy of Germans roared past us on the way toward Ville sur Tourbe.

It was as close as we had come, I think, to being caught. If the Germans' truck had had brighter headlights, surely the metal bicycles would have reflected our whereabouts.

After waiting awhile, the cyclists repositioned our blindfolds, and we continued our journey with only short breaks for rest.

"We have to watch for more convoys," my cyclist said. "Because of all the strafing in southern France, the Germans have reorganized their forces into units of only six soldiers. Now when the bombers come in, the Germans won't suffer as many losses at one time. And they move the units at night, when the Allies aren't running missions."

"Merci," I said. For what, I didn't know exactly, except that the fellow was thawing a little since the convoy incident, and I appreciated the information.

We rode up a pretty steep road and finally arrived at a village. "This is La Placardelle. We're at the edge of the forest. You'll be meeting with members of the Resistance here."

The fellows removed our blindfolds, then led Burnie and me up a path to a house. We were told to wait in the foyer, where we over-heard softly spoken words.

"What're they saying?" Burnie asked.

"I don't know," I said.

He asked me again and again and earned the same reply, but neither he nor I needed fluency to understand that the Maquis were discussing the risk of bringing us into the forest with them.

A man with gold-rimmed glasses came out to the foyer and gestured us into the main room. A dozen men, all members of the Maquis, sat around a long wooden table. Two empty chairs awaited us at the end. At the opposite end, the man facing us was a gen-darme. I swallowed. Our friends in the Underground had consis-tently warned us that many French policemen were collaborators, so I was more than a little wary. This gendarme was clearly in charge of the meeting.

Burnie and I were questioned. As requested, we told them of our capture and escape. As we listened, the men debated whether or not to take us into the forest. Ultimately everyone stood, and we were blindfolded.

"You are going far into the forest," the gendarme said.

Someone took my hand and placed it on his upper arm. He was my guide, and in a group we walked and walked and walked. At times we were on a path where sharp stones bit into the soles of my inadequate shoes. Then we moved into an area where soft forest detritus provided a cushion underfoot. Limbs brushed against my arms, lifted the tam off my head—snatched up and replaced by whoever was walking behind me—and whacked my legs. The leaves and needles released their fragrant oils as we passed over them, and the piney smell was invigorating. I felt grateful I did not have an allergic reaction to anything growing in the Argonne.

We walked at a good clip. I picked up a few words, including *ammunition* and *parachutes*. The men's voices carried a sense of urgency, and I gathered from the conversation that the Maquis had explosives, rifles, machine guns, and ammunition hidden at our destination, as well as magnetic mines for slapping onto moving trains. We were going to see plenty of action in this forest, and I was glad for it. I had told McKnight that my duty was to fight the Germans, and now, with these men, I would have an adventure of a lifetime and fulfill my intentions to be a soldier.

Deep, deep into the forest, they removed our blindfolds. I looked around. I was in a forest dreamland, where the moonlight slid down the heavy slope of the pine boughs. Never had I seen anything so beautiful. These savvy fighters were dead serious about preserving the secrecy of all of their bases of operation, and they had succeeded with us.

As we continued through the forest, I noticed what appeared to be a trench from World War I. In contrast to the enveloping darkness, the dug-out channel appeared bright. My dad had dug trenches during the First World War. Pop could have been at this very spot thirty years before. I went over to the trench, jumped in, and dug my fingers into the soft soil. I grabbed the dirt and came up with handfuls of spent fifty-caliber heavy brass shells that were from World War I. I shoved some of the shells into my pocket, to show Pop when I returned home.

My father's father came to mind. He had fought in the Boer War. Realizing I was upholding a tradition of Irish-American soldiers serving their country, my journey took on an even greater personal importance. I knew that seeing myself as one man in a line that spanned generations would comfort me through some difficult moments.

I jogged back to rejoin the others, who had kept moving except for Burnie and one other, who hung back and waited for me. The column was walking down a long hill to a flowing stream. We jumped across and came to the entrance of a rough, well-camouflaged shelter of logs and debris. The roof, supported by posts, extended from the slope, and its steel sheets were covered with dirt and plants. Someone could walk above it without ever suspecting a shelter existed below. Adjacent to the shelter was a cave that I guessed had been chiseled out of the mountainside during the First World War. Its interior was dry enough to store ammunition and rifles.

Other men were already at the shelter, at work enlarging the cave. Burnie and I joined them, with two other Maquis, hammering and slicing at the embankment while another fellow held a flashlight.

The work exhausted my reserves. The muscles in my arms and shoulders burned like fire, and I worried I might collapse. I thought about giving up, but I did not want to appear weak or inferior to our hosts. I knew Burnie felt the same way; we were both determined the Maquis would never regret bringing us into their ranks.

The next night an air of intense purposefulness filled the camp. We all walked a long distance to a farm, and everyone scooped up armfuls of brush and carried them to an opening in the forest. Burnie and I and other Resistance fighters made many trips between the farm and the clearing, while some men stayed in the lea to pile up the brush into three mounds that grew to the size of a barn. To avoid a paroxysm of sneezing, I wrapped a cloth around my nose and mouth.

"What are we doing?" I asked a man who had fallen in step beside me, but he did not speak English. I pointed at the brush, then gestured my not understanding what we were doing.

The man brightened and nodded. He pointed at the brush at our feet, then used his hands to indicate a large mound. Then he pretended to open a jar and pour something atop the mound. He pantomimed the striking of a match against the heel of his boot, then showed an explosion with his hands flying apart.

I nodded understanding, but he held up his index finger. *Wait.* His arms akimbo, the man became an airplane that banked left, right, left. I nodded. Now the Frenchman pretended to heft something large from the plane. Again I nodded. Taking on the role of a man on the ground, he pumped his arms, running to the delivery on the ground. He pried it open, pulled something out, and used it as a gun.

Got it. I pretended to applaud, and he took an extravagant bow.

Almost on cue, I heard an airplane coming in low. A man in our group turned on a flashlight, which signaled another man to light the dry timber. The breeze carried the smell of kerosene, and a moment later, three huge burning piles illuminated a white parachute as it billowed out of the plane. I saw a large crate attached to it.

Burnie and I and several others dashed toward it. Others worked to extinguish the blaze. My heart pounded from the thrill as we recovered the crate. We also took along the parachute. We could cut it up and use it for warm blankets and socks—certainly the most luxurious socks I could ever wear.

A long day and night had passed since leaving Madeleine's house, but we had to keep going. Burnie and I helped to haul the heavy crate back to the base. The Maquis gathered around to see what was inside. Christmas in July! It was packed full of Allied munitions.

Pairs of hands brought Burnie and me to the center of the circle next to the crate. As we unpacked the munitions, we identified them for the Maquis.

"Tommy guns, M-1 rifles," Burnie said.

"Magnetic bombs," I said. "You can attach these to a moving train or truck."

"Composition C," my friend said. "To blow up bridges and railroad tracks."

"One heavy machine gun." And a partridge in a pear tree.

It felt great to have these familiar weapons in our hands!

"Burnie and I will be more than happy to teach our new compatriots how to use them," I said, and the men crowded around us, thumping us on the back, inspecting the weapons, "tousling" our half-inch-long hair.

I knew everything was going to be all right. I wasn't with my buddies in the Screaming Eagles, but I was back in the battle, shoulder-to-shoulder with brave rebels from my mother's country. I was now an official and trusted member of the Maquis, and my home the dense Argonne Forest.

CHAPTER 12

While I was a prisoner of the Germans, shuffled from one miserable compound to another, I heard some Americans gripe about the French collaborators. Of course I was sensitive to complaints about the French because of my own heritage, and I took the insults personally. My mother's loyalty to the United States and to France could not have been stronger or more genuine. In my opinion, the French were strong allies, steadfast supporters of our shared objective to rid Europe of the Nazi invaders. They were worthy of Americans' trust.

I chose not to enter the conversations and explain my beliefs. The Germans had taken my freedom and ruined my physical health. All I had left was my thoughts, and I did not want to dilute them by sharing them with other prisoners. Nor did I want to exhaust myself by arguing, or introduce any more negativity into our downtrodden group.

Living now among the Maquis gave even more weight to my

beliefs. Men from all walks of life joined the Maquis for any number of reasons. Still, the diverse gathering—lumberjacks, farmers, hunters, teachers, and cooks, respected leaders in the community—had but a single goal: the country's freedom. The commitment to this cause came with a heavy price: Each man lived a double life and harbored very dangerous secrets. Much of the time they camped in the forest, away from their loved ones. That meant their family lived at home without a man to protect them. While the guerrillas plotted how to thwart the Germans and carried out secret missions, their farms and businesses languished. To avoid suspicion, they returned periodically to their normal life, worked at their trade, and spent time with their family.

The group that adopted Burnie and me and invited us into their encampment had two factions. There were the men who maintained a supply camp in the forest. They were well organized and made calculated strikes at the enemy. The head of that segment was the gendarme who had sat at the head of the wooden table in the house at Placardelle before we were allowed to enter the forest. He proved to be a firm leader and a gentle, thoughtful man. The other faction was the French Forces of the Interior (FFI), a more radical, aggressive group. In our camp the FFI faction numbered fifteen.

The FFI, yearning to get even with the Germans, went on undisciplined killing sprees that targeted enemy soldiers. The rampages always backfired because the Germans, provoked by the so-called bloody acts, exacted fierce retribution on innocent French citizens.

Not surprisingly, the Resistance was not universally supported in France.

Most of these partisans spoke little or no English, but a common language proved less important than our shared camaraderie. We had surprisingly little difficulty making ourselves understood by the others. Obvious to Burnie and me were the men's abiding love for and pride in their beautiful country and its culture. They valued and cherished the forest as a national treasure and knew exactly what was edible and what could be used medicinally. We lived off the land, and the local farmers supplemented our diet with gifts of vegetables.

One partisan who was the camp's cook befriended me after I told him my mother's maiden name. "Munier?" he said. *"Vous êtes mon cousin!"*

All during my stay in the forest, I never learned his name, but from then on, he called me his cousin and made sure Burnie and I had abundant servings of vegetables.

Also camped in the Argonne Forest was a band of Russian fighters. They survived by stealing food or demanding it at gunpoint. The French farmers hated them. Perhaps they would not have minded had the Russians cooperated with the Maquis in their efforts against the Germans, but that was never the case.

Because we lived off the land, most of our meals consisted of hunted game. We ate "delicacies" I would never have imagined, such as cow udders. The udders were delicious—definitely different, but delicious—the way my cousin prepared them. (Or was I just really, really hungry?) If we had a taste for fish, we implemented my mother's method and threw hand grenades into the stream, then gathered the dead fish on the surface for cleaning and cooking.

When we needed meat, the Frenchmen were experts at trapping the wild boar—*le sanglier*. Boars are big, heavy animals that can be extremely dangerous. They are also creatures of habit who follow the same trail every night. When a boar finds two trees growing close together, he likes to stand between the trunks and give himself a good rubdown on the bark. If the boar finds two trees whose positioning suits his size, he will usually return to that spot every night.

Armed with that knowledge, my French friends showed me how to make a wire noose and hang it between the trees to capture *le cochon sauvage*. The boar gets his head caught in the trap, and his struggles tighten the noose. Thrashing about to get free, the boar kicks at the ground and quickly digs a hole almost a foot deep. In the morning, we would travel to the trap and collect the dead animal. For the next few days we would have delicious meals of stewed boar.

As straightforward as this method seemed to me, the *best* way to fashion the noose and hang it between the trees sparked fanatical arguments among the Maquis. They also argued with great emotion about America, the Allied forces, and how best to defeat the Germans. The Frenchmen's reputation for being passionate was, I decided, well deserved. They debated stubbornly, rarely giving an inch, each trying to convince his compatriot of his own superior logic.

Burnie and I watched the men argue while we calmly ate boar stew from vintage, army-issue, World War I tin lunchboxes with a folding handle—a gift from the Maquis. When I finished my meal with time to spare before Burnie and I reported for guard duty, I carved my name and the initials *U. S. A.* on the bottom of the lunch box.

For our first three weeks in the forest, my buddy and I accompanied the Maquis on a number of offensive forays. We also had guard duty every night at the cave, where the airdropped treasure was stashed. Protecting those crates was the group's most immediate responsibility. Their overriding concern, however, was learning how to use the stockpiled equipment and explosives. The freedom fighters were unfamiliar with the weaponry.

The Resistance's contribution had become ever more crucial to the war effort. Having gained a foothold on the continent, the Allied

Army now needed to penetrate enemy lines and sweep across France. American and British forces counted on the Maquis to clear the way by destroying critical targets such as train tracks, bridges, and communication wires.

When we joined the Resistance, the Frenchmen were making the transition from committing isolated acts of sabotage—basically depending solely on their own inspirations and plans—to joining cooperative, coordinated wartime efforts. They had established clandestine radio communications with England, and the British supply drop we had helped to retrieve was the result of international support.

Our first important mission for the Allies was to destroy a large German ammunition dump filled with mortar shells and bombs. By this time Burnie was willing to concede to the miracle of our being available to the Maquis at this precise moment in this particular place. He and I had been trained to use most of the sophisticated weapons, and we were able to share our knowledge with the Maquis and answer all their questions.

These very able young and middle-aged men had grown up hunting and were familiar with firearms, so showing them how to use the sophisticated American rifles was not at all difficult. The French had no idea how to use the explosives, however, and that was where Burnie and I were most helpful. Without our assistance, the Maquis would have figured out eventually how everything worked, but they probably would have lost a few fingers, arms, and lives in the process.

We taught them how to use shaped charges and Composition C, how to mold the explosive, and how to direct the force of the powerful blast in one particular direction, which made their covert efforts much more effective.

For a few nights we joined the Maquis in reconnaissance missions at the ammunition dump. We crouched in the darkness, staying about three hundred yards from the target's outer edge. One of the compatriots, whom I had secretly nicknamed Scarface, was beside me in the brush. He spoke a little English and was eager to learn more.

We noted that the Germans always changed the guards around midnight. On that night we timed how long the replacement guards needed to walk to their post. Those few moments would be our only opportunity to carry out our plan.

As we walked back to camp, Scarface warned me that if anything went wrong and the Germans pursued the Maquis into the forest—this had happened from time to time—the Frenchmen would scatter, work their way back home, and resume their normal activities. No one would be in the forest when the Germans arrived . . . except, possibly, the Russians. Scarface grinned evilly at that thought.

"Who will take Burnie and me?" I asked.

"No one," Scarface said sadly. "That is why I tell you now."

"We'll have no place to go," I said.

Scarface nodded. "So you know now. You tell your friend."

I didn't like the idea, but I understood. They had to protect their family. That gave me the idea of asking my "cousin" for an invitation when we got back to camp, but not even he would agree to shelter us.

I decided to tell Burnie when we were alone, on guard duty, but I didn't have the chance. The gendarme accompanied us to the cave, and we went inside to look at the stash.

"Nous avons exactement quarante-sept secondes," the leader said to Burnie and me. *"Que devons-nous utiliser?"*

"Forty-seven seconds isn't much time," I said. "You won't be able to plant the charges and get the hell out in that amount of time."

"They'll only have enough time to sneak out of hiding and get down to the fence posts," Burnie said. "But planting charges is the way to go."

The Frenchman came up with the idea of his men falling in step behind the guards as they passed by on the way to their assigned locations. The Maquis would quietly plant the explosives as the guards walked on.

"Je reviendrai à l'aube," he said. *"J'amènerai six hommes pour faire le travail. Vous leur direz ce qu'ils doivent faire."* Then he melted into the darkness.

The next morning he returned, as promised, with the six men. Among them was Scarface. I liked the gendarme's selection; I knew these men to be the fastest runners in the camp, with outstanding eye-hand coordination. They'd perform the dangerous tasks like well-oiled machines.

Burnie and I had passed the night discussing how much matériel the men would require to do the job and had already separated the items from the large shipment. Once the group reported to the cave, we spent the morning making sure they understood what to do: stick the Composition C on the stacks of bombs and munitions, then rig the charges with thirty-minute acid-type fuses.

One of them, a fellow I had nicknamed Smoky because he always had a hand-rolled cigarette hanging from his lip, eyed the roll of fuse. He pointed at it, pantomimed igniting it, then pointed at his watch and finally indicated an explosion.

I turned to Scarface. "Tell him he will have enough time to get a half mile away," I said. "But tell him not to stop on the way to roll himself a cigarette."

The men laughed and poked at Smoky after Scarface gave my answer.

Of course Burnie and I wanted to go with them, but our leader told us to remain behind for this foray. One of the men promised to tell us all about it. Then we all returned to the main camp for a day of rest.

I wasn't even aware when the men left for the ammunitions dump or when they returned. At some point in the night, while I was on guard duty, I became aware that the breeze carried a distinct smell of sulfur. I looked over at Burnie, and his white teeth shone in the moonlight as he gave me the V for Victory.

———————

Word got around camp that Burnie and I had wanted to go on the big mission but had been told to stay behind. To make up for this disappointment, Scarface came looking for us a few days later to go on a spur-of-the-moment FFI raid against the Germans at the nearby village of Vienne le Chateau.

Scarface found Burnie, but neither of them could find me—I have no idea where I was at the time—so they left without me. I felt really frustrated when I found out. I wanted nothing more than to pick a fight with the Germans. I ran through the forest, hoping to cut them off, but I was minutes too late. I saw them far, far ahead, three vehicles with five men each, two in front and three in the back.

Oh, it looked like fun, like a bunch of fraternity boys racing off to the nearby women's dorm for a panty raid. The reality was that the vehicles were loaded with hand grenades, machine guns, and other automatic weapons.

I walked back to camp in a black mood. My cousin intercepted me, and I shared my aggravation that the men had not waited for me. He explained that the attack was planned for noon, when all the local citizens would be safely inside their homes, having lunch or taking a midday nap. Had they waited, not knowing where I was or when I might return, their countrymen's lives could have been jeopardized.

Once I understood that, my anger faded. I would go on the FFI's next raid, maybe.

At dusk, I went to stand guard at the cave. Burnie had not returned to the campsite, but I figured the raiders had gone to celebrate their wild afternoon, and he would find me at the cave when he came back. A few others came with me, to keep me company until my pal returned. They fanned out, and I sat under a bush. The sound of rustling leaves told me someone was approaching, and I cocked my weapon.

"Jimmy! Jimmy, it's me! Burnie!"

"Hey, Burnie, how'd it go?"

He emerged from the brush, out of breath and looking like crap. "We gotta get the hell out of here," he said. "The Germans are coming!"

"They don't come into the forest, Burnie."

"They will this time," he said, pulling at me. "We threw grenades and shot at everything in sight. We killed a mess of soldiers. The Germans aren't going to let us get away with that! Now, let's go!"

It wasn't sinking in. I looked around. "We have to wait for the Maquis to come back, so we can tell them we're leaving."

"They went home, Jim!" he shouted at me. "They all went home!"

All at once I understood. This was what Scarface had warned me about. We no longer had any safe haven with the Underground.

Shots rang out in the distance, and I heard the harsh, deep barking of big dogs. I grabbed my musette bag, and Burnie and I took off and ran all night. Racing through the forest, we left behind everything we had enjoyed with the Maquis—protection, rest, and being part of the cause.

Even without a compass, Burnie was able to navigate our way through the dark, unfamiliar woods. He was a natural woodsman and kept us pointing south by occasionally checking tree trunks. "Moss doesn't grow on the south side of a tree," he said again and again as we crashed and lurched through the Argonne Forest.

To put a safe distance between us and the Germans, we ran the rest of the night and through the next day. We had regained our strength during our weeks with the Maquis; otherwise we would not have been able to run as fast and as far as we did.

We went through a section of forest where all the trees were brightly illuminated, as if phosphorescent. Wood chips glowed at our feet. It was magical, and Burnie and I were so awestruck, we couldn't speak. We both took chips from the trees and stuffed them into our pockets, then ran on.

We came to the lower part of the forest by daybreak, far enough from the Germans' point of entry for us to move onto one of the cleared trails. At last we burst out of the forest, into the intense July heat. Even in the first hours of sunlight, I knew the day would be a scorcher.

Reality settled in. How would we sustain ourselves? We had no food or water. We had lost the protection of the forest and all friendly contact. Very likely we would never see our friends of the Maquis again. Worst of all, we were escaped prisoners on the run.

CHAPTER 13

B urnie and I didn't talk much as we walked along the trail. My thoughts were consumed with figuring out what to do next, and I'm sure his were, too, as our few exchanges focused on that. The only thing of which we were certain was that we had to start again from zero. I realized that as much as Burnie's and my expertise was a miraculous gift to the Maquis, our being adopted by their community had been no less wondrous for us. I believed they had literally saved our lives. Surely the Germans would have closed in on the Camus household, if Madame Camus had not forced us out first.

The gash on Burnie's head was healed, as was the shredded skin on my knees. The healthy diet and uninterrupted sleep had built up our physical strength, and the camaraderie and sense of purpose had restored our spirit.

"Pssst," Burnie hissed.

I looked up from the trail and was startled to see a young boy, perhaps nine years old, within twenty feet of us, coming in our direction. His short pants revealed birdlike legs with outsized knees, and his arms were similarly thin, with knobby elbows—a pup who needed to grow into his body. He wore a French tam and a huge smile. We smiled at one another but exchanged no words as we kept on walking.

"*Pssst,*" Burnie hissed again and surreptitiously pointed behind us.

I glanced over my shoulder to see the boy was now following us and still grinning.

Was he laughing at our socks, cut from the parachute silk of the Allies' munitions airdrop? I wondered if the funny white wraps might have blown our cover.

After a few moments, the kid started whistling, and after a few notes, I recognized the tune as "Yankee Doodle Dandy."

"Holy shit," Burnie said. "He knows we're Americans."

"We better try to talk to him." A child being aware of our nationality but not of the necessity to keep it secret was too great a risk to go unchecked.

Burnie and I sat down on a pile of logs alongside the road. The boy sat in front of us and crossed his legs, Indian style, and grinned. In my best French, I asked him to bring his father to us: "*Cherchez votre pere.*"

The boy seemed to talk to himself, then he jumped up and took off running. Burnie and I retreated to a wooded area just off the trail and waited. When an hour had passed, we began to worry. We did not know if Germans were prowling the area or if the boy would even return.

Before we came to any decision, the child appeared with his father, a barrel-chested man with bright pink cheeks. He introduced himself as Monsieur Berger and his son as Etienne. "*D'où vous avoir deux messieurs viennent?*" he asked.

We pointed north, through the forest, and he seemed to understand.

"Nous voulons aller à la Switzerland," I said haltingly.

He nodded, smiling. *"En Suisse?"* he corrected.

"Oui."

"Vous pouvez rester avec moi et ma famille," Monsieur Berger said, and led us out of the woods.

I felt astonished at our luck as we followed Monsieur and Etienne down the road. I jammed my hands into my pockets as we walked—a lifelong habit—and rubbed the glowing wood chips and the heavy brass bullet shells from World War I between my fingers. I was happy to have my souvenirs, but I regretted abandoning my tin lunch box. Pop would have gotten a kick out of it. And I had lost my jump knife in our dash through the forest.

"When I was Etienne's age," I said to Burnie, "I had a nun who always ordered me to keep my hands out of my pockets. I never realized I was doing it, so I forgot to obey her. One day, she sewed up my pants pockets."

"You're kidding me, right?"

"No, I'm serious. She did it herself, with a kit from her desk drawer at school. I couldn't understand why she would bother—or even care. And I was sure my parents were going to throw a fit when they found out."

"And did they?"

"Not in the way I expected. When I went home, I told my mom that the nun had sewn up my pockets. When Mom told Pop, he got mad at *me*, and I got a whipping."

"Why?!"

"I had no idea, till years later. I found out that Sister Agnes thought I was playing with myself when I kept my hands in my pockets. I swear, I never understood that as a kid."

"Hey, you don't have to convince *me*. *I* don't care if you were playing with yourself or not." He veered over and bumped me off balance, joking around. "I'm warning you, Jimmy, if we don't meet some women soon, I'll be playing with myself." He added, "So don't go looking for a needle and thread."

We continued in companionable silence for a while. Then I heard Burnie chuckle. "Now what's so funny?" I asked.

"I was thinking about that forced march from Hot Springs to Fort Benning. Do you remember it?"

"Walking a hundred thirty-six miles with full field equipment in tow is not something I'd be likely to forget. Ever." I laughed, too. Then I sobered. "It led up to one of my proudest moments in the service."

"Yeah." Burnie knew exactly what I was talking about.

Just before Christmas 1942, I officially qualified as a paratrooper, earning my wings and an extra $50 each month for jump pay. All qualifying jumps took place at Fort Benning—five in three days: two jumps on the first and second days, and one on the third day. The army told us that if we completed our qualifications, we could go home for Christmas with our wings, our uniforms, and $50 bonus to burn a hole in our pocket.

My first attempt was successful; both the jump and landing were clean. The prevailing conditions deteriorated in time for the second. Guys were coming in fast and landing all over the place because of high winds. I had looked down from the plane and tried unsuccessfully to find a soft spot. I jumped, had a high oscillation, and came in hot, landing on my left heel. Searing pain shot up my leg. I knew I had fractured or cracked my heel. A meat wagon pulled up and transported me to the hospital.

The jump in that kind of wind had put more than fifty of us in the hospital that night. We were so disappointed! We had been all puffed up with pride and committed to doing whatever was necessary to complete the jumps and head home for the holiday.

My platoon sergeant and friend, Al Engelbrecht, went out of his way to visit me in the ward. I thought, "Whatta guy!" He asked how I was feeling, then got to his real concern . . .

Now I turned to Burnie and asked, "Remember when I was laid up after that second jump and Sarge came to visit?"

Burnie snorted. "You mean when he didn't have enough money to go home to Syracuse and hit you up for a loan since you'd be laid up for Christmas?"

"Yeah," I said, shaking my head and laughing. "I figured there'd be no sense holding on to my dough, so I gave Engelbrecht what I had."

"Then what happened? I can't remember," Burnie said, "except it was really screwy."

"The doctor came in the next morning and asked me what was wrong. When I told him I'd sprained my ankle, he told me to try hopping on it."

"I remember now!" Burnie said. "You hurt your *left* foot, and you hopped on your *right* foot so the doctor would discharge you!"

Now we were both laughing, and Monsieur Berger and his son turned back and looked at us. Burnie and I smiled and waved, and Monsieur waved back and continued walking.

"The jump master allowed me to finish my three remaining jumps. I made a point of landing on my right foot, but still they were painful as hell. I earned my wings in time to go home for Christmas. The only problem was that Engelbrecht had my money. I requested aid from the Red Cross—"

"Which loaned you the money to get home!"

"Jesus, I was proud to lace up those shiny boots and wear my wings," I told Burnie. "I felt invincible."

Never would I have imagined that I would be one of the first soldiers captured, photographed, and interrogated. The depth of my humiliation shocked me. I thought I had forgiven myself, but apparently it would take a long, long time.

––––––––––

Monsieur Berger headed a large and affectionate family, with children ranging from late adolescence to the little boy we had met on the road. As soon as Burnie and I stepped inside their house, love and hospitality enveloped us. The Bergers, poor in terms of money, were rich in love and generous in spirit. Monsieur's wife, their comely daughters, and their strapping sons eagerly offered assistance despite the considerable risk. Dinner was a feast in our honor, featuring a generous array of food and drink that otherwise would have lasted the family for many days.

At the end of the meal, the eldest daughter's fiancé came in to join us. He was the life-of-the-party sort, and when he heard about the child whistling "Yankee Doodle Dandy," he encouraged the gathering to sing American songs. Everybody immediately looked to Burnie and me to carry the tunes, but we didn't have the talent or the nerve to take the lead. Nevertheless the singing commenced, fueled by large quaffs of calvados, wine, and every other drink the Bergers could find in their cellar.

The more everyone drank, the more we sang, and the more excited we became. Eventually the fiancé, already too far gone with the drink, tried to tempt Burnie or me to sing a solo in exchange for spending the night with his fiancée.

Burnie jumped up from his chair and belted out, "Put your arms around me, honey, hold me ti—"

I jabbed him hard with my elbow, which came close to breaking a couple of ribs. Fortunately no one took offense, and the party and good spirits continued well into the night.

"Cet homme a un permis," Monsieur Berger said the next morning as he introduced us to a young woodsman who had stopped by the house. He nudged the fellow, who obligingly held up some sort of permit for our inspection. *"Il peut travailler n'importe où sans être interrogé."*

I recognized enough words to understand that *I* would like such a permit, which allowed the fellow to travel anywhere without being stopped for questioning. We would have the next best thing, however. The woodsman, Andre, would escort us from the Bergers' house to our next destination.

We sat around the table, and Andre made reference to my mother and father and their marriage in Domremy. Apparently I had told my parents' story the night before—perhaps between the fifth bottle of red wine and the first bottle of calvados, because I had no recollection of it.

The Berger family took a few photographs with us outside the barn, then we said our farewells with thanks and followed Andre to the village of Belval, where a local administrator welcomed us into his home for the night.

The next day we continued our journey south, through the strategic town of Bar-le-Duc. The more time we spent with Andre, the more I doubted his being French, but I couldn't pinpoint his country of origin, and I was reluctant to ask.

The streets of Bar-le-Duc overflowed with German soldiers, all drinking heavily and not paying any attention to their surroundings. I had no idea what they were celebrating, but the festivities eased our way through the settlement.

Andre brought us to a path with a steep upgrade, and when we had climbed to a dark, out-of-the-way spot, he stopped and gave us directions to our destination. We were expected at the house of the postmaster in a village beyond Bar-le-Duc. We were to go up another hill, and when we crossed train tracks that aimed toward Paris, we should look in the distance for the steeple of a white church. The postmaster's house would be next door.

Again we said a grateful farewell, and Andre surprised me by remaining with us until we were officially outside the limits of Bar-le-Duc.

From the Bergers to Andre to the postmaster. Now I suspected Burnie and I were being passed along by the French Underground's network. Meeting Monsieur Berger had been a fortuitous event ... or had it? The Maquis knew our goal was to reach Switzerland, which would have placed us on a southward track through the forest when we fled. Possibly the Maquis had gotten word to everyone in the area to look out for us.

Had Monsieur Berger's entire family been searching for us? The possibility went a long way toward explaining why Etienne grinned like a little fool when he saw us and why he whistled "Yankee Doodle Dandy." *Hmmm.*

A warm feeling expanded in my belly. After living and working with the Resistance and forming friendships with the men, I had felt angry when the Maquis went home and abandoned us. That they ran home *and* made provisions to protect us smoothed out my feelings on the matter.

———

At nightfall we knocked softly on the postmaster's door. His big, beautiful house had been easy to find. The family was extremely well-to-do, and the wife, a wonderful hostess, was able to feed us better than at any of the other homes. The couple showed us to our small room in an attached barn. We spent a comfortable night there, and the next morning we had the opportunity to take a much-needed bath in a little brook behind the house.

We had not been able to cleanse ourselves fully since jumping off the *Ugly Duckling* over Normandy some two months before. With great relief, Burnie and I stripped off our clothes, which needed a serious scrubbing, and leapt into the stream.

Our enthusiasm was cut short when we noticed two girls a little younger than we were walking toward us, laughing and taunting us and pointing. We didn't know what to think.

"I'll show you how to get rid of them," he said.

I did not like the look in his eyes.

He turned toward the girls and said, "Screw," using hand gestures that left no room for doubt. They took to their heels, and we ran after them. They were shrieking with giggles. They led us to a pond where other teenagers were swimming and washing their clothes. My friend and I stopped short, to check out the situation from the relative safety of some bushes before committing ourselves.

After hanging back for a few moments, we decided we couldn't stay there all day. Burnie left the cover of the bushes just as two other girls came forward to pull us out.

"Look at them, Jimmy," he said, breathless. "They look beautifuler and beautifuler—more beautiful than Hollywood movie stars—the closer they come!"

He jumped out with a yelp worthy of a Cherokee warrior and let the girls chase him into the water. "Augh!" he screamed. "Cold!" He looked at me with his index finger high in the air, then curled it down, showing me the effect the cold water just had on his penis.

One of the two girls turned out to be the postmaster's niece. Her name was Huguette. In any country, by any standard, her beauty would have gone undisputed. Her blue eyes reminded me of twin pools of ice-rimed water. Her hair, thick and blond, flowed over her shoulders. She had a figure that was nothing less than magical.

"*Serez-vous de la partie ce soir?*" she shyly asked Burnie.

How can a buck-naked girl be shy about going to a party? I wondered, but France was different from New Jersey in a lot of ways.

"*Oui. Oui, oui. Oui,*" Burnie answered. This was the first time I'd heard him try to speak French.

"*Bon!*" she said, and clapped her hands. Then we watched her butt as she ran back to her friends.

Burnie turned to me. "So what'd she say?"

That evening the postmaster and his wife hosted a big party. Neighbors and kin came carrying trays and earthenware dishes brimming with food. Burnie was distracted and impatient until he saw Huguette come in with her mother and father. That was the last I saw of my friend and the beauty for the rest of the evening. Later, though, after the party was over and just as I was trying to go to sleep, I heard some amorous moans outside our window. I put the pillow over my head to block the sound and prayed Burnie wasn't thinking of bringing Huguette inside.

Suddenly I heard her mother's voice calling, "Huguette, Huguette."

A few minutes later Burnie bounded into the room and launched himself onto the bed, landing on top of me. "I'm in love!" he cried out, and started to hump me.

"Get off me!" I yelled, and pushed him away. He landed on his ass on the floor.

Our private heaven continued through the next day as we enjoyed the postmaster's hospitality. Precedent had taught us to expect another escort to appear for the next leg of our trip, so we relaxed. At sunset my friend and I were lying on the grass under a large willow tree, as content as could be, talking to the ravishing local girls.

After three days, our host became concerned for our safety and told us to prepare to leave. He was ready to pass us on to another contact along a route to Switzerland. With an air of great seriousness, the postmaster gave us thorough directions to follow and offered a detailed description of the farmhouse where we would meet our next contact. It would be on the right side of the road, he said, with a set of wooden steps leading up to the entrance.

He was nice enough to accompany us for a short distance and point out the road we were to take. We said goodbye and struck out along the narrow road, once again on our own.

Burnie had always been a man of few words, but on that day he was even more silent, and morose. I believe he had left a piece of his heart with Huguette. ·

Eventually we arrived at the farmhouse. We knocked on the door, and the owner, a farmer, quickly introduced us to another man staying with him. The boarder was a Russian news correspondent working behind French lines. He was the first Russian I had the opportunity to speak with, but he seemed guarded. He did not come forward to shake hands, even though we offered ours, and his chin tilted in defiance as he looked down at us through his wire-rimmed spectacles.

Our first few minutes there were a distinct departure from our previous experiences. Neither the Russian nor the farmer smiled, and the atmosphere was tense. Burnie and I felt extremely ill at ease; we had become accustomed to congenial and warmhearted hospitality.

I tried to thaw the room by striking up a conversation with the correspondent. "I've heard the Russians are making great progress on the northern front," I said. "Congratulations!"

"The Americans are surprised always when my country shows its strength and ability," he said with unmistakable hostility. "You think a communist society is backward? You think we are all peasants who know nothing except how to grow potatoes? We are as smart as you! Smarter, even! You will see. It is Russia that will win the war, not America and not England."

"Hey," I said, annoyed, "I just wanted to say I think the Russians are doing a fine job up north, and I'm glad we're allies."

I tried to calm down. I was not at boiling point, but the pot was simmering. "We don't have to accept each other's political system or way of life to be allies in a war or even guests in the same house."

"You know nothing if you think America does not consider the whole world inferior! America says always she is right and everybody else wrong about everything. Should you live and go home, you make time to learn about America so you will know what you talk about!"

"We didn't invite this conversation," I told him.

"Drop it, Jimmy," Burnie said quietly. "Let's just get some rest." He pulled at my arm.

I glanced at the farmer, to see if he had intention of intervening, but he proved hardly neutral. When he saw me looking at him, he took a step forward and said, "The Americans don't like socialism or communism. American politicians do not believe in people taking care of people. All they want is to make money. In America, it is my dog eats your dog." He was indignant, as if he had suffered some immediate and personal harm.

"Where will we be sleeping?" Burnie asked in an even, calm voice.

"Upstairs." The farmer pointed in a general direction.

"Thank you," Burnie said quietly. "Good night."

When we got to the room upstairs and closed the door, Burnie and I sat on the edge of the bed and looked at each other. We knew we were in trouble.

"We have to get out of here," I whispered.

He nodded. "Tonight. As soon as possible. Otherwise I think we may be trapped here."

"Or they'll kill us themselves," I said quietly.

We lay down to rest, fully clothed, our eyes wide open. When we could no longer hear any movement in the house, we both sat up.

"Wanna leave a note of apology on the bed?" Burnie asked. "Or do you think they'll excuse our bad manners because we're American."

We tiptoed downstairs and crept away from the house into darkness. We walked at a quick pace, continuing farther along the narrow road we had taken to get to the farmhouse. At dawn we came upon a wooded area.

Suddenly we heard the hum of a motor, then we made out the outline of a motorcycle approaching us. As the noise grew louder, we saw the driver was a German officer. We knew he had spotted us when he reached down on his right side. Germans carried Luger pistols in a black holster with a flap across the top, and I watched as he loosened the flap.

"Burnie, get to the other side of the road, so he'll have to ride between us. If I holler, swing your musette bag as hard as you can, and we'll take him down. Don't do anything unless I yell."

Burnie strolled casually across the roadway.

I watched the officer carefully as he got closer. He never moved to draw his pistol. He went past, staring ahead, ignoring us, so I did not give Burnie a signal. I breathed a little easier when the German rode past.

As we continued to walk, however, I heard the motorcycle turn around and come toward us. "Same plan, pal!" I said.

We walked, turning slightly toward the center of the road so we could see the officer coming in our peripheral vision. I could see his hand still on the gun. The motor got louder, and he did maintain his speed. When he was within yards of us, I saw his pistol hand move.

"Now!" I yelled.

We turned and swung our bags hard. The German flew sideways off his motorcycle and landed in the road. Burnie and I jumped him. He fumbled with his pistol and kicked at us, but we knocked his weapon out of his hands, held him down, and strangled him. There was no other way.

Burnie and I dragged the motorcycle into the woods and carried the body deep into a wooded area where we covered it with detritus. We hurried back to the roadway and smoothed over all signs of the scuffle.

Soon the farmer and his Russian friend would find us gone, and the officer would be reported missing. The Germans wouldn't have to be geniuses to make the connection. We had to get off the road and as far away as possible.

CHAPTER 14

Neither Burnie nor I had ridden a motorcycle before, but we learned fast. We sped down the road, not knowing where we were, as far as the gasoline carried us. After carefully burying the motorcycle in the woods, we sat on a log to consider our next step.

Now that we were on our own with no friend to guide us, I took out the silk map the British paratrooper had given me on the prison train and spread it across my knees.

"We were there in Bar-le-Duc," I said, pointing. "Then we went south to the farmhouse with the Russian correspondent."

"We were just about here when we met the German officer," Burnie said, "then we rode the cycle to here." The map seemed to indicate we had traveled along the perimeter of the Foret de Vov.

I studied the map, trying to make a decision. Something half jumped out at me. "Hey, Burnie, move your finger a second."

When my friend complied, I was shocked to see the village of

Domremy-La-Pucelle, where my own mother had been born and raised and the home of Joan of Arc.

I was jubilant. It appeared to be only four or five kilometers away.

"What do you see?" Burnie asked, peering over my shoulder. "Passaic, New Jersey?"

I laughed. "No, my friend, but it's the next best thing!" I explained my happiness. "If we can get to Domremy, we'll be safe."

"Do you know anyone there? Family?"

"Not exactly, but my mother said people rarely move from the village where they are born. When we were kids, she didn't have much to say about France, but she did tell us we were probably related to Saint Joan of Arc because people did not leave Domremy."

Burnie stood. "Well, Saint James, my appetite is in the mood for a family reunion."

We set off over a rocky terrain toward my mother's village. As we walked, I thought about the mystery that surrounded my mother's life. I knew hundreds of stories about my pop's youth and had met many of the players. When something triggered a memory for Pop, his eyes would get a certain warm look, and the corners of his mouth would lift, and sometimes he would laugh out loud. When he had all the details in mind, he would vividly recount the incident, and we kids would feel as if we had been there with him.

When Mom remembered something, her small chin would drop, her lips thinned to a tight line, and her whole body seemed to wilt. What had happened to her, she would not say. Whenever we asked Pop to explain, he would answer, "Ask your mother." He respected her privacy, and plainly the story was hers to tell. We did not press her, trusting her to reveal the great unknowns when the time was right. Which left me with one of the knottiest dilemmas of my young life: When Burnie and I were in Domremy, should I learn as much as I could about my mother and then bring the information home to my sisters?

My friend and I climbed a steep hill and at the top looked out over a vista of lush green fields interspersed with rows of swaying wheat and other crops. A blue river sparkled on the horizon. We knew it could be the Meuse. No more beautiful or welcome scene could have met our eyes. I felt as if we had found the Promised Land. Anticipation quickened our step and eased our ascent to the top of the next hill.

Several graceful trees bearing ripened yellow fruit surrounded us. I jumped to grab a sturdy limb and swung up into the tree. "My God, Burnie," I called down to him. "This is a miracle! I know they are *les mirabelles*, the plums my mother said grow only around Domremy, and only in July."

Burnie scampered up the tree and straddled a nearby limb. We picked several plums and ate them ravenously, as if they held the answer to all our problems. The sweet juice ran down our chins, and soon we felt full.

We climbed higher into the tree, steadying ourselves by holding on to sturdy branches, and gazed out over a field. Movement caught my eye: a man crossing the field with such an exaggerated limp, he was almost hopping.

"We could talk to him," Burnie said after watching the man. "At least he won't be able to run after us."

"Haven't you ever seen a mummy movie?" I asked. "Fay Wray runs full speed, and Lon Chaney always catches her, even though he's wrapped up in bandages and dragging his bum leg."

"I'll take my chances," my friend said, "although you have made an excellent point."

We climbed to the ground and approached the man. I saw he had a wooden leg fitted with a boot whose sole resembled a snowshoe so he would not sink into the mud. When we met, I looked him confidently in the eyes. *"Connaissez-vous Lucie Munier?"* I asked.

The man looked closely at me. *"Lucie? Oui, je connais Lucie. Nous sortions souvent ensemble."*

"Je suis son fils."

In broken French, I told him our story from the day I parachuted from the *Ugly Duckling*. I concluded with our having lost all contacts, then added, *"Mais ici nous sommes dans la ville natale de ma mère!"*

The man struggled to comprehend what I was saying. Aside from my slaughtering his language, he may not have heard my mother's name in twenty years. I felt encouraged, though, because he looked as if he wanted to believe me.

"Entrer dans les bois et cacher," he said, pointing. *"Je me retournerai."*

We found a good place in the woods to hide, in case anyone came walking across the open plateau. It was a low-lying area where we fashioned a little shelter and dug a foxhole using sticks and our hands. The day grew dark. Threatening clouds moved in quickly, but the cooling air made us comfortable for a few hours before dusk.

The intense flavor of the luscious *mirabelles* stayed with me all day, and I felt good. Burnie and I talked about the guys more than we had in weeks. We laughed about Al and Neeper and Huff and imitated Captain McKnight giving us a speech while dressed up with his silk neckerchief and shiny Colt .45.

"I wonder how Johnny Simpson is doing," I said, remembering the last time I saw him, with his hand amputated in the German compound. "Did you ever notice how he never talked about his family or showed up for mail call?"

Burnie nodded. "I don't remember his name being called for a letter. I figured he was an orphan."

"Yeah," I agreed. "I wrote to my parents about Simpson's smarts, how this one guy in our unit was so worldly and sophisticated but never wanted extra attention. I mentioned in my letter how Simpson never got mail. Not long after that, Simpson got a letter from Pop."

"You're shitting me," Burnie said. "Your dad sounds aces."

"He is. He and Simpson exchanged a few letters. I don't know what they wrote to each other—Simpson never mentioned it to me—but he acted more relaxed and was more open with me after that."

"I think Simpson kept himself to himself because of his promotion. He probably felt awkward to jump over us like that."

Burnie had a good point. One day Simpson went to the captain with some ideas about how we could use the machine gun better. If he had followed protocol, he would have talked to me about it first. Not long afterward, he won a promotion to corporal. The promotion—combined with his flat, hollow voice, which did not motivate anyone when he gave orders, and his superior intellect—inspired his nickname, King Corporal.

As if reading my thoughts, Burnie laughed and said, "King Corporal. Whatta name." He sighed happily, his arms folded under his head. "Let's find your family and live the farmer's life in Domremy."

"You can begin your new existence," I suggested, "by harvesting some *mirabelles* for dinner."

"I'm too comfortable," Burnie said. "Why don't you go instead?"

"Because I'm not very hungry."

"I'm not, either. I'm tired, though. Long day, huh?"

I flashed on killing the officer. "The longest of my life, maybe."

We sat in silence for a few minutes. Maybe Burnie was thinking about him, too.

"Let's cover the dugout," my friend said, and hauled himself to his feet. "I smell rain."

"That's serious," I said, "when an Indian smells rain."

"Never doubt a Cherokee's woodlore."

I stood and helped gather leafy branches, then watched Burnie weave the branches into a canopy. It proved to be a poor ceiling. The rain did fall, and our trench flooded. I rode hard on him for being an Indian who, for all his woodlore, couldn't build a proper shelter.

After a few hours we grew impatient and uncomfortable. We abandoned our hideout for the plateau, where we gathered a few *mirabelles*. We did not speak much. I began to wonder about the peg-legged man, but I kept my doubts to myself. I tried to raise my spirits with thoughts of my mother's reaction when I told her I had eaten her mythical yellow plums.

Finally, at dusk, the farmer returned alone. A companion of few words, he led us closer to the village and stopped at the ruins of a burned-out house. The walls were charred, and the air smelled of a recent fire.

"Vous deux attendez ici," he said, but did not indicate when he would return.

Burnie and I were hopeful he would be back soon, as we could not find a place to sit that was not thick with soot. We stood around or leaned against the skeleton of the house. Night fell, leaving us in total darkness. Time hung heavy. We waited in silence for hours. The gloomy environment gave birth to worry and more doubt. Had my hopes of finding friends and safety in my mother's village been misguided and naïve?

Once those fears took root, they mushroomed. Had the peg-legged man told a German sympathizer? Had he been killed? Coerced into leading us into a trap? I began to connect my mother's reticence to bizarre happenings in her village. Maybe some curse had struck her and her family a generation before, and I would be the next victim. Chills ran up my spine.

My faith in finding help among my mother's people had been complete and unwavering. Now my discouragement was equally deep. I began to cry.

"What's wrong?" Burnie asked.

"I'm sorry," I wailed.

"What for?"

"For leading us into this mess!" I continued to weep.

Burnie hit my arm. "Jimmy! Hush!"

I stopped crying and heard the murmur of voices.

"Someone's coming!" he hissed.

I heard footsteps. We crept from where we had been standing to an opening in the side wall, whence we could run if necessary.

A flashlight beam pointed into the house, and in the shadows I could see several people. None wore the helmet or uniform of a German soldier. More flashlight beams slanted into the interior, and an old woman, surely in her eighties, came forward. She shone the light into Burnie's face and then into mine.

At once her eyes widened, then crinkled into a smile. She nodded and affirmed, *"Oui, c'est le fils de Lucie Munier!"*

I looked closely at her.

"Je suis Madame Blondeau. Je voyageais dans le train avec votre mère quand votre père l'a vue pour la première fois!"

Madame Blondeau did not speak much English, no more than I could speak French. *"Vous devez être très prudent. Une grande concentration de soldats allemands est dans le secteur,"* she warned.

I promised we would be careful not to attract the Germans' attention.

She smiled at me with such affection, I could feel how dearly she loved my mother. She reached a little, bony hand up to my cheek, and her eyes filled with tears. *"Vous ressemblez à votre mere,"* she said.

"Yes, I have her eyes and coloring," I said.

"Mais vous ressemblez à votre père, aussi."

"His nose and mouth," I agreed.

"Vos parents sont-ils en bonne santé et heureux?"

"They are both well, *merci*. And they are very happy together."

"Bon! C'est tout j'ai voulu pour votre mère. C'est tout ce qu'elle a mérité, après ce qu'elle a souffert."

After all the misery my mother had suffered? I wondered what Madame Blondeau meant by that.

————

My mother had described Domremy as being at a crossroads. For centuries German soldiers as well as French had come to worship at the Basilica of Bois-Chenu, built on a hill overlooking the village to honor Saint Joan of Arc. I didn't know how many soldiers were usually there, but when Burnie and I arrived, the Germans were everywhere.

Enemy occupation was unimaginably stressful, and we did not want to add to our hosts' anxiety. We stayed in Madame Blondeau's cozy house for only one night, but the stories flowed for hours, and I soaked them up as we sat at her tiny round table and sipped tea sweetened with peach preserves. She told the stories in French, and I translated them as best I could for Burnie.

At times I recognized my mother as the heroine, and at other times, Madame could have been describing a stranger because Mom had changed with maturity and the responsibility of raising a family.

According to Madame, my mother had a strong will, and she disobeyed authority whenever she believed it was necessary. On one occasion, her best friend's older brother became ill. He dragged an old couch under the steps of his house, lay down on it, and refused to budge. He was only twenty-one years old, and no one in the village could figure out what was wrong with him.

My mother had heard about a very good doctor, a major in rank, in charge of the American army hospital in Neufchateau, and she bicycled there with a girlfriend to fetch him. The doctor said he would come to the house to look the boy over, but my mother insisted he go with her immediately, before it was too late. The two young women refused to leave his office without him.

The next morning, the major saw that the young women had camped overnight on the floor outside his office. Impressed with their determination, he agreed to accompany them to see the sick boy.

Lucie had worried her parents sick by staying out all night, Madame reported. When she came home, her father pretended to give her a good licking. Madame said he whipped my mom with a wet noodle.

"And the boy?" I asked.

Gravely ill with an infection, she answered. The doctor immediately took him back to the army hospital and amputated his leg, saving his life. Madame wiped tears from her eyes as Burnie and I sat in somber silence.

Suddenly Madame began another tale about my mother. After the war, an epidemic of swine flu swept through the village and quickly killed several people. Whenever someone contracted the fever, my mother bicycled ten miles to Neufchateau and summoned the doctor, even though he lacked a flu remedy.

But then my mom herself became so sick with a soaring fever, she was barely able to crawl into bed. Living alone and feeling too ill to call for help, she simply left the door open and prayed someone would find her.

"Lucie still had the pet goose her parents had given her when she was a child," Madame told us in French. "The goose was quite attached to Lucie and would follow her around in the manner of a devoted dog. While Lucie lay in her sickbed, the goose somehow realized something was wrong. He waddled into the village, honking and making a commotion."

Madame's eyes shone with humor. Some of the villagers recognized Lucie's goose, she said, and when they brought it back to the farm, they discovered Lucie burning with fever. They gave her the only remedy they had—a pint of whisky—and wouldn't leave until she had drunk the whole pint.

"La pinte entière de bourbon?" I said, amazed. I had never seen my mother drink more than a single glass of wine.

"Aussitôt," Madame assured us. *"Elle a été complètement remise."*

"Recovered completely," I translated for my Cherokee friend.

Our hostess shooed us to bed like a couple of chicks, then took her leave.

Early the next morning Madame led us to our next resting place.

We followed her up the hill and into the forest, to a tiny stone shelter that surely was several centuries old. It had three walls, and the roof was so low, Burnie and I could not stand beneath it. The shack provided us with a decent space to lie down, however, and would afford us a little protection from heavy rain—better than Burnie's leafy lean-to, I told him.

"On a dit à Jeanne d'Arc de venir ici quand elle a voulu être seule pour prier et étudier," Madame explained.

"I doubt we'll do much studying or praying," Burnie murmured, looking around.

"But I can see how it would have been an excellent spot for young Joan," I added quickly.

Madame added that my grandfather Jules Munier and his sons and friends rested there when they hunted. My mother had fought to accompany the men, the old woman said. Lucie hated being excluded from any of their outdoor activities and adventures.

"Your mother had a wild streak," Madame told me in French. "She was never one to be limited by her skirts."

As a young girl she begged to go along, but later, after she had proven herself, the other hunters welcomed her presence and contribution.

The little refuge became our home for a few days while Burnie and I lay low and replenished our strength. Despite her advanced age, Madame Blondeau trekked up the steep hill each afternoon, bringing stewed rabbits, crusty bread, cheese, and always a little wine. While we ate—she never ate with us—she kept us company and talked about the town, the war, and my family's history.

Madame spoke as if I already knew all the stories. In fact, although my three sisters and I had always been curious about Mom's life in France, we had never heard much about our French grandparents. I had no idea if she was an only child or had siblings. Now I learned that my mother was closest in age to her two brothers, Eugene and Albert. She had one married sister, Helen, who was much older, and another sister much younger than she, who went to live with Helen in Paris. I did not catch her name.

"When your parents met, your mother and I were on our way to Paris to find your aunt Helen," she recalled. "We hoped to bring her back to the farm, to help your mother."

Why would my mother need help with the farm? I wondered. Where were her parents and brothers? Why had they not been with her when she was bedridden with the swine flu? I had to leave those thoughts unanswered, for Madame changed the subject and was telling stories and teaching us new French words. I looked forward to telling my parents all about the visit. I knew my mom and Madame had been close, and I felt a growing fondness for the elderly woman.

But for all her conversation, Madame never mentioned any plans for moving Burnie and me closer to Switzerland, and after a few days of seclusion, he and I felt restless. Madame clearly enjoyed the vista of Domremy and the Meuse River—and the view was spectacular—but that only added to our frustration. We wanted to get closer to the river. We wanted to jump in the water, especially when the sun was at its peak.

We could see girls from the village swimming in the river and washing their clothes.

"I'm going down to the river, Jimmy," Burnie said. "And if you don't want to, I'll tell you how it was when I come back."

"I want to go with you, but I don't want to offend Madame Blondeau."

Burnie looked at me as if I had grown another head.

"We're connected through my mother," I explained weakly.

"Jimmy. Where is your mother?"

"New Jersey?"

"Where are you?"

"France."

"Does your mother even know where you are?"

"No . . ."

"Do you think your mother would really care if you went swimming right now?"

I looked down at the girls splashing in the Meuse and finally agreed we should investigate Domremy's feminine attractions. I wanted Madame to know about it first, though.

That afternoon, during Madame's visit, I asked her to bring scissors the next day so Burnie and I could cut off our pant legs and go swimming.

One eyebrow shot up. She made a remark about respecting whomever we saw at the river and, of course, being careful of any suspected Germans and German sympathizers. Madame saw through me as if she were my own mother, then apologized for behaving like my guardian.

"I was more an aunt than a teacher to your mother," she explained. "I was her parents' friend, and I stayed with Lucie during that terrible time after their death. I made it my duty to protect your mother from pain. If anything were to happen to you while you were my guest . . ."

"*Je comprends,*" I said, then took a risk. "*Ma mère ne m'a pas parlé de sa famille.*"

She looked surprised. "*Non? Pourquoi pas?*"

"*Je ne sais pas. Vous m'en parleriez?*"

I watched as she weighed my request to tell me about my mother's family.

"*Peut-être. Peut-être que non.*" She reached for her cane, and I moved to help Madame to her feet. "*Je ne voudrais pas qu'elle soit fâchée avec nous.*"

"I wouldn't want her to be angry with us, either." I tried to hide my frustration. "I didn't mean to place you in an awkward position. Whatever you decide will be fine with me."

―――――――

The next afternoon, Madame Blondeau brought a serious-looking pair of dressmaker's shears almost as long as my forearm. She told me that sewing had brought her and my mother together. Madame had been a respected teacher in Paris. When she retired, she, like many other Parisians, traded an expensive Paris apartment for a place in the country. She settled in Domremy-La-Pucelle and was hired right away by the villagers to supplement their children's education each day after school. This was especially crucial for the girls, whose education was limited to home economics, taught at a "finishing" school. One of these schools was owned by my mother's aunt, so she not only had to attend, she was expected to set a good example.

"Was she?" I asked. "A good example, I mean?"

Madame laughed and shook her head indulgently, then answered in French, "Rarely. More often she was in trouble for stealing peaches and pulling other pranks."

In those days, she said, boys and girls went to separate schools run by the Church. When my mother was eleven, the government closed the schools because they wanted to remove the Church from what was viewed as a responsibility of the state. By then my mother was already "finished," having mastered the cooking and sewing skills that would serve her throughout her life.

That afternoon our guest did not stay as long as usual, and she had nothing else to say about the Muniers.

Burnie and I impatiently hacked at our long pants and turned them into swimming shorts, and then we made our way to the river. Lucky for us, a few girls were already down there, washing clothes. Burnie ran full speed and then stopped behind a tree. We felt timid about getting any closer. We were so accustomed to hiding, any interaction, no matter how appealing, seemed dangerous to us.

We watched the girls from our spot for the next two days. On the third day, I noticed an older man fishing about fifty feet from where we stood. I knew a lot about fishing from watching Pop and his friends at the Jersey shore, so I was interested in what this Frenchman was catching. He pulled in what looked like a pretty large pickerel— about twenty inches long. He put it in a basket beside him.

I ventured a little closer and made eye contact with him. He waved and seemed to welcome my company, so I walked over and said hello.

"Je suis Monsieur Faerbus," he said, pointing toward the village, *"et j'habite à Domrémy."*

"Ma mère est Lucie Munier," I said. *"Vous l'avez connue?"*

His face brightened. *"Lucie? Ah, oui! Et j'ai connu votre père, aussi!"*

Since Monsieur Faerbus had known my father, I told him about my going fishing with Pop. Monsieur asked about him and our family and our life in America. He said he could never leave Domremy and would die there, even if it meant being killed by Germans.

Burnie wandered over and watched as Monsieur caught a few more pickerel. My sharp-eyed friend pointed to bass in the stream, and the Frenchman said he had come that day with the hope of catching some.

He ended up talking about my grandparents and the great farm they once had. He knew my grandfather had been educated at the Sorbonne and told me that he had held my grandfather in great esteem.

"He was a very fair man," Monsieur Faerbus said, then asked if I would like to hear a story about my family.

Of course I said yes; I still had not found out what had caused my mother's sadness. Perhaps his story would reveal it.

"Your grandfather," he began, speaking in French, "told each of his sons that they could have their own horse when they were old enough to assist at the birth of their foal and take full responsibility from that moment."

He paused, chuckling. "Your mother was always one to run with the boys. Lucie made sure her father understood that he had set a precedent for all his children, and she fully expected to have her own horse when she met the qualifications."

"Did she?" I asked.

"When she was thirteen," Monsieur answered. "With help from four other farmers from Domremy, Lucie and her father pulled a foal out by its legs. As soon as the handsome little rascal was born, he stood on all fours. Right away Lucie showed it great affection and devotion."

We waited while the man pulled another pickerel from the river and put it in his basket. "That one is for you, boys."

We thanked him, and he continued with the story. "Her father said to her, 'From now on, that's your horse, Lucie, and your responsibility.' She fed and groomed him and made sure his mother took good care of him. Every day Lucie brushed him and fed him a lump of sugar. She played with him the way people play with a dog. She would lie down on the ground each morning"—here, Monsieur lay down on the bank to illustrate—"and he would gallop right up to her! She always hid a lump of sugar under her arm that he would sniff and find."

He sat up and flapped his jacket to loosen the leaves and grass that had stuck to the fabric. "One day she decided that he was old enough to ride, and in her usual headstrong manner she plunged right in. She tried to break him by jumping from a fence onto his bare back. The horse was so shocked, he immediately threw her over the fence! Lucie was indignant. She said, 'How can you do that to me? I'm so good to you!'"

We all had a good laugh.

"Her parents forbade her from riding the horse until he was properly broken in by her brother Eugene," he went on.

"Did that happen?" I asked.

"Ah, yes! Eventually she rode him without a saddle and went over hair-raising jumps." Now he stood, arms out to the side, as if he were balancing. "She even taught herself to stand on his back while he galloped! She never did this where anyone who might report back to her parents could see her."

"Did they ever find out?"

"No, I don't believe word got back to them. They would have worried that their daughter tried such stunts."

He fell silent and shook his head mournfully. *"Tragique!"*

My breath caught in my throat. *"Que?"* I asked when he did not explain. *"Qu'est-ce qui était tragique?"*

Again Monsieur Faerbus sighed. "When the war broke out—this was World War I—the French military swept through each village, confiscating horses for the cavalry. They were so impressed with Lucie's horse's training, they paid her four thousand francs for the four-year-old—double the amount her brothers received for their horses. But that did little to ease her devastation.

"Also, boys, these were the days before tractors. Horses were essential to farming. But then the government forbade the Muniers to grow crops because their farm was only five miles from the front line."

"They didn't want them feeding the enemy?" Burnie asked.

"Exactement." During the First World War, he explained, the Germans plundered big farms like theirs, so the government allowed them to raise only the food the family needed to survive.

"Because Domremy-La-Pucelle was the birthplace of Joan of Arc," Monsieur Faerbus continued, "whenever a French regiment passed through the village, it always had a full-dress parade—complete with music—to honor the patron saint of soldiers. At the first sound of music, Lucie and her friends would run to the main road so they could see the soldiers and feel the excitement. During one parade—I believe Lucie was about seventeen at the time—she noticed a handsome French lieutenant who was suddenly unable to control his horse. He looked completely bewildered that his horse would not stay in line.

"As he moved closer, Lucie lay on the ground, and the horse came straight to her and began to nestle under her arm. It was her beloved horse, looking for the sugar cube!"

"You're joking," Burnie said.

"I'm serious," Monsieur assured him. "The lieutenant was on his way to the front line. He would be stationed only five miles from Domremy, so he asked Lucie if he might visit her and bring the horse. Of course she liked that idea! They wrote letters back and forth—a lucky fellow, I thought."

"But did she like him or his horse?" Burnie asked.

Monsieur Faerbus shrugged eloquently. "The lieutenant visited a few more times when he was sent from the front line for a rest. But their romance was short-lived."

Lucky for me, I thought.

"About six months later, one of her letters was returned. The envelope was marked Missing in Action, and then another was returned, marked Killed in Action. Knowing how the cavalry fought, Lucie immediately knew her horse had died with him on the battlefield."

He fell silent for a moment, deep in thought. When he looked at me again, his face was etched with sorrow. "But we must keep things in perspective, yes? As big a grief as it had seemed at the time, it could not compare with what befell her next."

Monsieur had no more to say. He had talked quite a bit, and I didn't want to ask for more of his time and memories. He packed up to go home, gave us two of the fish, some food he had brought in his basket, and the promise to bring us more the next day.

I knew I would ask him to tell me stories about my mother. I was on the brink of hearing my family's deepest secrets, and I had to be patient. In the meantime, Burnie and I were becoming the best-fed guys in Domremy.

CHAPTER 15

My plans to see Monsieur Faerbus did not materialize, for Madame Blondeau had made other arrangements. When Burnie and I returned to our stone hut, we found our friend waiting for us.

"J'ai localisé votre cousin Jean Gossot," Madame said happily. *"Il vous emmènera dans son camion demain."*

I was very relieved to hear she had arranged for our departure and excited about meeting my cousin. Would he and I look alike? Would he resemble my mother? I would find out the next morning, when all Burnie and I had to do was walk down the hill to the main roadway. My cousin Jean would pick us up there.

We said our farewells, and Madame started out for home before her path fell into shadow at the day's end.

Burnie and I packed up our clothes and food at dawn, and as promised, Jean arrived . . . in a truck unlike anything I had ever seen. Behind the cab was an overlong wooden flatbed, which he needed to transport lumber from the forest to builders. The truck's cab resembled most others, but its combustion system was powered by a charcoal burner. An unusually long stack on the driver's side pointed skyward to protect the driver and passengers from the fumes.

We rode in silence for over an hour through the picturesque farmlands before reaching Jean's large home. His land stretched for well over one acre, and his three young daughters seemed to play on every foot of it. He had a pond behind the house, and a stream flowing under the house generated electricity. His irrigation system also served to enhance the setting. The grass was thick and the wooded area, fertile and lush. I learned early that Jean valued his independence.

My cousin introduced us to his wife, Marie-Madeleine, the niece of Cardinal Eugene Tisserant, a Frenchman who was at that time the dean of the College of Cardinals in Rome.

We sat down at their big wooden table, and Jean immediately broke out some wine. Like many French farmers we had met, he made wine from the grapes of his own arbors and was very proud of it. He explained how meticulous he was, every stage of the process. The very best wine was saved in the basement, he said, and a lesser table wine was served with meals.

Once he relaxed, Jean proved to be quite a talker. The more he said, the less I cared for his company. My cousin claimed to know how the world worked. He counted among his friends many famous people, and they all depended upon his sage advice on a wide range of important subjects. I was surprised France had fallen to the Germans, when my cousin probably could have single-handedly prevented it.

He asked little about my mother and nothing about her life in America. He had never been to the United States, but he spoke as if he knew all there was to know about it. He said he would get there someday.

I felt disappointed. I had hoped my cousin and I would feel an emotional connection, but we began with a distance between us. I held little faith we would close the gap. I did, however, gain a little understanding into his character when Jean told me he had lost a newborn son. The death had embittered him, and he did not hide his disappointment from his wife or daughters. He had always wanted a son, but the one God gave him was sick.

Jean kept his own hours, and the rest of the family accommodated him. He conducted much of his work under the watchful eye of the Germans. He delivered logs from the forest to the railroad station, from where the invaders would take and ship them for their own use. Unlike other Frenchmen who showed contempt or sorrow about such forced labor, Jean seemed indifferent. He claimed to go about his tasks with little emotion and was never afraid to communicate with the enemy when he had a question or when they confronted him.

Marie-Madeleine confided that he frequently disappeared into the forest and did not return until sometime between midnight and dawn. I thought of the men in the Argonne Forest who tried to shield their families from their activity with the Resistance. I suspected that Jean's logging was a front for nighttime missions for the Maquis. In the time we spent at his home, however, Jean remained secretive about his work. He never took Burnie or me with him, so my friend and I spent our days cutting wood for Jean at the house or helping Marie-Madeleine with chores.

One morning about a week after we began our stay with him, my cousin received a call: The Germans had heard about someone harboring two Americans, and soldiers were on their way to search his house. Jean's extraordinary composure made me suspicious. Showing neither fear nor hesitation, he told Burnie and me to hide in the woods until further notice. How could he be so bold? Should I feel calm or wary? Was he telling the truth? I did not know.

His conviction could be extremely convincing. It worked with the Germans who searched through his house: They found nothing to suggest our presence and soon left.

Jean spoke repeatedly about getting us *cartes d'identités,* and the Germans' search prompted him to action. A couple of days later, he took us to Monsieur Buboney, the owner of a crystal factory in Vannes-le-Chatel, a twin city to Allamps, where many local residents were employed.

The factory owner was a handsome and gracious man who, despite his apparent wealth and comfortable life, assumed huge risks by issuing false papers and working alongside the Resistance. Buboney with three other men created the identity cards.

"You weell have to wait a day or so before receiving zee official seals and stamps," one of the fellows, Christophe, explained. "Zay are processed een a town not so close to Allamps." He held up his index finger. "But zee seals and zee stamps make zee cards . . ." He searched for a word. Suddenly he smiled. "Jenuine. Zee Germans never trace one card back to find eet ees not jenuine."

They took our photographs and filled out some information for us. For occupation they wrote *ouvrier agricole.* I was now a registered farm laborer. My work on my cousin's farm the week before made that statement true. I helped fill in the rest.

Jean read one question aloud. *"A-t-il une barbe?"* He and the other men looked at me and laughed.

Christophe slapped my cheeks and joked, "He could not grow a beard eef he wanted to!"

Our receiving official-looking documents allowed my cousin to feel more comfortable about Burnie and me staying with his family. As soon as we had identity cards, he invited us to accompany him on errands. No longer were we confined within the boundaries of his farm.

One morning Jean had to deliver a truckload of logs to the railroad station. He asked Burnie and me along, and we jumped at the chance. When we arrived at our destination, I was amazed to see the bustling activity at the acre-wide train yard. German soldiers stretched shoulder to shoulder across its width, and they had to step out of the way to let the truck through with the delivery.

Jean led us to an area that had a hand crane we could use to unload the logs, which would be shipped to Germany. The job really was suitable for four men, but we were only three. Had Jean ever managed this by himself? I wondered.

My cousin hopped on the flatbed and positioned clamps on each end of a log. Burnie stood on one of the train's flatbed cars, to direct the logs as they swung onto the platform. My job was to operate the crane. The mechanism was designed with two handles, for two operators. I did my best to work both sides, but I struggled with them. Soon a German soldier strolled over, smiled, pointed to the other handle, and made a circular motion. Apparently he could not speak French, a shortcoming for which I was intensely grateful.

I nodded, and grasping the second handle, he helped unload the entire flatbed in about half an hour. Then Jean, Burnie, and I piled back into the truck and drove out of the rail yard.

"Vous êtes fou!" I yelled at Jean. "With a wife and three kids at home, you can't afford to be so nuts! If that German had heard me make even one sound that did not seem French, your whole family would be dead!"

He did not respond.

"Or did fooling the soldiers give you some weird kind of satisfaction?" I demanded.

He just kept driving. He was not a worrier, and he probably understood the situation better than Burnie or I could. I continued to huff and yell on the way home.

"Vous êtes fou!" I repeated, and Burnie began to laugh, and soon Jean was smiling wryly but did not say a word. I wanted to believe his silence had a meaning—that he saw things my way and agreed he had done something stupid.

When I calmed down, I had to acknowledge we had not encountered any problems with the Germans, and after we got home, Jean and I never spoke of the incident. I believe my cousin tried to smooth things over with me, for that same afternoon, he asked Burnie and me to help him in the barn. He wanted to kill a veal-sized calf for a special dinner. I never asked what the occasion was, but I lent a hand with the preparations.

We slaughtered the calf and delivered it to Marie-Madeleine's kitchen. We three men drank some fine wine in the barn until we all felt really pleased with ourselves and happy with one another.

"Getting tipsy in the barn is a proud tradition among the men in my family," Jean said in French. "I always thought I would do it with Eugene and Albert, just as our fathers and uncles had."

"Quelle relation avec moi?"

He looked at me, puzzled, then replied, "As your mother's brothers, they would be your uncles."

"Would you tell me about them?" I asked.

Jean refilled our glasses as he spoke. "They both served with the French Army on the front line, so we saw them only sporadically during the war. Albert had been badly wounded early in the conflict, and the surgeons put a silver plate in his head." Jean shrugged and smiled sadly. "And yet as soon as he was able, he returned to the Western Front and continued to serve."

"Ma mère a aimé ses frères?"

"They were fishing and hunting buddies," my cousin answered. "All three were very close, and she fervently prayed they would survive the terrible war."

My mother and her parents had struggled to maintain the land and house after Eugene and Albert enlisted. The oldest sister, Helen, married and moved to Paris. The youngest sister lived with the newlyweds. When Lucie's strength waned or when her grief threatened to overcome her, she concentrated on the day Eugene and Albert would return safely to the farm, marry, and raise a new generation of Muniers there.

Jean heaved a sigh. "But it was not to be."

Eugene died in battle a few days before the Armistice was declared.

"Et Albert?" I could hardly breathe.

Jean explained that Albert's regiment was stationed on the front line about ten miles from Domremy. Early the morning after the Armistice, Lucie jumped on her bicycle and pedaled to his camp. She found her brother's best friends, and they turned away, refusing to make eye contact. Desperate to find her brother, she cycled to army headquarters, where she learned that Albert had been killed in a skirmish two hours after the Armistice was declared.

Jean shook his head, then took a long drink of wine.

Just as I was going to ask about my grandparents, Marie-Madeleine called to us from the yard. Dinner was on the table.

"Merci, cela a répondu à beaucoup de mes questions," I said as Jean, Burnie, and I left the barn. *"Vous m'avez donné une famille."* ("Thank you. This has answered many questions. You gave me a family.")

He stopped walking and looked me in the eyes. *"Donc beaucoup de misère,"* he whispered. *"Donc beaucoup de mort."* ("So much misery, so much death.")

———

Two days later Jean was up to his old tricks. He invited Burnie and me to join him on another expedition. When he loaded extra charcoal into the truck's engine burner, I knew our ride would take us farther than the train station.

He had a habit of letting the charcoal burn off each night. On this day a few embers must have remained, for when he poured the charcoal in, a big explosion erupted in smoke and flames. Jean staggered out of the conflagration, covering his face with his hands and cursing roundly.

"Are you okay?" I asked him.

"Take your hands away so we can see you," Burnie said, and Marie-Madeleine and the girls came on the run.

"Ne vous inquiétez pas, ne vous inquiétez pas," Jean said, and dropped his hands. *"Je suis beau."*

He *was* fine, but his eyebrows were gone, and his face was as red as a lobster in August.

The girls stopped in their tracks and stared at their father, who stood in the midst of the swirling smoke, mumbling with anger. He was steamed! Marie-Madeleine tried to keep from laughing at him, but she could not control herself, which was rare. I began to applaud, first slowly and then louder and faster. Burnie put his fingers in his mouth and whistled, startling the girls even more than they already were. When they felt they could laugh with impunity, they did, loudly, and pointed at Jean, who managed to chuckle when he wasn't cursing. By the time the three of us finally left in the smoky truck, we were all laughing hard and wiping the tears from our eyes.

We rode for over an hour, and despite repeated inquiries as to our destination, Jean revealed nothing.

Another hour passed, and a number of large buildings behind layers of barbed wire came into view. When I realized he was driving toward a prison camp, I burned as hot as his charcoal engine. "Where in God's name are you taking us?" I demanded.

Jean replied it was a Polish prison, and he was doing a favor for a friend. We were there to pick up an alembic, a miniature still, which was stored at the prison and worth good money.

"Of all the places you could take us, a prison is the worst!" I shouted. My heart was pounding just looking at the German guards standing at the gates, their weapons at the ready as Jean pulled to a stop.

The prison guards asked for our *cartes d'identités*. After careful inspection, the guard handed back my card as he peered into my face.

Accompanied by a pair of soldiers, we drove around the back of the prison camp, to an area of locked storage garages. The commandant had probably stolen the still (among other valuables) from local residences and intended to take the loot back home to Germany. Jean's job was to get it to the railroad station. The German soldiers assisted us in loading it onto the truck. The alembic was a beauty, made of solid copper.

We breathed a sigh of relief when we drove out of the camp without a confrontation. I sat back, trying to relax.

We drove another two hours in silence. I believed we were headed for the railway station, but Jean surprised me by turning down a secondary road and stopping at a padlocked garage. He unlocked the door, drove his truck inside, and with our help unloaded the still. Then he went out into the darkness and began digging a hole behind the garage. He did not ask us for help, so Burnie and I stood by and watched with interest. Was my mysterious cousin burying something or retrieving it?

When we heard the shovel make contact, Burnie and I moved forward to see Jean brush dirt from what proved to be a wooden crate. He pried up the lid to reveal a stash of World War I French rifles and some ammunition. Grinning, he handed one to each of us. Within ten minutes, the crate was hidden, the garage was locked, and we were speeding away in the truck, heading back toward Allamps.

Closer to the village, we saw German soldiers running and racing away in trucks.

"*Ceci est étrange . . .*" Jean murmured, looking around.

The Germans looked utterly disorganized, which *was* strange for them. Some were on bicycles, some on motorcycles, and a few on horses—anything that moved faster than their own two legs had been commandeered.

"*Je me demande où ils vont si rapidement,*" he added.

"*La gare?*" Burnie ventured.

"That's my guess," I told them. Where else could the Germans be going in such a hurry but the train station?

The more Germans we saw on the run, the more excited we got.

"*Je me demande si les Alliés sont plus près que nous avions pensé,*" Jean said. His eyes glittered.

Perhaps the Allies *were* closer than we had expected. My heart was pounding so hard, I could feel it hammering against my ribs.

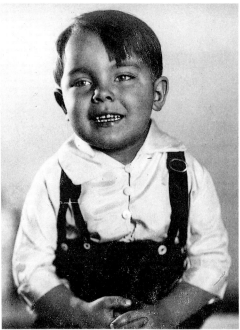

Jimmy at age three, on his way to being dubbed "The Holy Terror."

Jimmy after graduating Parachute School.

Jimmy's mother, Lucie Sheeran

October 1942. Lucie Sheeran visiting Jimmy at Camp Taccoa Jump School. She's wearing the fur coat he bought her when he enlisted.

Madame Blondeau.

Lucie Sheeran's family.

Jimmy's father, John F. Sheeran.

John F. Sheeran, a charismatic leader, and comrades from Passaic.

Al Engelbrecht and Jimmy posing with a U.S. Army Recruiting Office sign.

Spring of 1944 in Scotland.

My Mademoiselle From Domremy

I saw her first on a speeding train;
Since then she's reigned as Queen in my brain.
This glorious darling smiled at me,
It was in France this happened to be.

We left the train but my heart stayed on;
To earth's end I would have gladly gone
To meet this girl who had stirred my love,
But our Army orders ranked above.

Sad I was when the train started up,
Never to meet her — a bitter cup.
I treasured the smile she sent to me,
Thinking I'd have but a memory.

Drab days followed; my spirits were low,
Nothing was right wherever I'd go.
Even the solace of good French wine
Could not erase this girl from my mind.

Came Christmas Eve, I was really blue —
No place to go and nothing to do.
While drinking in the local cafe,
The orders came — we were on our way.

Five trucks the detail, with thirty men.
I cared not where we landed, or when.
I sat up high on a pile of gear;
Feeling no pain, I was crocked I fear.

Arriving in St. Joan of Arc's town
The word was here, our new home we'd found.
In an open door I saw there framed
The woman God for me had ordained.

I rolled off that truck filled with delight
Fearful the vision would fade from sight.
Sweet Christmas Eve our romance began;
She was happy, too, to find her man.

'Twas five months later that we were wed
In Domremy, where St. Joan was bred.
Thank Thee, God, for these thirty-three years;
Joy has greatly exceeded our tears.

Lucie, my sweetheart, Mother of four,
Three girls and a son we both adore;
God has been good in our married life.
Thank you, my love, my wonderful wife.

                    To Lucie with all my love,

                            Jack Sheeran

July, 1952

John (Jack) Sheeran's poem about Jimmy's mom and family.

Jim (first from left, standing) with his 101st Airborne buddies at Camp Taccoa, 1943.

Fall 1945. Johnny Simpson and the Sheeran family. Notice Johnny with his artificial left hand and wrist. From the *New Jersey Herald* newspaper.

The Secretary of War desires me to express his deep regret that your son Private First Class James J Sheeran has been reported missing in action since six June in France if further details or other information are received you will be promptly notified.

Outside Forest D'Argonne with the Maquis. The Cadet Family. The plaque Jimmy is holding states 14 July 1944 – French National Day. One British pilot and one Canadian pilot were also there, but did not join the fight with the Maquis. This photo was taken behind the house of the oldest brother of the Cadet family (not shown), who was the Gendarme sitting at the head of the table when Jimmy's blindfold was taken off after arriving at Placardelle, Argonne Forest.

Serge Berger's family in front of their wooden barn in Senard, Argonne. Wooden structures were rare.

Burnie and Jimmy at the bank of Meuse River. They had asked Madame Blondeau for a pair of scissors to cut off their long pants, so they could join girls swimming in the Meuse River.

Jimmy's false Identity Card made by Monsiur Boubonney, the owner of the Crysterrie at Vienne Le Chatel.

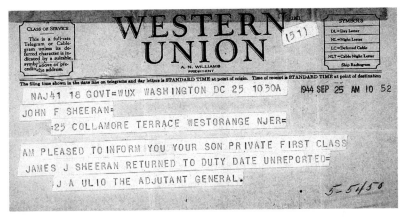

Am pleased to inform you your son Private First Class James J Sheeran returned to duty, date unreported.

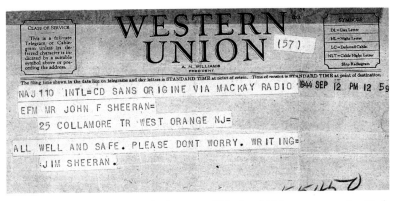

"All well and safe. Please don't worry. Writing." Telegram sent by Jim's West Orange High School buddy Bill Hill at the request of Jim after he and Burnie returned to the Allied lines in France on September 11, 1944, but before the completion of their debriefing.

Jim's French cousin, Marie-Madeleine Gossot, visiting Jim and his mom, Lucie, in West Orange, New Jersey, in the 1950s.

In France in 1994 with Burnie Rainwater at the fiftieth anniversary picnic with the Maquis in the Argonne Forest.

At the French Ambassador's official residence in Washington, D.C., January 31, 2007. French Ambassador Levitte, Jimmy, his wife Lena, and his daughter, Josette.

January 31, 2007, Jim receiving his medal from Ambassador Levitte of France, naming him a *Chevalier De La Legion D'Honneur*, the highest honor given to a civilian by the President of the Republic of France. Wife Lena looking on with admiration.

We'd be able to reunite with the Allies, get back to our company, and join in the fight!

Burnie reached to grab my arm. "If we can find our company, the army will send us home, Jimmy. *Home!*"

Jean downshifted the gears, slowing the truck, then gripped the steering wheel with one hand and his rifle, beside him on the seat, with the other. Burnie took hold of his, and my instincts told me to do the same. If the Germans were beating a hasty retreat, who knew what might happen? They might want to kill as many Frenchmen as possible while they still had the chance.

Even as I sensed a serious threat from the mob of German soldiers, I watched my cousin closely because I knew him to be foolhardy and unpredictable. His fingers were curled so tightly around the rifle, his knuckles turned white. Jean was an excellent shot, and his hatred for the invaders was unfathomable. He, too, would want to exact revenge while he had the opportunity.

Of course I understood his excitement. My own trigger finger was twitching. The idea of picking off a few Germans as they fled Allamps was tantalizing . . . but *I* could enjoy the temptation without doing anything about it. I couldn't say the same thing about Jean. How often had my cousin walked casually into danger, dragging Burnie and me with him?

He took a detour off the road and up a hill where we could get a wide view of the train station and village. He stopped the truck, hopped out with his rifle, and found himself a spot in the tall grass to aim his old weapon. Burnie and I ran after him.

"Jean, what are you doing?" I cried.

"*Restez calmes!*" he shouted. Shut up!

"Hold on! Don't shoot, Jean!" I lunged for his arm. Burnie positioned himself between Jean and the village.

I lowered my voice and pleaded, "Not like this, Jean. We don't know what's going on yet. Please! Wait."

He wheeled on me, and the barrel of his weapon was aimed at my gut. His eyes blazed, and spit flew from his mouth as he screamed, *"Ceci ne vous concerne pas!"*

I let my rifle drop from my fingers into the soft detritus. Over Jean's shoulder, I saw Burnie creep toward my cousin.

"Think of the consequences if you do this. It will—"

His chin went up, and he squinted at me warily. *"Pourquoi avoir si peur de la sécurité allemande?"* he demanded.

"Jean, I don't give a flying shit about the Germans' safety. I'm thinking about Marie-Madeleine and the girls and the three of us! Even if you pick off a bunch of Germans, others will come after us and go straight to your house."

Burnie stopped just behind Jean and, poised to strike, watched for my signal. I waited, my eyes locked on Jean's. My whole body throbbed with my racing heartbeat. Suddenly my cousin blinked, and I saw the fire in his eyes go out. He did not smile or nod, but I saw he understood. My gaze flicked to Burnie, who reached to take Jean's rifle. My cousin did not resist.

"C'mon, Jean, let's find out what's going on," Burnie said.

We followed Jean back to the truck. He turned the vehicle around and sped down the hill and toward home. We were all silent for a few minutes. The sharp smell of acrid sweat invaded my nostrils.

"I will keep the still," Jean finally proclaimed.

"Sure, Jean, keep it to remember this day," I said.

"Yeah," Burnie seconded. "It should belong to a bon vivant like you." He punched me lightly on the shoulder. "I guess being sophisticated connoisseurs runs in your family."

We laughed harder than his joke warranted, but we managed to release some tension and restore camaraderie. The rest of the ride was pleasant, and soon the house came into view. Marie-Madeleine, waiting on the doorstep, was bouncing up and down on the balls of her feet and clutching her hands over her heart.

"*Les Américains! Je pense que les Américains arrivent!*" she cried, running out to the truck. Her face was wet with tears, and after delivering the news, she broke down and sobbed in earnest.

Jean brushed past her and ran to the phone. We were at his heels. Marie-Madeleine trembled in my arms as we watched Jean listen to the news. A huge grin split his face.

"*L'armée du général Patton est juste à quelques villages d'ici!*" he told us, then walked stiffly to the table and sank into a chair.

Marie-Madeleine wept, and the girls came on the run to jump up and down and shriek and clap their hands. Jean just sat looking at us, tears running down his cheeks.

Burnie and I hugged and slapped each other on the back. "Looks like we're going to live through this war after all, Jimmy!" His dark eyes shone bright.

"Thanks for back there," I said quietly, referring to Jean and the hilltop.

Burnie nodded. "That's all right. It would have been a pisser, though, if you survived the Germans but were taken out by your French cousin."

We grabbed a baguette, a hunk of cheese, and a handful of olives, then climbed into the truck to see what was going on at the train station in Allamps. A low rumbling overrode our conversation.

"*Quel est ce bruit?*" Jean asked.

"I think it's a Sherman tank," Burnie said.

Jean turned the truck toward the sound. In a few minutes we rounded a curve, and from the top of a slight incline, I could see one of

Patton's tanks turn a corner and head toward us. A couple of GIs gripping machine guns stood in the door in the roof. They did not see us.

"Stop!" we screamed, and Jean pulled the truck over to the side of the road.

Burnie and I jumped out and took off running toward the tank. "We are Americans!" we screamed. "We're from the 101st Airborne!"

We stopped within a hundred yards of the tank and looked straight into the barrel of the cannon. Other vehicles pulled up behind the tank.

"Halt!" an officer up top hollered. "Halt! Put your hands up, or I'll blow your ass off!"

"But we're Americans! From—"

Burnie shook me off. "He's serious. Put your hands up," he said.

We walked slowly toward the tank, showing our weaponless hands in the air. The machine guns aimed at my skull quickened my speech. In about ten seconds I explained myself to the guys standing up on the tank. One of them hopped down to check us out, and we finally convinced him we were Americans from the 101st Airborne Division.

"Hiding since D-Day?" he said, incredulous.

"When we weren't fighting alongside the Resistance," Burnie mentioned casually, picking at an imaginary callus on his thumb.

"Jesus H. Christ! Welcome back, men!" He pumped our hands, grinning. "This is really exciting!" He pointed at Jean, who had caught up with us and was standing off to the side. "Who is—?"

"This is my cousin," I said, and waved Jean forward.

Jean beamed, shaking hands with the GIs.

"Men!" The tank commander scowled down. "If you recall, we're on a mission!" He pointed at us. "Can you lead us to where we might find the enemy?"

"My cousin can!" I called up. "He knows the terrain better than any of us."

"Then hop in that jeep," he ordered, and I interpreted for Jean.

My cousin slid into the passenger seat, while Burnie and I sat in the back. Jean directed our driver through town, pointing out where Germans had been living and eating. Next we drove to the train station.

The Germans had vanished without a trace.

Jean climbed from the jeep and looked around the station, scratching his head. He strode toward a stack of papers spread out on the station floor and found a map. He picked it up and brought it to the driver. Jean traced the route on the paper with his finger, then pointed down the track.

The soldier stood on his seat and looked out from the jeep. "Thank you, sir," he said graciously, and handed Jean a pack of Lucky Strikes. "Thank you very much."

Jean looked at the pack of cigarettes as if it were a Bronze Star.

The soldier radioed his lieutenant as he drove back to Jean's truck. "Where should I take the newcomers, sir?"

"I want to get them to England immediately," he ordered. "You know where the new airstrips are near Allamps."

"Near the prison camp for captured German soldiers, sir."

"Right. Take them there."

Burnie and I grinned at each other. *Home,* he mouthed.

I looked at my cousin. When we had jumped into his truck, I thought I'd be having dinner at his house with his family.

"S'il vous plaît dire au revoir au Madeleine-Marie et à vos filles pour moi," I said.

"And *moi,* too," Burnie said.

"Merci pour tout," I added.

"Yeah, thanks, Jean," Burnie said.

Then Jean and I quickly, emotionlessly, parted company. He was not an effusive man, and I was feeling so exhilarated, I couldn't get choked up about anything. I was going back to the troops! I wanted to find Lud and Simpson and Neeper and find out about the other guys. All my energy was flooding in that direction.

Funny, I thought, looking at the French countryside on the way to the airport. Some relationships that begin suddenly, like with Lud and Simpson and Neeper, would last forever. Others, like with Jean, end just as abruptly as they start. I hadn't offered to stay in touch, hadn't invited him to visit the U.S.

I looked over at Burnie. Of everyone in our division, he and I could not have had less in common, and I wasn't even thinking of our backgrounds. Burnie was a man of few words. He kept himself to himself, always. Despite months of going through training together, being in the same company and assigned to the same aircraft, I knew almost nothing about him. Now, after living with each other for all this time, he still remained a mystery, mostly.

One thing I knew for sure, though—he was the reason I was alive, and I was the reason he was. Burnie always knew what to do when I had no idea, and I inevitably could fill his gaps. He had the knowledge of his Cherokee nation behind him, and on the most fundamental level, from recognizing a cow's cough to possessing an inner directional compass, he got us through the forest and cross-country, and he pushed me through my periods of despair.

As for me, I provided the bold ideas, the linear strategies, and the impetus. I was the sociable one, the conversationalist, our connector to other members of our species. I could not call myself a linguist—not with my father as the standard setter—but I managed to pick up enough of the language to make us understood.

Because Burnie and I were so mismatched, we were the perfect pair.

CHAPTER 16

The United States Army had recently poured one long strip of concrete that could handle light airplanes. The area still stank of fresh tar, but orange blossoms could not have been more fragrant to me. Groups of GIs sitting or standing outside the hangar watched us with curiosity as we sped past them and rocked to a stop inside. I felt great seeing our guys.

German prisoners stood inside two guarded enclosures within the hangar. These areas had no solid walls, so some interaction between the Americans and their captives was unavoidable. They could hear what we said, and we could hear what they said.

While waiting for an officer to give us our orders, Burnie and I struck up a conversation with a few GIs. As we talked, I looked more closely at the enclosed sections. I was surprised by the number of German prisoners. They clearly outnumbered our own men.

"Hey, Burnie," I said. "See the showers over there?"

"Sure." He snorted in derision. "And steam rising from the hot water."

"A regular Ritz," one of the GIs drawled, and chuckled.

"That's pretty close to the truth," I told the soldier, "relatively speaking." We had expected the same amenity from the Germans after we were imprisoned in St. Lo. "I haven't had a hot shower in almost four months."

The soldiers, as one, took a step back from us, and we all laughed.

"Let's get you permission to take one," the Southerner offered, and off he went to find a commanding officer.

The officer immediately ordered all the Germans out of the shower so Burnie and I could clean up. "Take your time," the lieutenant said. "And that's an order."

As the hot water drummed on my back, I couldn't help but think about how badly the Germans had treated us. By the time I had dried off and realized I didn't have fresh clothes, my righteous indignation had superheated into rage. I shrugged on my French garments and fumed some more.

By the time we came out of the shower, I was feeling confrontational. I muscled up to a few Germans. "I want your watch," I demanded of them. "Your officers stole my watch when they captured me. And a medallion that had great value to my family. It's only fair that you replace my belongings."

The Germans hung back.

"Now!" I shouted, and a few shuffled forward, unbuckling their watchbands. "You're lucky I'm not taking your boots," I yelled, fastening the spoils of war from my wrist to my elbow. "The Germans stole my boots and my friends' boots, then marched us barefooted to a prison camp. Our feet were raw and bloody and infected. But did the Germans care? Hell, no! They were wearing our boots, so they had no problems."

Burnie also took watches from several and lined them up, showing them off. Some of the captives became angry and shouted at us.

"Ich gebe nicht Ihnen irgendetwas!"

"Sie Dieb! Sie können meine Uhr nicht stehlen!"

"Gehen Sie fickt sich und Ihre Mutter!"

"Hey!" One of the guards came rushing over. "Shut up in there!" He motioned the Germans to move back from Burnie and me, then he looked at us and shook his head. "What're you guys trying to do? Start a riot? Get outta there!"

The lieutenant came striding up. "Take off those watches!" he commanded.

"But—"

"Drop them!"

"Yes, sir!" I knew he was right, now that I was calming down. I was, in fact, startled by the intensity of my feelings.

We sheepishly left the enclosure under his stern glare. "Go outside and sit down." He lowered his voice as we neared him. "I know you've been through a lot, boys, but I don't want any trouble here. We'll get your debriefing going as soon as possible, then move you out. Until then, you are not to demand restitution from our prisoners. Do you understand?"

"Yes, sir."

"Yes, sir."

"Good."

Burnie and I sat on the concrete wall and talked with a few soldiers.

"Looks like you was purt' well nourished whilst you was hidin' out," one GI remarked, and stared at my midsection.

"We were lucky," Burnie said.

"Jimmy Sheeran! You son of a bitch!"

I looked around.

"Sheeran, where the hell is your uniform?"

I turned to see Bill Hill, a buddy from West Orange High School. We slammed into each other with some old football maneuvers, then gave each other a hard hug. He picked me up off the ground, then I did the same to him.

"I think they may already know each other," Burnie observed, and everyone laughed.

I pulled Bill over and introduced him and Burnie.

He motioned me to hurry. "C'mon! Tell me all." He raised an eyebrow. Why are you dressed like a Three Musketeer?"

"I'm not," I said, indignant. "I'm a top-level spy, and my cover is Maurice Chevalier. You are the first to suspect this isn't my true identity."

"You jerk," Bill said, laughing. He turned to Burnie. "And who're you s'posed to be? . . ."

"Claudette Colbert," the Cherokee replied.

Bill shook his head and laughed. "So what really happened? Quick." He jabbed a thumb over his shoulder, where an officer sat in the jeep, waiting impatiently.

I quickly recapped our experiences.

"So you're going home?" he asked.

"Yes," Burnie said immediately.

"We don't know what's next," I said at the same time. "We've heard our regiment is back in England."

"You guys need anything before I skedaddle?" Bill asked.

"Yes!" I said. "Could you see that my folks get a telegram ASAP? Just say I'm well and safe."

"You got it, Jimmy. I'll do that right away. For you, too, Burnie."

"Thanks, Bill."

Bill waved to his officer, then wrote down our addresses. We quickly shook hands, and he trotted back to the vehicle. "I'll look for you when I get back. Don't go too far, Jimmy. Stick around West Orange!" he shouted as he and the officer roared off.

"Okay!"

"Sheeran! Rainwater! On the double!"

We turned to see a corporal beckoning to us. He ushered Burnie and me into an office where several officers were gathered to interrogate us. We started at the beginning and explained how we'd gotten to where we were. I did most of the talking. The officers stopped me to request details and when I launched into a subject that did not interest them they asked me to skip over what we did in the forest and in Domremy, but they wanted to know all about the prison train.

"When did the train leave Paris?"

"How many prisoners were taken to Germany?"

"Where did you jump from the train?"

"Who jumped with you?"

"Describe the terrain you crossed."

"When and where did you see Germans?"

"Describe every interaction you had with them, no matter how inconsequential it may have seemed at the time."

"Where was your cousin's house?"

"What did you do in Allamps?"

"What were the Germans loading onto trucks and trains?"

"How many Germans do you estimate remain in the area?"

"Where do you think they might hide?"

At last the questions trailed off. The commanding officer leaned forward to look at his men. "Is everyone finished?" he asked.

I glanced at the clock on the wall. I had been talking for ninety minutes, almost nonstop, while a corporal was taking notes.

"You men are extremely fortunate," the commander said. "I'm sure you know that."

"Yessir," Burnie and I said as one.

"You have fully earned an honorable discharge from the army"— the corner of the commander's mouth twitched—"as well as a new uniform."

"Thank you, sir," we said.

"Tonight you can relax." His eyes sparkled. "You must have been born under a lucky star. Bing Crosby and Fred Astaire will be performing tonight for the troops. It's a surprise, but I'm letting you in on the secret to lessen your disappointment about not leaving immediately."

Burnie and I really got pumped. Crosby and Astaire!

"The army will fly you to London tomorrow morning, and then you can hop on a transport to the States. I expect you to stay out of trouble till then," he concluded.

"Yes, sir. Can you tell me where our company and the 101st Airborne are now, sir?" I asked.

"Ramsbury, England," he replied.

"Thank you, sir."

I still had not made a decision to go home. I would talk it over with Burnie once we arrived in London. Nothing prevented us from making different decisions. Now we didn't have to stay together.

———

We stood around talking with more soldiers to get a better sense of how the invasion was going.

"Jimmy! Burnie! Special delivery for you!"

I turned to see Bill Hill standing up in the jeep and heading straight for us. Sitting in the back were none other than Fred Astaire and Bing Crosby.

"Jesus," Burnie said. "No wonder his lieutenant was impatient!" Obviously the officer's assignment had been to pick up the two entertainers and chauffeur them to the airstrip.

The jeep screeched to a stop. "I told them all about my high school buddy being behind the lines since D-Day," Bill said, grinning.

Bing jumped lithely out of the jeep, his hand extended. "Burnie," he said, and grasped my partner's hand, then slung his arm across my back. "And you must be Jim."

Fred vaulted out of the backseat and landed on the concrete as if it were rubber.

Everyone cheered, including Bing, who stepped back to make room.

Fred put his arm around us. "I was expecting American soldiers, but from their clothes, I'd say these men are French paupers," he teased.

One of the GIs looked horrified. "Oh, no, Mr. Astaire, sir! These men had no choice but to dress like bums!"

Bill barked a laugh. "Is that what you'd call defending them?" he hooted.

The movie star held up his hands. *"Je n'ai pas fait d'offense! Je m'amusais un peu avec ces hommes généreaux. Comprenez-vous?"*

"Huh?" the soldier said.

"Our friend Mr. Astaire was just trying out a new comedy routine," Bing explained. He turned to Fred. "It still needs work."

Embarrassment flamed red in the soldier's neck and burned in his cheeks. "Ohh. I get it. Sorry." He forced a laugh. "No, it was real funny, now that I understand."

Bill smoothly guided Burnie, our famous visitors, and me away from the crowd. We sat down in the Spartan cafeteria and had some coffee while we just shot the breeze and Bill jogged off to let the brass know their guests had arrived.

Both celebrities asked about my "catching up with the family" in Domremy and "hiding out with the Maquis" somewhere in the heart of France. They focused on Burnie and me as if we were the only people in the hangar, and they sincerely cared about what my pal and I had experienced.

"Man," I thought, "these are two special guys!"

"What's your next stop?" Fred inquired.

"London. Tomorrow morning."

His face brightened, and his eyebrows shot up. "I insist you visit my sister, Adele, Lady Cavendish!"

"Aw," Burnie said, "I don't know about that . . ." He winced. "We really do look like bums."

"Nonsense! You're warriors!" Fred told him. "Right, Bing?"

The sleepy-eyed crooner nodded. "When heroes come home from work, they always need to clean up. It's the desk jockeys who stay neat and clean."

"That's right," Fred put in. "Desk jockeys and golfers."

Again we laughed, this time at Bing's expense.

He chuckled and shook his head. "Too true," he admitted. "Too true."

Fred leaned forward and spoke confidentially. "This wouldn't be strictly a social call," he continued. "I need you to deliver a top-secret message for me."

Burnie and I exchanged glances. I didn't know much about Fred Astaire's elder sister except she and her brother had been vaudeville kids, and she had retired from show business before he'd made it big in Hollywood. She had married a duke and moved to Ireland to live in a castle. Maybe his message had to do with the war, and he was counting on Adele to relay it to the king and queen?

"Sure we'll do it," I said. "Right, Burnie?"

"Excellent!" Fred whispered. "Tell her I'm wearing my long johns."

"You're wearing your long johns," Burnie repeated, concentration knitting his brow.

"What does that *really* mean?" I asked. "If you are able to divulge it, that is."

"Certainly," he said with alacrity. "She was worried I'd catch a cold over here and made me promise to wear the long johns."

I struggled not to laugh. "I dunno," I said, pretending to think it over. "Before I can carry military secrets across the English Channel, I need proof. Can I trust your word?"

He laughed and rolled up his shirtsleeves. "One hundred percent army-issued long johns. Satisfied?"

"Yessir."

"Then promise me you'll see Adele. She would love to meet you fellows. I'll call her after the show and tell her to expect you."

As he gave me instructions, Bill reappeared at the head of our table. "I hate to drag you away," he said when Fred had finished, "but the commander would like to meet you. He's waiting in the tent where you'll be performing. We're expecting about seventy soldiers."

We all stood and shook hands. "Repeat it one more time, Burnie," Fred said.

Burnie puffed out his chest and stood at attention. "Your brother is wearing his long johns."

"Perfect!" Fred said, then took Bing's arm and waltzed him from the room.

Burnie and I set foot on London soil at midday, September 15. A driver greeted us and said we already had hotel reservations. When we registered at the front desk, the clerk handed us a fancy envelope of heavy, creamy stationery. Inside a matching card informed us that Adele Astaire would come for us at eight P.M. sharp.

As I read the note, the clerk rang for a bellboy.

"I don't think we'll need help," Burnie told him. "We don't have our duffels, and I'm pretty sure we'll be able to find our room without any problem."

The clerk smiled stiffly and dropped our key in the Cherokee's outstretched hand.

Upstairs, we went to sleep for a few hours, and then got back into our French farmer's clothes again. "Funny," I said to Burnie, who was standing at the door, "how the same clothes that make you invisible one day can make you conspicuous twenty-four hours later."

"Would've been nice just to get a pair of socks," he said, watching me wrap the parachute silk around my feet.

I pulled on my sliced shoes, set my tam at a jaunty angle, and said, "Let's go." The clock on the nightstand read 7:52.

Exactly eight minutes later, a chauffeur entered the hotel lobby. With French-accented English he asked the clerk for Private Rainwater and Private Sheeran.

"We're right here," I said, cringing under the driver's appraising stare.

"Ah, *messieurs*," he exclaimed, "you are making me homesick!"

He escorted us outside, where an absolutely gorgeous, shiny Rolls-Royce was parked at the curb. The vehicle's elegance was exceeded only by its occupant when the chauffeur opened the door. Adele Astaire greeted us with a hug and a kiss.

Boy, was she something! She was the definition of *regal*, and much too refined, I decided, for Hollywood and motion pictures. Adele was probably in her forties, but she looked no older than Burnie and me. I could not stop grinning at her. No one could have slapped that grin off my face. I was glad Burnie could vouch for her beauty. Otherwise who would believe me?

Adele Astaire, I kept thinking, and two Depression kids from America.

Her limousine allowed us to sit opposite our hostess. I leaned and whispered in her ear. "Fred's wearing his winter underwear, just like you told him to do!"

"Long johns," Burnie confirmed.

She laughed melodically and hugged us again. I breathed deeply. She wore a fragrance that reminded me of a world that existed beyond the carnage.

"I'm taking you out on the town," she said.

"This is awfully nice of you," I said. "Going to all this—"

"Not at all!" she replied. "You're doing me a favor! I work all day as a Red Cross volunteer at Rainbow Corners, in the heart of London. Since my husband, Charles, passed away a couple of years ago, I don't have much opportunity to go to clubs and listen to American jazz. So you see? This is a treat all around."

We visited several nightclubs. Each time, we walked through a separate entrance and were guided to a booth reserved for us, and we turned heads wherever we went. Adele knew everyone, and the people she did not know still recognized her.

She wrapped one arm around each of us the whole night, skipping and dancing as we pleased, and never let us go.

"You're a heck of a dancer, Adele," I told her.

"I miss dancing," she confessed. "Our mother enrolled Fred and me in dance class when we were very young, and we became professionals soon after that. Dancing became as natural to me as walking."

"Then why did you quit?" Burnie asked.

"To get married," she answered. Her eyes took on the look of remembrance. "I met my husband right here in London. He was waiting for me outside the stage door after one of our performances."

"Jimmy's parents had a good start," Burnie offered, and jabbed his elbow into my ribs.

After not too much prodding from Adele, I described their meeting on the train to Paris, then told her the rest of their story: Almost one year after Jack Sheeran had first laid eyes on "the most beautiful woman in all of France," he and his buddies were celebrating Christmas Eve, the Armistice that had been signed a mere six weeks before, and the certainty they would soon be going back to the States. The more champagne Pop drank that night, the more morose he felt, for while the beautiful woman continued to live in his heart, he had never spoken one word to her.

"Oh, that's so sad," Adele said as Burnie rolled his eyes.

"There's more," I said.

"Of course there is," Adele said pertly. "You're here, aren't you?"

"Uh, right. Anyway, a lieutenant and his orderly walked into the bar to announce their departure within the hour for Domremy-La-Pucelle, where the soldiers would soon be processed to return home."

"Domremy-La-Pucelle is where Jimmy's mother lived," Burnie added. "Before she was his mother, I mean."

"That was very helpful, Burnie." Adele smiled graciously at him.

"The few sober men in their platoon helped Pop, his friends, and their gear into ten trucks. Pop rode in the back of the truck bed, so he could look outside and have fresh air. While the truck was moving, he felt okay. But when it stopped at their destination—the farm where American barracks had been built to process troops returning to America—Pop tumbled off the truck and landed on the ground. He looked up, and who was standing there but my mother!"

"What was she doing there?" Adele asked. "How did she know he—"

"She didn't know!" I replied, laughing. "That's what was so amazing! Her family had owned that farm for generations!"

Now Adele was laughing. "What did your father do?"

"He declared triumphantly to my mother, 'Here she is, the most beautiful girl in all of France!'"

"And what did your mother do?"

"She poured a pail of cold water on him. But only after she and her sister sobered him up with coffee. Pop demanded a kiss goodnight before he rejoined his buddies at their barracks."

"She didn't kiss him, did she?" Adele asked.

"Not at first, but Pop wouldn't give up, and he delivered his Irish blarney in perfect French. Her fascination with this American rascal was quickly rekindled—"

"And your mother finally gave him a kiss!" Adele said, her eyes shining. "I approve wholeheartedly." She raised her flute. "To your parents!"

"To my parents!"

Completely comfortable in one another's company, we listened to great jazz that night, and then we strolled arm in arm down the streets of London, totally crocked and in love with life.

———————

Burnie and I said goodnight to Adele at our hotel. I wondered if I would be able to fall asleep after all the sudden changes and excitement of the last thirty-six hours. Long after I heard Burnie's breathing deepen with slumber, I lay awake. My heart ached for my parents and home and a return to a normal life. I wanted to see my mother and Pop and tell them everything that had happened to us. If I said the word, I could probably be sleeping in my own bed within a couple of days and then wake up and get dressed in clothes from my own closet.

But I also wanted to join the guys and be with them in battle. That was the whole point of enlisting in the Airborne. Sure, I had seen action and done my bit for the war effort while Burnie and I were in France, but for me, it wasn't a topped-off experience. I wasn't a Frenchman, so helping the Maquis was not, for me, the same thing as facing danger with the men from my company. All my training had prepared me for that ultimate experience, but then things did not turn out that way. Usually we don't have a second chance in life, but this once, maybe I could make it happen.

How would I get to Ramsbury? Could I get there before my unit set out to accomplish its next assignment? If that were possible, then I could fight alongside my brothers.

The decision felt right. My heartbeat slowed, and tension drained out of me every time I exhaled. I flapped my blankets a couple of times to straighten them, then sank into the down pillow. Now that I had direction, I knew I would fall right to sleep.

When I opened my eyes the next morning, Burnie was already dressed. His black hair was still wet from the shower, and steam from the bathroom was diffusing into the room, giving it the clean smell of hotel soap.

"Are you going down to breakfast?" I asked, sitting up.

"I have already eaten," he said, grinning, "while you were catching up on your sleep."

"Aren't you as exhausted as I am?"

"No," he said. "But we weren't staying with *my* relatives."

I laughed, then got serious. "Do you know what you're going to do? I'd like to hear your decision first."

He sat down on the edge of his bed. "I want to walk around London today." My friend paused and looked at me. "And then I will accept the army's offer and go home."

I nodded, understanding.

"I wasn't sure until breakfast," he continued. "I was eating alone, and a man asked to sit down at my table. He'd seen us with Adele last night." Burnie flashed a grin.

"He wanted the scoop?"

"Yes." Burnie shrugged. "Along with everyone else in the hotel. He ended up doing all the talking, though. About Adele."

"What'd he say?"

"How she seemed to have special blessings. When she met her husband and retired from show business, she was only thirty. Already she'd been on top of the world, a Broadway star."

"Marrying a duke seems like a fairy tale, too," I said.

"Sure, when you consider she and Fred were from Nebraska, and their parents weren't rich or anything."

"I didn't realize that."

"Adele and her husband had three children," he continued, "a daughter and twin sons."

"I didn't hear her mention her kids," I said.

"She didn't," Burnie said. "Her daughter died in childbirth."

"Oh, that's rough. The twins?"

"Died shortly after they were born."

"Oh, Jesus." I sat stunned, thinking about our beautiful, vivacious hostess from the night before. "And her husband died, too! Two years ago."

"He was only thirty-eight," Burnie said. "She's had so much misery and sorrow, after a life filled with luck and riches."

"A steep drop."

Burnie nodded. "That's why I decided to go home. I started thinking about us, Jimmy. How we were sick and starving, on our way to die, probably, and now we're here." He spread his hands. "Everything changes so quickly and drastically—not just for me and you but for everyone, all the time."

He leaned forward, and his eyes were intense, burning. "I want to be home before everything changes again. I want to be with my people, living the way the Cherokee have lived since time beyond beginning. That alone makes sense to me in a world where nothing else does."

"I understand," I told him, and meant it. "The man at breakfast brought you a gift."

"He gave me the gift of seeing things clearly," he agreed.

I told Burnie what I planned to do, and he was not surprised. He waited for me to get dressed, then we said goodbye outside the hotel in the way soldiers say goodbye to each other.

"Hey, Burnie," I said, pounding him on the back as I hugged him, "take care of yourself, and remember moss don't grow on the south side of trees."

He laughed and stood back. "I know that, Jim! Don't *you* forget it!" He grinned. "Hang tough, all right?"

"Yeah."

"And say hi to the guys for me."

"Will do."

"Well, I guess I'll put an egg in my shoe and beat it."

He turned and walked away to do his sightseeing. I went back into the hotel to have breakfast and figure out how to get myself to the army base.

I took the stairs to the dining room two at a time. I was happy Burnie was going home. I felt fortunate he had been with me in that boxcar. Burnie Rainwater had been a gift to me. I knew I would not have found myself in the forest or in my mother's village without him.

CHAPTER 17

During my walk to the train station on the north side of London, I felt out of syncopation with life. Having spent so many weeks in the forest and French countryside, I felt overwhelmed by the frenetic urban landscape. My army pass allowed me to be out of uniform and unrestricted in my movements, and yet although surrounded by city crowds, I felt odd and conspicuous without my stripes. People stared at me on the street and glared at me after I boarded the train.

I was on my way to Swindon, the closest stop to Ramsbury, and a reunion with my company. I could not get there fast enough. Without Burnie at my side for the first time in months, I felt alone and vulnerable.

At last the train stopped in Swindon, and I jumped into a taxi to travel the few miles from the depot to the camp. My anxiety rose. Who would be there? Who would not? My buddies' faces swam before me: Lud. Neeper. Johnny. Huff. So much could have

happened—*had* happened!—in the hundred-plus days since D-Day.
I wiped my moist palms on my shirt and tried not to worry.

At last the taxi stopped at the camp gate. Even as I paid the driver,
I searched for a familiar face. I displayed my pass and walked in. I
recognized no one, even after wandering around for twenty minutes.
I looked at strangers, and occasionally they glanced at me.

I had to take a leak and found a latrine with walls of corrugated
steel. I was standing alongside some other guy taking a piss when
something shot past, just over my head—*zing! zing!*—and hit the
side of the latrine.

"Holy shit!" I yelled, and as I ducked, I felt a projectile whiz past
my right arm—*whing! whing!* It punched exit holes in the steel just
two feet from my shoulder.

"What the fuck was that?" I shouted to the guy who crouched
next to me.

"F-f-f-fuck if I know," he said. His teeth chattered.

I ripped out of the latrine and immediately spotted a real slick guy
with a very thin mustache. He was holding a crossbow. I squinted at
him.

"Baron?" I asked. "Baron Duber?"

"Oh, shit! Did I hit you?" he asked, and hurried toward me. "I
accidentally released the trigger!"

Baron was from the original 506th. Someone had given him the
nickname back in Camp Toccoa, and it stuck because he was very
suave and dramatic looking, and his clothes were always pressed.

"What the hell are you shooting at, Baron?" I yelled. "You nearly
killed two of us in the latrine!"

"Jimmy?" He was bug-eyed. "What the fuck are you doing here?
I thought you were dead!"

"Shit, no. Haven't even been close to it—till now. Taking a piss near you is much more dangerous than being trapped behind the lines with the Krauts." We hugged and slapped each other on the back, laughing. "You still collecting old garbage?" I pointed at the crossbow.

Baron collected antiques, and crossbows were one of his favorite items. In his free time, he searched for crossbows and primitive ammunition to buy from the locals. He paid almost nothing for these "treasures." He would hurry back to camp, very excited, and fire them while we watched. I had been impressed by their power, which wasn't much different from a rifle's.

"You bet. Isn't this a beauty?"

"Yeah," I said without enthusiasm. "You'd be better off if you stuck with being a ladies' man," I said. "You were never the best shot in the army."

He pretended to be insulted. "I've improved, I assure you."

"I'm glad to hear that," I said. "So how many wives do you have now?"

Every place we had been stationed, Baron found himself a wife. When we were in training in the States, he married a Southern girl and lived with her. When we got to England, he married a girl the same night he met her in a barroom. After producing evidence of his marriage, Baron got permission from the officers to live with her.

"I'll ignore that remark." He wiped his little waxed mustache. "Let's talk about you. And your getup." He pointed at the latrine. "Are you done in there? Want to walk around with me?"

I laughed. "Yeah, I'm finished. Tell me about the guys. Where's everyone hiding?"

The fear of learning the fate of my friends caused me to regret my question as soon as it left my lips. Baron and I were not in the same platoon, but he told me about the guys he knew in I Company, particularly the Third platoon—*my* platoon. I listened without asking about anyone specific.

Baron, holding his crossbow, named a lot of guys who had been killed or seriously wounded. Others, he said, were captured. "Engelbrecht is around here somewhere," he said.

Relief and gratitude filled me. "Can you help me find him?"

"Sure."

He guided me to the barracks and pointed out Lud, who was sleeping in the top berth of a triple bunk at the far end. "I'd better go stash this, Jimmy," Baron said, indicating the crossbow. "I'm sure you guys have a lot of catching up to do."

After he and I shook hands, I turned and yelled, *"Hey, Lud!"*

Sarge's eyes flew open, and as soon as he saw me, he jumped off the bed. "Jesus, Pruneface!" he cried out, hurrying toward me. "What happened to you? Where have you been?"

I quickly recounted the jump and how Freddy Hoffman and I were surrounded by Germans and taken prisoner. I described carrying Johnny Simpson after his hand was blown off. I told him about Paris, the prison train, and Captain McKnight ordering us to remain in the car. I got choked up saying how Burnie and I jumped anyway, later to connect with the Underground and find my mother's village. Finally I told him about watching Patton's troops roll through town.

"I couldn't fall asleep last night in London until I decided to find the platoon," I concluded. "Now tell me what happened to the rest of the guys."

Lud filled me in, telling me how many and which ones of our close buddies were gone. "Right after I realized you were missing, we were ordered to establish bridgeheads across the Douve River. We attacked a little past midnight, and by dawn we encircled St. Come du Mont, and the Germans got the hell outta there. With the enemy hunkered down in Carentan, our focus turned there. Once the Germans had crossed the bridges and causeways on the way to Carentan, they blew them up. Only one causeway was intact."

"So did you get there?"

He looked at me. "Nah, we gave up and went home."

"Shit, Lud, just tell the story."

"Whaddaya think we did? The engineers worked under heavy enemy fire to repair them." He cringed. "I saw some really gruesome stuff. The Germans kept blasting away at us. We finally managed to get across the causeways but not into the town. For two days we fought against massed machine-gun and heavy artillery fire. It was unbelievable."

"Wasn't anyone sent around to the east, to attack from behind the Germans?"

"Oh, yeah," he said. "We had Carentan surrounded and were attacking the Germans from two sides, but the sons of bitches held. I couldn't believe it."

"So what happened?" I asked.

"You don't know?" he asked, surprised.

"No."

"You must be bullshitting me! How can you not know?"

"Lud! Look at my clothes! I've been completely out of touch."

"The brass ordered us to pull back, so they could begin a massive bombardment—artillery and naval gunfire. *That* went on for two more days! Finally the bombardment stopped, and we were sent back in from the east, west, and south. We made quick progress and seized the town, but, oh, man, we paid a very high price."

"What's the outfit doing next?"

"We're going to carry out a very bold assignment," he said in a

213

low voice. "The Allied armies aren't getting supplies because France doesn't have enough port facilities for distribution."

"It's not a shortage of supplies, right?"

"Right. The crates are piling up here in England. So the brass is targeting Antwerp—"

"Where's that?" I asked.

"Holland. We'll conduct a massive airborne assault on the Mass, Wahl, and Lower Rhine rivers, and simultaneously the Brits will launch a ground attack on Arnhem."

"When?" I could feel my heart beating hard. I wanted to be there with the Screaming Eagles, doing the job.

"Maybe as soon as tomorrow," he replied. "Guys have been resting and prepping for the last few days and getting their on-the-ground assignments. Now tell me your plans." He gave me a sidelong glance. "If you were in London last night, why are you in Ramsbury today? Why didn't you get sent home from London?"

"I could have gone. Burnie went. But no one told me I had to go home."

"So what the hell are you doing here?"

"I wanted to see how everyone made out—"

"Now you have," Lud shot back. "So get the hell out of here and back to London as fast as your ass can carry you." He took my elbow and steered me toward the door. "I'll go with you to the gate."

"Bullshit." I shook myself loose and turned to face him. "I'm jumping again."

"Forget that shit, Pruneface. No way you can. You're too late." He spoke with a finality that discouraged further discussion. "Go home while you can."

I followed him outside. "Lud, I'm prepared to jump again," I pleaded. "Look around! You need every guy you can get."

He wheeled on me. I'd never seen him so pissed off. "What the hell happened to you? You've fucking earned your trip home already. Don't screw up your chance to get out of here alive!"

My own anger exploded, and we stood toe to toe. "You're my top kick, but this decision is mine! You can either help me or fuck me over." I tried to reason with him. "For Christ's sake, how many guys do you have left with actual combat experience?"

He looked away without answering me.

"How many?" I pressed him. "Listen. We don't have time to fight about this. Just take me to General Taylor or Colonel Sink or whatever officer can make a decision."

"You don't even have a uniform or a rifle."

"I don't need a uniform." I showed him my pass. "I can jump like this." I had momentum. I suddenly felt reconnected with my outfit. "Just find me a rifle."

He seemed to relent a bit. "Let me talk straight with you about the operation and tell you a little about Holland. Will you hear me out?"

"Okay."

All the guys already had received their briefings, so Lud had to bring me up to speed. We went back into the barracks and sat facing each other on a couple of cots. The operation was called Market Garden. The men would be taking off early the next morning, September 17.

"Holland gives us better odds of success than Normandy did," he began. "First, we jump in daylight. Second, the planes will be at a higher altitude, so we can jump and land in layers. Third, the brass chose a drop zone that's not divided by hedgerows. That keeps us together as a unit at our target."

"Got it," I said, nodding. "I'm ready."

"If you've changed your mind and want to go home, I won't make no sound," Lud said.

"I didn't join this outfit to go home before the job was done. Only a medical reason could stop me."

"I doubt that," he said wryly. "Weren't you the moron with a sprained ankle who completed his qualifying jumps by landing on one foot?"

I laughed. "Jesus, I figured you'd forgotten that."

"Pruneface, I don't think I have the authority to bring you into the mission."

"Then take me to the company commander," I pleaded. "Let me try, at least. If he denies me permission, then I'll go home."

Captain Anderson, who had flown on the *Ugly Duckling* with me over Normandy, was a terrific guy in my book. He had given me a thumbs-up just before we jumped, and now as I stood before him, he was very happy to see I was alive. Like Al, though, he did not want me to jump again.

"You've got no uniform and no squad," he said, "and I have no authority to grant your request." He stood, came around his desk, and grasped my hand. "I have nothing but respect for your patriotism, Sheeran."

"Thank you, sir. But someone in this camp must have the authority to say yes. Who would that be, sir?"

Captain Anderson rubbed his chin and thought. "He might call all three of us lunatics, but let's see Colonel Moore."

Ned Moore had been with us since the birth of the 101st Airborne Division. While waiting for him to see us, I told Captain Anderson and Lud about going to nightclubs with Adele Astaire.

"I'm jealous!" Lud said, grinning.

"With Sheeran demonstrating such consistent good fortune," Captain Anderson said, "we should find a way to put him into combat somehow, regardless of what the colonel decides."

We were called into the colonel's office, and he immediately refused the request. "No. No uniform, no squad, no briefings," he ticked off on his fingers. "Dismissed."

I did not move. "With all due respect, sir, I believe that after spending three months behind the lines, I've earned the right to make another jump and won't take no for an answer."

I heard Lud choke behind me.

"Sir," I continued, "I'm tired of this—pardon me, sir—shit. Ever since I first tried to enlist, I've faced nothing but roadblocks. But I wouldn't give up, and when the army finally did let me in, I signed up from the start to be a paratrooper. I'm fully trained and experienced, and I want to jump. Can't somebody scrounge up a spare uniform around here?"

Colonel Moore squinted at me. "We did lose a lot of good men in Normandy . . . We are short on men with combat experience . . ."

"Well, sir, there you have it. I'm a combat veteran," I said, and shot a warning look at Lud so he wouldn't laugh out loud; he knew damned well I'd seen only a day and a half of actual combat before being taken prisoner.

But clearly the colonel was beginning to see things my way, so I kept my mouth shut. I sure wasn't about to correct his impression that I was an experienced combat soldier itching to jump over Holland.

"I'm going to let it happen!" he said. "Captain Anderson, I want you to promote Private First Class Sheeran to a squad leader and a sergeant. Sergeant Engelbrecht, assign him a squad."

"You are?" I asked in disbelief. "Thank you, sir!"

"Dismissed!" he said quickly. "And I mean it!"

Walking out, Captain Anderson slapped me on the back. "I have to laugh, Jim, thinking that last night, you were sitting with Adele Astaire in her Rolls-Royce and dressed like a French peasant—and now I'm making you a sergeant."

Lud and I had to join in the laughter.

"By tomorrow night," the captain added, "you'll probably be on the joint chiefs of staff."

"Yeah," Lud grumbled. "And won't his pals be happy for him!"

———

"Okay, Sheeran," Lud said, after Captain Anderson went on his way, "while you and Rainwater were sipping wine, enjoying the French countryside, and spying on skinny-dipping mademoiselles, we've been driving the Krauts back to Berlin."

We strode through the encampment and wound up in the map room and operations room. We sat down, and my private briefing commenced. Through the end of the summer, Lud explained, the Germans had been retreating across France and Belgium. Because they were on the run, the enemy couldn't set up an organized defensive shield in Holland.

"That being the case," my friend told me, "the Allies believe we can ram through Holland, invade Germany from the north, win the war, and be home by Christmas."

The offensive called Operation Market Garden had a goal beyond making ports available for supply distribution. An equally crucial objective was to secure a sixty-four-mile-long road so the British Second Army, which had already fought its way into Belgium, could join us quickly for the invasion of Germany. Lud called this "laying a carpet" for the British ground forces.

"This is a narrow road that runs northward from the Belgian border through the towns of Eindhoven, Zon, Veghel, Uden, and Nijmegen and then crosses the Lower Rhine into the town of Arnhem," he explained, and showed me the locations on a huge map on the wall.

As he rattled off the names of Dutch towns, I tried to repeat and memorize them, but I could barely pronounce them.

"The Allies plan to drop several airborne divisions simultaneously into Holland at selected sites along the highway," he continued. "As we move north, we'll attack, seize, and hold the towns and crossings in our sector of the highway. That's all-important," he emphasized, "protecting the road, railway, and several critical crossings over local rivers and canals. We don't want the enemy blowing anything up, like at Carentan. That was a tough lesson. If we allow it to happen again, we'd be dishonoring the lives of the men who died trying to repair the bridges."

I studied the map and traced the target with my finger. The Allies wanted to extend control along the entire road, I saw, from Eindhoven, near the Belgian border in the south, to Arnhem in the north. The strategy made perfect sense. It would allow the British tanks, trucks, and infantry to move quickly from Belgium, across Holland, and into Germany. Then the combined armies could mount the final assault into the German heartland.

"We'll have to do the job fast, before the Germans have time to organize themselves as we invade their country."

"Understood."

"The battles'll be sporadic and fierce," he warned. "Snipers will be waiting for us on the ground."

I turned to face him. "Yeah."

"If you've changed your mind and want to go home—"

"What stretch belongs to us?" I said, giving him my answer.

"Our division will secure the southernmost stretch of the road from Eindhoven north to Veghel and Uden."

"How long is it?"

"Twenty-two miles." He stood beside me at the map. "The Eighty-second Airborne is assigned the middle sector of the road, between Grave and Nijmegen."

"And farther north?"

"The British First Airborne, with help from a Polish paratroop brigade that's been barracked in England. They'll drop at Arnhem and secure the bridge there, plus the section of the road approaching Arnhem from the south."

"What do you know about the terrain?"

Lud blew out a long breath. "Flat. Too flat. Lends itself to delaying tactics by the enemy. Even though the Germans are backpedaling, they can buy time by holding on to the bridges and taking advantage of the terrain." He paused. "This will be the largest airborne assault of the war, Jimmy. Twenty thousand paratroopers."

"Twenty thousand and *one*."

Lud snorted. "Let's find you a uniform and some weapons and munitions." We walked outside. "Plus a needle and some thread."

"What for?"

"Whaddaya think?" He grinned and slung his arm around my shoulder. "To sew your three stripes and our regimental patch on your shirt and jump jacket, Sergeant Sheeran."

CHAPTER 18

September 17, 1944. The first day of the Market Garden offensive. Captain Anderson had made me a *floater*, a wild-card authorized to give commands, but I was surrounded by new faces in the squad. As I introduced myself, I tried to memorize their names. Leading these replacement soldiers would be a challenge for even the most experienced officer, like Lud, our platoon sergeant and commander. I was a stranger. Although I was one of the very few veterans on this mission, to the rookies I was the guy who just twenty-four hours before had been wearing civilian clothes.

I had no anxiety about the jump, the landing, or the fighting that lay ahead. My only concern was that the guys respect my judgment and respond to my commands. Some of the replacements looked as tough as nails, but they lacked experience. The only way they would be effective against the enemy and have a chance to survive was through instant, unquestioning obedience to their superiors. Would they trust me enough to respond to my orders? Could they have enough faith in my decisions to obey?

Lud and I strapped each other up with about fifty pounds of gear and equipment—ammunition, rifle, shovel, grenades, medical kit, gas mask, and a canteen. The men climbed into the C-47, and our pilot lost no time in taking off.

Lud was the jump master of our stick, so he stayed by the door. I sat in the back with my squad. The C-47s were reliable aircraft, but they had no more armor than an Oldsmobile and afforded no protection in combat. These aircraft were very slow, so they made easy targets as they bounced and swayed in the slightest turbulence. During the Normandy jump, flak had ripped through the *Ugly Duckling* and seriously wounded one of our guys. Now, however, we enjoyed a British Air Force escort as we traveled east.

We didn't have far to travel, but the flight would take two hours—long enough for the guys to get sick.

"Who needs a pill?" one of the flight crew called out, and more than a few guys raised a hand.

Continuing east, we squinted at the French coast in the distance, trying to find signs of destruction. Whatever we saw, we credited to our D-Day ground forces.

As we approached the Eindhoven area, we ran into flak. For about ten nerve-racking minutes, hot metal fragments ripped through the plane's thin shell. Miraculously no one was hit. I hoped that was a good omen for the whole operation.

The red light flashed. "Stand and hook up," Lud yelled.

I knew my squad was watching me, following my example, as I took my static line and attached it to the cable running down the center of the aircraft. The crew took care to deliver us precisely to the jump zone and to monitor carefully the timing of the jump. Unlike our haphazard landing at Normandy, we would hit the ground as a tight fighting unit. The calculations made certain the machine gunner and his assistant would land only fifty to a hundred feet from each other.

I knew the weight of my gear would cause me to come down pretty hot. The ground rushed up to meet me, and I landed rough, on the run, weapons loaded, near the town of Zon. From there my men and I would work our way south to Eindhoven and hook up with the armored divisions of the British Second Army, which was advancing northward from the Belgian border. The joined forces would "lay the carpet" northward, toward Arnhem.

I cut my chute loose and looked around. The guys were already hundreds of yards ahead, running swiftly, and I took off after them. Our entire Company One quickly regrouped, which was exhilarating.

Gliders carrying the heavy equipment such as jeeps and cannons landed in an adjacent area. We lost only a few minutes collecting our equipment and vehicles, but the Germans took full advantage of the delay. As we moved on our first objectives—to cross and secure the bridge over the Wilhelmina Canal—the enemy destroyed the span. Even as we approached, we heard the blasts and watched the thick smoke billow skyward.

The canal was about twenty-five meters wide. Huge chunks of partially submerged concrete could serve as steppingstones to the far bank. We quickly stretched ropes between the shores in preparation for a nighttime maneuver.

Using the dark to shield us and the ropes to stabilize us, we leapt through the frigid air, from boulder to water-slick boulder. The last man set foot on land at midnight, but we were in no mood to congratulate ourselves; we were shivering, soaking wet, and dog-tired. We took whatever shelter we could find, but sleep eluded many of us. The rain continued to fall and the temperature dropped, and we had no chance to dry off. Lots of guys asked around for cigarettes. Few men had been able to keep their pack dry, and the air stank of wet tobacco.

Weighing heavy on my mind was the knowledge that the Germans' hours-long head start would get them back to their homeland and give them time to organize their defenses against us.

Early the next morning we headed into Eindhoven, an area of enormous importance to us and to our enemy. The light industry of the town manufactured goods that were critical to the war, and both sides wanted control of its output. Thick black smoke rose from the factories' chimneys into the mud-colored sky as we attempted to enter, secure, and hold the town.

German snipers were waiting for us everywhere. A heavy concentration hid on the north side of town, our intended point of entry. As soon as we entered the outskirts of Eindhoven, expert marksmen picked off five of our guys. Seeing them lying there on the ground once we had found cover . . . it was a sobering experience.

One of the dead was a young replacement soldier in our squad. A sniper had hit him early, and the rest of the guys were so jittery afterward, I wondered if their ability to fight would be severely impaired. Beyond snipers' reputation for being effective, efficient, and destructive, they are morale breakers; you try to take each step seriously because it could be your last, but no matter how careful and logical you are, if the sniper notices you, you're a goner. The utter randomness of death and the stress of knowing you might already be in a German's crosshairs can be your undoing, can make you stupid and careless.

Lud Engelbrecht knew that. He hung around the recruits, who tended to stick together. He tried to provide them with some protection, reassurance, and direction. This would be our squad's first real combat assignment, and it was an extremely dangerous one.

I heard him tell them to fire off more shots at the enemy, then he came to hunker down beside me. "We've got to take out those snipers," he said. "So long as they keep us nailed down, our equipment can't move ahead."

I nodded.

"I want that to be your responsibility, Pruneface. We can't fail."

"All right, Lud." I looked him in the eyes. He was a great rifleman. I was fairly good, but not nearly the shot he was.

Many of the sharpshooters were in trees, in the bell towers of churches, and on the roofs of other tall buildings. We would have to locate all the snipers, pick them off before—I hoped—they could fire at us, then disable and capture or kill them.

This was the uneasy moment I knew would come sooner or later. Lud had given me command of a contingent of replacement troops whom I knew nothing about and who knew nothing about me, either.

"Good thing you're a patient man," I said, and gestured toward the rooftop of one of the factories. "This'll take a few hours. The Krauts are well placed."

"At *least* a few hours." He shook his head grimly. "And I was counting on making up the time we lost at the canal. Shit."

I scanned the no-man's-land between our position and the rooftop lookout. I saw several square plots of land bounded by brick walls only about three feet high. I turned to my friend, but before I could verbalize my idea, he said, "Yeah, they're not much, but they'll give us some protection."

Lud and I figured out how we could make life very tough for the snipers by laying down a heavy fire and sending one, two, or even three guys—replacements among them—into a flanking position to fire at the snipers and take them out, one by one. As soon as the plan was set, I went to find the leader of the platoon covering a position adjacent to us.

"Ready for some action?" I asked him.

"Why? Ya find a pool hall?" he asked sarcastically.

"Oh, this'll be much more exciting than pool," I told him, "and it'll get us out from behind the eight ball."

The fellow shook his head. "Now he's tryin' to kill me with humor. All right, I asked for it. Go on."

"We're going to maneuver around the Krauts and then get rid of 'em. Engelbrecht and I'll take our squad to the right of the road, and you'll lead your men to the left. One squad'll stay here and put down a heavy field of fire."

He rubbed his chin and nodded. "I guess anything's better than just sittin' here."

Word went out down the line: *We're gonna get the Germans the hell out of wherever they're hiding! Let's go! Move quickly, and keep your head down. Be prepared to hit the ground at any moment.*

I expected this maneuver to resemble my missions in the forest with the Maquis. I had heard many GIs as well as members of the French Resistance compare combat training and offensives to hunting wild game. Sportsmen were experienced gun handlers and good shots, adept at sneaking up on their prey, be it deer, rabbit, squirrel, or, now, sniper. I used that analogy as I explained the mission to the young recruits, and they seemed more confident.

I was not a hunter, but I had seen the Maquis use surprise to its advantage in combat. Our plan did the same thing.

We closed in on the Germans from behind and caught them

unaware. The strategy worked. We were able to fire off good shots from different directions and pick off snipers on the factory rooftop and in a bell tower. Now that the replacements had earned their chops, I expected them to become much more aggressive soldiers.

We halted fire, but we were still just starting our mission in Eindhoven. Our soldiers regrouped, and Engelbrecht and I dived into an empty foxhole, ready to move on to the next clot of Germans. As we hunkered down in that trench, we heard horrific shrieks. We looked out from the foxhole, and no more than fifty feet from us an American lay on his back, screaming in pain and trying in vain to move. A barbed-wire fence separated us from him, but despite that obstruction we could see he was in very bad shape.

He spotted us, his eyes bulging with fear. "Don't come near me!" he shouted. "The place is booby-trapped. Stay away! If you try to help me, you'll be blown sky-high!"

"I can't stand watching this guy die," I told Lud. "We've got to try and get him."

Lud quickly agreed. Although the soldier said he had stepped on a mine, we figured snipers had shot him and that it had happened so fast, the guy didn't realize what had hit him. He kept screaming that the place was mined, but Lud and I took a careful look around and did not see evidence of that. Feeling even more certain of our sniper theory, we decided to loop around the soldier and bring him in. Lud ordered the squad to lay down a heavy field of fire.

Keeping to the low spots in the terrain as our men's bullets whizzed overhead, he and I made for the fence. Barbed wire ran horizontally across the top, middle, and lower third of the posts. I dived headfirst to the ground and scrambled under the wire, with Lud on my right. Gunshots exploded all around us.

"No!" the soldier shrieked. "Stay away from me!"

As I pulled myself forward under the wire, I heard a bullet whistle over my ass, then clip the lowest wire just over my butt. Miraculously the barbed wire split apart with a *pop*. Al hooted, realizing what had happened.

He and I crawled closer to the soldier and searched for mines as best we could. Not seeing any, we were ready to take the ultimate risk. We dashed to the soldier's side, grabbed him by the shoulders, and dragged him toward the fence. Our squad's field of fire intensified. The split wire proved a blessing; we were able to move the wounded man under the fence without too much trouble, and within a few moments we were lowering him into our foxhole.

Obviously we couldn't leave him there, nor could we stay with him. He needed immediate medical attention. Mickey, one of the guys in the squad, ran to a nearby barn and found a wheelbarrow, which he brought back. As we lifted the soldier into it, Lud asked if Mickey had seen a medic.

"Not a one," he said, "but a GI at the barn offered to take care of the patient until a medic arrives."

I hoped that time would come soon—the soldier was barely conscious—but Lud and I couldn't hang around to find out. We had taken a lot of Germans out and rounded others up, but we knew more were lurking in the shadows. We downed some quick rations, then continued the sniper offensive.

By the day's end, many Germans had surrendered, some faster than we could shoot. Our men were exhausted but exhilarated. We had worked well together, and the replacements had fought tenaciously alongside the others and had proven themselves in battle. They got to know and trust me as a leader, and I knew they would continue to follow my orders without hesitation.

As I settled down for the night, I felt great, knowing I had made the right decision to stay in Europe. Lud was a couple guys down from me, snoring, and I grinned at the racket he was making. I finally had done what I'd enlisted to do—fight the good fight with my friends.

Only a couple of days had passed since our first encounter with snipers, and about eight GIs wanted to take confession. I wanted to attend the service.

A group of us entered a church nearby in Eindhoven, and I wondered about the appropriateness of being in full combat gear, our loaded rifles at the ready, inside a house of worship. We stood quietly against the wall in the back of the church, and all eyes turned to us. The church was filled with women in traditional Dutch garb—long black dresses and stiff white caps that reminded me of the wimples worn by the Catholic nuns back home. We GIs were the only men present, and I realized how terrible a toll the war had exacted from the Dutch.

"Do you mind our being here?" Lud whispered to one of the women.

She shook her head and gestured that we were welcome to stay. Many women looked glad we were there, although no one talked to us. We probably would have discouraged conversation anyway. Although we surely must have made progress clearing Eindhoven of the enemy, our situation was extremely dangerous, and we were on full alert. Just because we were inside a church did not mean the Germans would ignore us. Snipers might be hiding inside and, knowing we were within easy range, fire on us.

As a survival tactic, we never stayed anywhere too long. When we left the church through the front doors, we covered each other, watching nearby buildings and looking back and up at the church tower for the enemy. We did not let down our guard as we returned to our camp just outside Eindhoven.

Over the next few days we cleaned out the rest of the snipers, but in a sense the Germans had achieved their goal. They had slowed us significantly.

On September 22, we moved out on Hell's Highway, as we called the road leading north to Arnhem. The Germans were not just defending themselves. In the five days since Market Garden began, the enemy had recovered from their initial disorganization. No longer were they in full retreat. Now, with the fervor that comes with defending one's homeland, they stiffened their resistance and counterattacked with armored tanks farther north, at Veghel.

Members of the Dutch Underground warned us: The Germans had amassed a veritable army of artillery at several locations near the road and inflicted heavy losses among the other airborne forces up and down the line. They targeted the four bridges in the area that, if taken, would effectively break the Allied supply line up the corridor. Our mission was to join the fight and prevent the Germans from succeeding.

Outside Veghel we soon found ourselves digging into foxholes to withstand a strong firestorm, one of the toughest the 506th had encountered. The Germans attacked us with heavy artillery, one of the worst barrages the 101st had seen. Never had the replacement troops seen anything like it. We were pinned down in an area about the size of two football fields. Moving forward or backward was unthinkable. We could not abandon even the foxhole's meager protection in the midst of continuous fire. The situation was tense, and I had lost track of my friend Lud.

"Lud!" I yelled over the whistle and blast of the German shelling. No answer.

"Lud!" I yelled over the roar of tanks. I feared the worst.

Finally I heard a response from about twenty feet away. I looked more closely and spotted him in a foxhole, eating some limburger cheese his parents had sent over. I had watched him stick it inside his pack in England.

"You goddamned Dutchman!" I yelled out. "You son of a bitch!"

He responded with just a wave, too busy eating his lunch and avoiding a bullet in his ear.

I hustled over to his foxhole. "What the hell are you doing?" I demanded.

"Here, Pruneface." He broke off a piece of cheese for me. "It's good for you."

We had no choice but to wait out the barrage in his foxhole and eat limburger cheese. We did not get out to move until the very early morning, when the night became quiet.

We crossed the field without major damage and continued the advance into Veghel while the Germans counterattacked along Hell's Highway. We gained little ground in town before getting bogged down again in rifle and machine-gun fire. In response to the enemy's strong firepower, we adopted a defensive posture and looked for secure positions in churches, basements, and attics. We would be stuck for a little while. Our job was not to shoot but to wait and watch.

Lud and I got into the basement of an abandoned warehouse—a strong building with cement walls. Soon other GIs joined us. Through a small basement window we watched the enemy's 88s roll by, then the panzers, with uniformed German infantry walking alongside the tanks and securing their positions.

After Al and I finished the cheese, he pulled a deck of cards from his parents' package. "Pruneface, you play pinochle?"

"No."

"C'mon. I'll teach you."

We sat on cement stairs, and Lud explained the rules. We played for what seemed like the whole afternoon. Occasionally he or I got up to check on the other men and to watch German tanks roll by. We continuously monitored the Germans' position through daylight, but just before dark, we paid more attention, with the hope of seeing where the enemy might be during the night. If the Germans saw us, they would throw potato mashers and blow up the building with us in it. One of the German 88 tanks—the Tiger—could have destroyed the side of our building and left us unprotected.

Had we climbed to the second or third floor, we could have picked off some Germans. Tempted, we did aim our rifles a few times, but we never shot. Good sense prevailed, and we remained quiet the whole night rather than risk exposing our position.

The fighting continued until late afternoon the next day, when we finally cleared the road. The Germans had penetrated Veghel very close to their four target bridges, but the Allies successfully defended the crossings.

On September 24, our regiment proceeded farther north along Hell's Highway to Uden, where our assignment was to relieve an advance party already established there. The next day, however, the road was again cut at a point south of Veghel and had to be reopened. Every order reminded us that if Market Garden was to have any chance of success, we had to keep the road open. The only alternative would be disastrous.

For the next two months, we continued to battle the Germans for control of Hell's Highway and some of the adjacent areas. At some points we got bogged down in machine-gun fire similar, I imagined, to the trench warfare my dad had endured during World War I. This struggle began at sunrise on September 25, when Colonel Robert Sink ordered the 506th Regiment southward from Uden toward Veghel. I marched with the Third Battalion on the left of Hell's Highway; the First Battalion marched on the right; and the Second brought up the rear. In the early afternoon we encountered strong enemy forces south of Veghel. By noon on September 26, the Second Battalion performed a flanking maneuver, which drove the Germans back to the right side of the road and cleared Hell's Highway again.

Once, as we moved up the line, we spotted an American Sherman tank advancing in our direction. We dug ourselves into a trench on a line that was taking on a German infantry unit. Next to me in the trench was my good buddy Walter Lukasavage. He had excelled in combat training, been in Normandy with our company, and proved himself to be a good, smart fighter. As I'd gotten to know Walter, I learned he had played Triple-A baseball and minor-league ice hockey before enlisting.

Walter and I kept our eyes on the Sherman tank. It did not signal or in any other way attempt to communicate with us.

"Think its crew is British?" someone asked.

"No," Walter answered. "I don't see a commander in its turret."

The tank simply rolled in, and something about it struck all of us as strange.

"Someone throw an orange-smoke grenade," we hollered down the line, to indicate that we were friendly troops. That was accomplished, but the tank continued to advance without returning a friendly signal.

Then we saw thin machine guns pointed at us. The tank suddenly opened fire, making clear these were Germans soldiers.

"Those sons of bitches!" Walter roared. "What right do they have to use our tank?"

And with that, he jumped up, a rifle in one hand and a grenade in the other, and started running directly for the tank.

"Holy shit!" someone yelled.

"Lukasavage!" Lud shouted.

"Is he nuts?" Mickey cried out.

I gawked at him. I wanted to shout at him, but no words came to my brain. I knew Walter was so enraged, he was not seeing a steel tank but looking through it, directly into the eyes of our enemy.

"Get your ass down!" we hollered.

I knew he could not be stopped except by a bullet. A rifle came around about twenty-five feet from us, pointed at our friend, and fired. *Bam!* Walter went down hard.

We all stared at him lying there. Walter Lukasavage, a guy everybody knew and respected, a superior athlete serving his country before getting back to the ball field and becoming a household name in pro sports.

"Give us a full field of fire!" I shouted, and Lud and I crawled out to get him. When we reached Walter's side, I could see that most of his jaw was gone.

"Oh, Jesus," Lud said, and yelled for a medic as he and I dragged Walter back under the intense field of fire.

While the Germans kept up their assault from within our own Sherman, we dragged our friend about ten feet behind our critical position, until he was safe from the enemy's bullets. I was sure he was going to die there on that field.

"Get us some help!" Lud shouted. "Get us a medic!"

Soon Walter was in a medic's care and in God's hands. Our guys were more than fired up now. Using mortar and bazooka shells, they forced the tank back, for our country and for Walter. But that isolated, albeit satisfying, victory was not the end of it. We and the Germans continued to battle for control of the road. They were based on the upper side of the road, we were below the road, and water separated us from them. Whenever we needed to move along the line, we walked—we never piled into a truck.

We hunkered down into classic trench warfare for short, intermittent episodes of fighting that reminded me of a football scrimmage. The opponents each had a line of defense and offense. Between the bursts of conflict, we endured long periods of sitting and waiting—enough to drive us all mad from the pent-up tension. Staying focused and sharp was a challenge, but mostly we were able to rally and do whatever the moment required of us.

Of course some men were better at handling their anxiety than others. A few GIs went a little mad and became reckless or worse. Once, a German soldier appeared, walking unsteadily toward our line, his hands held high, apparently intending to surrender. We called down the line, "Hold your fire!" and stood, watching him.

Suddenly a shot sounded, and—*bang!*—the German hit the ground like a sack of potatoes.

"Hold your fire!" Lud roared.

Maybe the shooter had gone temporarily nuts, but we were shocked and angry. Soldiers had a right to surrender safely. We had been trained never to fire upon an enemy who was giving himself up. Our mission was noble, and it demanded high-minded deportment. Also, if the Germans learned that Americans were shooting their prisoners, fewer would surrender. Worse, the Germans might exact vengeance by murdering their captives.

"Who fired that shot?" men cried out.

"Who shot the prisoner?" everyone demanded.

The felled German managed to get to his feet, and a few guys ran from the foxhole to help him to our line. Miraculously, the bullet had entered the soft flesh of one cheek and exited through the other cheek. He had not sustained serious damage to his face—just the two holes.

Later we learned that the shooter was a replacement lieutenant who lost control of himself. Feeling sure the fighting would continue for a while, the commanders felt justified in making an example of him. They removed him from the line and disciplined him harshly. Not many people felt badly for him. We couldn't afford that kind of action, and we couldn't tolerate officers who modeled it.

The tough battle continued along Hell's Highway between Uden and Arnhem. We spent several weeks in tough, static fighting, just trying to hold the line. We no longer thought in terms of being on the offensive. Each day our purpose was simply to defend, patrol, and gather information. Fire came at us from all directions, so obtaining good intelligence about the Germans' movements was ever more important. Reliable information came to us through the Dutch Underground, and we ourselves got into the routine of going on patrols.

Every day at sunrise, we would improve our position, gain control in waves, and wait for British tanks to go on to the next area. While some troops stayed behind to keep the road open, the rest of us moved up beyond the Nijmegen Bridge to an area along the Lower Rhine.

When I heard that the colonel had requested a patrol of three quick and nimble soldiers, I volunteered. The GIs were still revved up four, five, six weeks into Holland, and usually all the men would volunteer every time. Before we jumped, few of us had ever been on a patrol. In Holland, we became experienced at it and drew a lot of satisfaction from each successfully completed task. The desire to perform these missions well was contagious.

We raised our hands to go out, and choosing was easy for officers because most of the men were either good or quickly becoming good. I was lucky enough to be chosen for the colonel's mission.

Robert Sink's distinguished career with the Airborne began with his assignment to the 501st Parachute Infantry Battalion at Fort Benning in November 1940. He went on to command the 503rd Parachute Infantry Battalion and the 503rd Parachute Infantry Regiment. In July 1942 he was named as commander of the 506th Parachute Infantry Regiment at Toccoa, Georgia; Fort Benning, Georgia; and Fort Bragg, North Carolina. I learned his name during my training in Georgia. When the army sent our regiment to Europe in September 1943, he assumed its command, and we figured he'd be with us until the war ended.

By this time we were not far from Arnhem, and endless green fields stretched to the horizon and thatched-roof houses stood out like blocks of wood in the fertile countryside. The pastoral beauty was a superficial overlay for the realities of war. As we trekked from place to place, we saw the grim evidence of failed attacks: dead soldiers from the 101st, Eighty-second, and British Sixth lying in the dirt. In the night we heard pigs squealing and knew they were feeding on the soldiers' corpses.

The colonel had the three selected volunteers report for a briefing in a makeshift operations room in the field. I felt confident about the two others chosen for the patrol—Chivas and Chovan, two good soldiers I'd known since Camp Toccoa days. Both were athletic and could move well at night. They'd already gone on a lot of patrols in Holland, and they were often linked in field combat.

"This is the most exciting patrol I've organized since the operation began," Colonel Sink told us. "If I were younger, I'd be the first in line for this one."

The colonel was probably in his sixties, but he had the hardened physique and barrel chest of a much younger man. I had no doubt he could have successfully completed the patrol.

"Members of the Dutch Resistance have been lobbying the Allied forces to plant land mines deep into German territory," he explained. "They've reported a high concentration of German soldiers along the Lower Rhine who'll be caught off guard by a nighttime attack.

"You'll be accompanying Captain Wojtowicz across the river." He nodded toward George Wojtowicz, an officer who worked from the colonel's headquarters. "Of course we want to take many Germans out of commission and terrify the survivors, but our goals are far greater than planting land mines along the road leading up from the riverbank."

Colonel Sink went on to explain that we were to make contact with the British whom the Germans had surrounded on the other side of the river. The Brits were trapped, and their position precluded mounting an attack to free themselves.

"You men must succeed in locating the British on this patrol," Sink said gravely, and his eyes locked on each of us in turn. "You present their only hope not to be massacred."

We nodded our understanding.

"Next I want you to locate the screaming meanies."

The *screaming meanies* were the Germans' large-caliber rocket launchers—eighty-eight-millimeter artillery with revolving barrels. They were capable of firing about ten mortars in succession, and the projectiles had been drilled to scream and howl as they rocketed through the air. The sound was terrifying, demoralizing. Disabling them would be a boon to our guys.

"Finally," the colonel said, "I want you to make contact with the enemy and bring back a German officer."

We applied black paint to each other's face, and instead of helmets we wore wool-knit hats. To cut down on weight and bulk, we took the stocks off our machine guns. Then we crept to the riverbank, to our boat. It was only ten feet long and barely large enough for the four of us. It was dwarfed by the Lower Rhine, which was fairly wide at this location, with a higher tide than we could discern from land.

For a while I felt safer in the river than I had walking along the embankment, where the moonlight had clearly defined our silhouettes. But then, as we crossed the river, a rocket lit up the sky. We froze and kept the boat as still as we could in the water until the sky darkened again.

Once across the river, we ran south along the bank and then up a five-hundred-foot incline. We believed the Germans were positioned at the top. Broken glass scattered all over the slope made climbing difficult and produced a loud crunch we could not muffle. Exerting great care, we reached the top and placed two land mines in the road. Our first objective was complete.

Crouching, keeping our heads down, we snaked deeper into the Germans' territory. Chovan stopped and pointed into the distance ahead. I looked in that direction and saw the distinctive red hats worn by the British armored division. We moved closer to locate their encampment and counted a few dozen British soldiers therein. We could not make direct contact with them—too many Germans soldiers separated us—but we believed Colonel Sink would be able to take action from the information we had gathered.

Soon after we sighted the British, another German rocket

exploded in the sky. We took advantage of its illumination and found the location of the screaming meanies. This fulfilled our third objective. Now our guys could destroy the launchers.

The last and most difficult objective—the capture of a German officer—still awaited us. We crept closer toward the crest of the hill, then along the top of the ridge. We were able to maneuver freely and use the terrain to our advantage and huge oak trees for cover. The sound of singing and merriment drifted to us, and we let it guide us to a house. Chivas and I led the way and found a party in full swing. Officers would be inside; rarely did enlisted men have the opportunity to whoop it up.

"We're going to get a goddamned prisoner," I whispered to Chivas, a bit awed by how this happenstance worked to support our goal.

He nodded his agreement, and his teeth gleamed whitely in the darkness. We circled around more towering trees until we gained a clear view of the house, then we crouched behind a two-foot-tall brick wall that enclosed the front yard. Beyond, one guard stood at the front door. To the left, two guards of lower rank stood along a walkway and chatted in a relaxed manner. Apparently we would witness the change of shift.

We four pressed ourselves tight against the wall and discussed possible strategies, all of which centered on surprising one of the guards.

"We could break our submachine guns down to small pieces," I suggested. "Our caps look like the guards' hats, so maybe we'll be able just to walk up to one of them and wait for him to challenge us. If we're lucky, we'll get close enough to kill him quietly."

"Use your knife," the captain said. "Shoot him only if necessary."

We nodded.

"We can raise hell with the officers in the house," Chovan whispered. "Make noise, create confusion, grab an officer, and get the hell out of here."

Chivas and I walked with confidence toward the house, but the first guard challenged us immediately. Still a good ten strides from knife range, we had no choice but to mow them down with our submachine guns. Both guards were dead before they hit the walkway.

The blasts from our weapons emptied the house. German soldiers burst through the door, and a couple of officers hurled themselves out windows. One came at us, but he lost his balance, tripped, and landed beyond us. Chivas and I exchanged a quick glance, then grabbed him under the arms and pulled him from the house and over the wall as Chovan and Wojtowicz covered us with intense fire.

Our captive kicked and yelled, but we beat him into unconsciousness and then dragged him toward the river. Chovan and Wojtowicz continued to shoot at the Germans, but no one seemed to be in pursuit. As we ran through the oak trees, I heard popping sounds that could have been the Germans shooting at us, but soon I realized the noise was acorns raining down from the branches.

We raced along the ridge and to the slope to the riverbank. As I approached the decline, I heard the unmistakable metallic *chink* of the bolt being pulled back on a machine gun. We stopped immediately and froze, anticipating the deadly tattoo of bullets. Staying low, I held my breath while my heart hammered in my chest.

Nothing. No one shot at us. After a few moments we ran again, even faster than before. We half slid, half bounded down the hill, trying to avoid the glass. Flares whitened the night sky, one after another, and as soon as one lit up, we froze, only to continue our escape when the flare was spent.

Our small boat was where we had left it—hardly big enough for four but now accommodating five. We punched the officer again and again, knocking him out for the ride across the Rhine. We laid him in the bottom, then crawled in.

"Looks like we got ourselves an officer," Chivas said.

"A captain, no less," Chovan said, flicking at the man's uniform. He turned to Wojtowicz and said, "Whaddaya think of that, Captain?"

Wojtowicz smiled and shook his head. "I think Colonel Sink is going to be very pleased."

CHAPTER 19

As I watched the new recruits mature into experienced combat soldiers, I had to acknowledge how much I myself had changed since enlisting—and not just because I'd made it through the tough times. I joined the 101st Airborne as a kid from New Jersey whose world encompassed his extended family and friends. I'd never met anyone from, say, Texas or Oklahoma. Then I started training and spent months with guys from all over the country. Now I was fighting alongside country dwellers who had been shooting guns since they were kids. I was bunking with fellas from Massachusetts and Maine, whose accents were unlike any I had heard before. I shared stories of home with guys from Washington and Florida. We were all around the same age, but some guys shaved, smoked cigarettes, and knew women—I mean *really* knew women—while others had a little peach fuzz on their upper lip, had never indulged in anything more wicked than Sugar Babies candies, and had been too shy to talk to a girl.

For the most part, we GIs created close bonds of friendship and learned from one another. Many of the guys had seen interesting places, done fascinating things, and possessed unusual abilities.

A lot of guys had won glory on their high-school football team, as I had done when West Orange High School won the state football championship in 1942 over Paterson East Side. I helped win the game when I lowered my head, gathered my strength, and tackled Paterson's star running back, Larry Doby, on the goal line, keeping him outside the end zone. I believed him to be destined for fame. Sure enough, he ended up playing professional baseball, in the major leagues with the Cleveland Indians.

Whatever our background, we developed as keen a familiarity with the terrain as if it were our own hometown neighborhood. We nurtured our awareness of the dikes and canals, the lakes hardly bigger than a puddle, the trees, and each thatched-roof house. One GI could mention a location, and everyone else would know where it was. (The same could be said for the Germans. They knew the terrain well from having been there for a long time.)

During this time of going on patrols and getting to know Hell's Highway inside and out, I began to develop a sixth sense in regard to combat. Every day I trusted it and relied upon it more and more. It had become indispensable. Other GIs had developed the sixth sense, too, and we shared this talent collectively, as if we all received the same intuitive transmission simultaneously. As a group we always knew when to fight and when to hide.

One cold, dry night Lud and I went on a patrol to "make contact with the enemy," which meant we would likely exchange gunfire with the Germans. With us were a medic and a rifleman, and Sam

Goodgall and Ed "The Face" Albers. His good looks had earned him that nickname.

Our officers wanted us to find out where the enemy was situated along the canal and how to lure the Germans into the open.

We set out, walking in knee-deep water. Our view limited by darkness, we thought we were walking in the canal but weren't completely certain. The five of us had trekked about a mile and a half when Sam spotted movement to our left. He signaled for us to stop and hide. In the thin moonlight I saw two German soldiers who had climbed from their foxhole: The first wore an over-the-shoulder antitank weapon, the other gripped a rifle. The pair looked out over the water but did not appear to be paying much attention.

We reasoned that because one of them was standing guard with a bazooka, many more Germans were probably encamped there, most likely asleep in their foxholes.

I really wanted to take the first shot. I had my rifle up and at the ready, but Engelbrecht was quicker than I. He raised his rifle and—*bam!*—knocked down the man with the bazooka. All I could do was stand there.

Lud stared at me. "Shoot, Jim, shoot!"

I fired and got the second guy.

By now the Germans had vaulted out of their foxholes, and we six took off at a run. We didn't notice that we were racing right up the thatched roof of a house that extended to the ground. We went right up one side, and down the other, not covering much ground for the amount of exertion.

At the bottom, we looked back, and a gaslight illuminated the interior. We peeked through the window at a Dutch family, all huddled in a corner and scared to death. The four small children were shrieking, and the parents looked exhausted to the marrow. The sight reminded me that the soldiers weren't the only ones stressed by the offensive in Holland.

We had found the Dutch to be good, kind people whose attitude toward us was consistently thoughtful and caring. We could always count on them to lend a hand.

We tapped on the window, and the family members looked our way.

We smiled and waved to them. "Everything is all right," Lud called out. "Please accept our apologies for running over your roof."

Then we took off for our line, but we had not gone far when we heard German voices coming from a house.

"Listening post?" Sam whispered, and Lud and I nodded. We had the same suspicion.

As one we changed direction and approached the house with caution, then crouched down by the front door and waited. Soon a German soldier came outside, and we dealt with him quickly and silently, with a knife. Next we readied our guns and positioned ourselves in the cold darkness, poised to shoot whoever came looking for our first victim. We did not have to wait long. Several more of the enemy came outside, and we dispensed with them quickly. When no one else emerged, we ventured inside and searched through the house. It was empty.

In the basement we found a cheery blaze crackling in the fireplace. We warmed ourselves, especially our hands. Certain more Germans would arrive soon to check out the house, we stayed in the cozy basement and pointed our rifles at the window and the stairs.

A humming caught our attention, and we all looked up, as if we might magically be able to see through the ceiling to the first floor. We were already familiar with the sound, though: The Germans' flashlights had hand-cranked generators that hummed distinctively. More than a few times during the Holland campaign those generators betrayed the proximity of their operators. Guys in our outfit spread the word to new replacements: "Listen for the humming at night. That'll be the Heinies."

Having heard that particular sound coming from the first floor, we knew Germans had entered the house. We crept up the stairs to engage them, but our advance was perhaps too aggressive. The soldiers quickly retreated. We decided not to fire at them in the darkness. Whoever took flight was likely to be German, but we had not seen anyone and did not want to harm a Dutch citizen or an ally who had found a German flashlight. Besides, we were on a patrol to gather information, not bodies.

We agreed to stay inside the house. In this sort of situation, we would take turns standing guard outside so each guy could get some rest while the sentry prevented a sneak attack. But the medic, a combat veteran named Growdy, spoke up.

"Oh, no," he said. "I'm not standing guard. As a member of the medical team, I don't have to carry a weapon or take part in any military action."

I looked at Lud. I was enjoying myself already, anticipating how he would respond. He knew crap when he heard it. While the others fumed, I remained silent, confident Lud would take care of it.

He nodded slowly at the medic, taking his measure. "Okay, you're right, Growdy. But you gotta get the hell out of the house."

Growdy rolled his head back and groaned in frustration.

"I don't have to keep you in the house," Lud said evenly.

"You'll need me for morphine," the medic objected, "and for bandages."

"We all know how to inject morphine and wrap gauze," Lud

responded. "Now, go stand outside the house without a rifle and let the rest of us know if you have any problems."

Growdy followed orders, but he did not stay outside for long. He came back into the basement, ripped off his medic's armband, grabbed a rifle, and took a turn at guard duty.

When the guard shift changed, Lud got Growdy alone, but I could overhear him. "You don't talk like that to anyone in this unit," he said, "especially not to a noncommissioned officer!"

When they returned to our group, the medic looked sheepish. From that moment forward, he evidenced a much-improved attitude.

The morning after we returned to camp, Colonel Sink called me, Chivas, and Chovan to breakfast. As I sat down to a repast none of us had seen in a long while—eggs, bacon, fresh bread, and coffee—I wondered if he had another patrol assignment for us. We three sat with him at a round table in his headquarters and listened politely as he reiterated, "I really envy you guys. I wish I could have gone on that patrol with you."

"We'd be happy for your company on the next one, Colonel," Chivas said, and earned a laugh.

"I'll keep that in mind," the colonel said, his eyes twinkling. Then he turned serious. "I brought you here for a specific reason, men. I sent another patrol into the area you penetrated. We made very good use of the excellent intelligence you brought back to camp and what we were able to learn from our unwilling guest, the captain."

Colonel Sink looked at each of us. "I wanted you men to know that the patrol established direct contact with the Dutch Resistance and rescued over one hundred British soldiers."

"The armored division that was surrounded by German troops,

sir?" I asked, thinking of the few dozen men in their distinctive red hats.

"The very ones. Our allies owe you a debt of gratitude. These men would have been massacred, every last one, if not for you. I'd call that a job well done, men, and I wanted to have the pleasure of telling you that myself!"

The rickety brick structure was situated on high ground on the opposite side of the Lower Rhine, about halfway between a dike and the Germans' position.

"That's the place," I told my squad, crouched beside me. "Our mission is to determine who and what are inside. If it isn't occupied, then it'll be a good place to establish a listening post along the river."

Orders had come down to Lud: He was responsible for setting up a listening post for the army, where radio equipment could intercept the Germans' transmissions. He had come upon this place and wanted it checked out. As structures went, it was a pretty good size. Measured against other factories, though—this place manufactured bricks—it was on the smallish size and so perfect for our purpose.

We crept out of hiding and approached the building. A thick layer of coal dust blacked out the windows, so we depended upon our ears to detect any occupants. Met by silence, we entered through a heavy unlocked wooden door.

The Face Albers went to a window overlooking the river and carefully wiped clean a small spot near the bottom, so we could see the out-of-doors. He left the solid coat of soot untouched over the rest of the window's surface, then he joined me to explore the rest of the ground floor. We froze when we heard a woman crying and another person talking.

The Face and I dropped to our hands and knees and crawled slowly in the direction of the sound. They led us to what had to be the warmest place in the building: the oven where a coal-fed fire baked the bricks. We peered down into the hole and saw two men and two women lounging on a pile of quilts. A closer look indicated they were a family. The daughter, a blond beauty, appeared to be about eighteen years old. Her mother was still quite striking. The father and son noticed us first and jumped up, interposing themselves between the womenfolk and us.

"We are Americans," I said. "We won't hurt you."

The father's face and posture relaxed, and he said in accented English, "Perhaps you can help us, yes? My daughter, she is hit by shrapnel three days past. Her leg is red and hot. I do not know what to do."

The mother's eyes glistened with tears. "You help? Yes?"

"Yes," I said, and The Face echoed my response. He and I hurried downstairs, found the front of the oven, and walked inside. I removed the streptomycin from my first-aid kit and cleaned the girl's wound, which was just above her knee. Her eyes glittered with fever, and red streaks of infection stained her skin above and below the shrapnel. I applied a tourniquet above the wound and instructed the family to loosen it and let blood flow once I was done.

I gathered my squad, and we carried the girl to the dike, where we could have Growdy treat her with his medical inventory, to which the contents of my first-aid kit could not begin to compare. As we walked, the family shared with us everything they knew about the brick factory, the Germans in the area, and everything else they thought might be helpful to the Allies. Armed with that information, I knew we could safely set up a listening post.

The Allies' ultimate goal for Operation Market Garden was to open a path across the Rhine, then cut deep into Germany from the north, to end the war by Christmas. Building on the momentum created by the Allies' successful summer campaign in France, American airborne forces won and secured a safe route to Arnhem's door, and the British First Airborne entered that city to secure the Arnhem Bridge. The British Army planned a swift advance along Hell's Highway to relieve the Airborne while more Allied troops gathered in Holland for the last big push into Germany.

Then the Germans surprised everyone with a strong counteroffensive. Arnhem and the land across the Rhine remained in German hands, and the British soldiers caught in the city were quickly evacuated.

The Market Garden offensive had failed. The world would have to wait for peace.

Our mood was as dark and dense as the lowering sky. October turned into November, and our tempers were short, like the early winter days. In our corner of the war, the fighting had become static. Little if any territory had been won by either side. So when we received word that we were being relieved by Canadian and British forces, the announcement could not have been more welcome. We had served our time, and new blood could come in to hold the line.

The 101st would head to France for a rest—hallelujah!—while awaiting our next mission. Word around camp said our destination, the city of Rheims, had a festive atmosphere where we could forget all about the war.

"I want you and your squad to travel ahead of us, Pruneface," Lud told me. "We're putting up at a military school outside Rheims.

Make sure the facilities are properly prepared and comfortable. The guys really need to recuperate from the last three months."

Nearly everyone had arrived in France from Holland, and the brass awarded us a number of unit citations for successful completion of our missions there. Formal recognition did little to ease the tension and touchiness in our squad after we left Holland, however. Our supplies were at their lowest. We had few rations left, and as for matériel, I had only two grenades and one round of ammunition. Most guys did not have even that much.

We also felt passed over. Replacement soldiers seemed to outnumber the original guys of the 101st, the guys from Camp Toccoa. Most of the original men still remaining had been promoted and now wore their stripes, but not us. By the time we left Holland, little distinguished us from the replacements, despite all the time we had served. It hadn't been easy duty, either. We had all seen war up close, had looked Germans in the eyes, and had seen buddies next to us die.

We couldn't do anything about that, and we weren't supposed to be glum. In Rheims our first step toward reenergizing ourselves was having fun and acting like guys our age . . . or younger. Rheims was in the Champagne region of France, the champagne center of the world. We could buy a bottle of bubbly for less than a buck.

As we lurched from one nightclub to another, I could have been on the streets of New York City, listening to live music, tossing back mixed drinks, and laughing till I couldn't even remember what had struck me funny in the first place.

One night as a few of us settled into a banquette table in a nightclub, The Face proposed a contest: Whoever could hit our waitress in the butt with the cork while opening a bottle of champagne would win a free bottle of the bubbly, courtesy of the less accomplished marksmen at our table.

That night I enjoyed uncanny aim. I got completely crocked and won three bottles and a dirty look from our waitress. Wearing a sixteen-proof smile, I stood and tottered from our table in search of some French people with whom to practice my fluency. I flirted with a few women, scuffled with a few men, and decided I had drunk enough and should catch the shuttle back to camp.

On my way to the truck, I decided on impulse to play the role of a French civilian again, as I had with the Maquis and my cousin's family. Walking ahead of me was a Frenchman about my size, and I talked him into trading his clothes for my uniform. I strolled happily along the avenues of Champagne, once again enjoying the sensation of being a Frenchman.

My happy thoughts ebbed when the shuttle driver refused to allow me on the military conveyance. I kept climbing up into the bed, but the guys kept throwing me off. Finally I convinced the others I was with the 101st Airborne, and I curled up on the floor under the folding seats so as not to raise questions or get the driver in trouble.

I gazed up at the stars. The night air was crisp and clean, reminding me of Thanksgiving and, inevitably, football season. I decided to see if I could get some touch football games organized at the military academy before our new orders came.

A football game between the 101st Airborne and the air force was set for New Year's Day. At first it was called the Champagne Bowl, then became known as the Pig's Asshole Bowl. I made the team and spent a lot of my free time in practice. We saw the first snow of winter while practicing for the game. The competition provided some diversion and a common topic for conversation, even for some of the officers. Both were much needed, for our stress level had reached a high point none of us had experienced together.

Lud Engelbrecht, the man we all loved and respected, inadvertently made the situation worse. He received orders to choose the best man in the outfit for a weekend in Paris. He assembled us for the announcement of his decision, and every man was hopeful he would be the lucky one.

"I have decided upon myself as the guy to go to Paris," he said without prelude. "Who better than me?"

Stunned, we stood staring at him. I could not blame Lud for choosing himself, but the way in which he did it pissed me off, as it did the rest of the men. He had always been honest with us—and that was probably why he informed us in such an abrupt manner—but it still rubbed us wrong, and he knew it. He split for Paris, and we went back to playing football.

This was only the second time my best buddy had caused me to see red. The first time was back in England, before the Normandy invasion. Neeper hatched a scheme that could have gotten us both court-martialed. Neeper and I were close. Like me, he was from New Jersey. He was three or four years older than I, already married to his high-school sweetheart. Neeper was so in love with Betty, he would turn her photograph facedown out of respect when we walked bare-assed around the barracks.

At that time we were staying at a medieval manor outside the quaint little town of Ramsbury. Warm, friendly villagers lived in thatched-roof homes around the manor house. Not long after we first got to Ramsbury, we noticed some forty or fifty baby chicks and a hen strutting and pecking at the dirt around the castle walls.

"Jim, keep your eyes on those chicks," Neeper told me. "They ought to be about frying size by the time we move out."

Just two months later the order came to pack all our gear and prepare for a long train ride. Neeper came looking for me in the barracks. "Jimmy," he said, and sat on the bunk next to mine, "let's get those fryers and cook 'em."

I stared at him. "How the hell are we gonna cook them? We're moving out today."

"In the officers' mess hall. I already got a bucket of frying oil from the chef."

We slipped out of the Nisson hut that had been our home and into the damp English night. The mist was so thick, it turned to water drops on my face as we went looking for the chickens. They were all there—about forty of them.

"How the hell do we kill them?" I asked.

"Nothing to it." Neeper gave me a demonstration. "Grab one, put its head between your legs, and jerk real hard on its neck." He ripped the chicken's head right off its body.

The fowl clucked and ran around in circles as Neeper and I popped the heads off. We threw some twenty of them in a large GI can and then lugged it to the officers' mess. In the kitchen we dunked the dead birds in boiling water to make the cleaning and cutting easier.

The aroma of frying chicken soon filled the mess.

"What are you doing, men?"

We turned to see Colonel Wolverton standing in the doorway. He had picked up the scent. Oh, shit, we're in trouble now, I thought, standing firm, looking straight ahead at the colonel.

But Wolverton smiled. "Cooking pigeons?"

"Yes, sir," Neeper replied, stabbing a piece to lift it from the sizzling pot before standing at attention. I couldn't help salivating as I glanced at the impaled chicken.

"Don't cook any more, men," Wolverton ordered.

"Yessir."

"Yessir."

As soon as we were alone, Neeper and I wolfed down four pieces each and packed the rest in large brown-paper bags before hustling out of the mess hall and back to the hut. We walked in the door, and a Texan named Lincoln exclaimed, "What the hell did you fellas do? For Christ's sake, what's on your pants?"

A roar of laughter and disgust from our buddies intensified as Neeper and I looked down at ourselves. The crotch of our pants was caked with grime and blood.

"Jesus Christ, Jim," Neeper said, grinning sheepishly, "I forgot to tell you that chickens keep pecking and bleeding after their heads are popped off."

"The order to move could come at any moment," Lincoln told us. "You better clean yourselves."

With our pants all messed up, we couldn't play innocent if the farmer came looking for the offenders. Neeper and I spent the next hour washing our pants and setting them over the barracks pot stove to dry. We were among the last to pile into the trucks that took us to the Swindon station.

All the windows of our long, long train were blacked out and curtains closed so as not to signal any troop movement out of Ramsbury. With everything shut tight, our car was uncomfortably stuffy. Once we finally got moving, the progress was unendurably slow. By lunchtime, everyone was in a lousy mood even before Lud handed out the dry, processed-cheese sandwiches to his platoon. The men complained loudly.

"If you don't like 'em, you can eat shit," he growled a few times.

Our sergeant's response got everyone all pissed off.

"Should we give him some fried chicken?" Neeper asked me, nodding toward Lud.

"Fuck 'im," I said, indignant. "Let *him* eat shit." Then we passed around the chicken to our best buddies.

The train soon returned to Ramsbury; the exercise had been a rehearsal for D-Day. When we got back, Colonel Wolverton summoned Neeper and me to his office and reamed us out. He said doing something stupid like stealing chickens could have blown the whole surprise of the invasion. It could have signaled the enemy that we were pulling out and were not coming back.

Of course we knew he was right, and that made us feel low. Security had intensified as possible invasion dates drew nearer. Any intelligence leak, or simply anything seen as out of the ordinary, could have helped get us all killed.

As punishment, through the rest of April and May, Neeper and I got assigned every miserable job that needed doing.

Now, while Lud was in Paris, I was playing football, living on a school campus, and feeling far removed from the war's front line. I enjoyed a feeling of normality, and I wanted it to last forever. Shortly after Lud returned from Paris, though, we got word we were being shipped out, and the timing forced us to cancel the much-anticipated football game.

Open-top trucks provided the transportation, and when we left, the weather was surprisingly balmy. We jumped onto the trucks with only our field jackets. A lot of the guys, myself included, wanted to shed bulk in any way we could, and among the first discards were our heavy, long, army-issue overcoats. Without much to pack in the way of ammunition or rations, we left in a hurry. No one briefed us about the assignment or informed us about the terrain. All we knew was our destination: Bastogne. Nothing more than a name.

Bastogne, Belgium, was a small town of only several thousand people, and yet it was the site of an Allied headquarters and the hub of a crucial communications network. Located between Berlin and Paris, it was a crossroads of seven highways and three railroads.

The Germans and Allies both considered the town integral to their strategy and success. Bastogne was the Allies' only position that prevented the Germans from advancing west in a straight line to the Meuse River. From there Hitler's army could push onward to retake Antwerp and then try to encircle the Allied armies in the north. Every officer, no matter which side of the conflict, was aware of this fact.

Now the Germans had momentum on their side. The Holland campaign in the fall had not realized its goal of penetrating Germany from the north and taking Berlin by Christmas. Instead the German soldiers proved how nimble and resilient they could be and how motivated when their very homeland was at stake.

On December 16 the Germans delivered a shock by breaking through the Allies' defenses in the Ardennes Forest and pushing westward across Luxembourg and Belgium. We expected our 101st Airborne to drop in and boost the infantry units on the ground by engaging in heavy combat to complement the tanks and armored divisions. In Bastogne, however, the airborne units made a less dramatic entrance than usual by walking into battle. General Eisenhower reluctantly committed the airborne units to combat, and then

General Middleton of the Eighth U.S. Army immediately assigned the 101st Airborne to get "behind his broken center."

The infantry commanders entrenched along the Belgian border gratefully accepted the airborne paratroopers as part of the ground force. Already they had exhausted their resources, and now the Germans mounted a new offensive. They had filled the area around Bastogne with heavy Panzer Corps artillery and were poised to take the main highway leading southwest toward Neufchateau.

We did not know how desperate the situation was at Bastogne when we climbed down from our transport trucks late on the night of December 18, 1944. The weather had already turned cold with rain, and the fog was so thick, I could taste it.

We stood around in the cold for what felt like hours, and certainly more than a few men were thinking about the heavy overcoats we had discarded in Rheims. We smoked whatever cigarettes we could find and asked one another about ammunition inventory. Instructions about our mission remained thin. Rather than anxiety, I felt the burden of the unknown, the weight of a mystery. What would happen before dawn?

"Jim," Lud called out. The fog distorted his location and disembodied his voice. "I want you and Albers to scout out the terrain ahead of our unit."

"Okay, Lud." Wherever you are.

The Face and I walked at a pretty good clip about one hundred yards ahead of the whole outfit. He took the left and I the right. At first huge pine trees dwarfed us, their upper tiers disappearing in the fog. The farther we walked, though, the more evergreens we saw that had been blasted from the ground and were lying on their sides. The Face and I exchanged knowing glances: The Germans' deadly artillery, the 88s, had done significant damage.

Through the milky haze I could see an orange luminosity—fires raging among the trees—and eventually I made out the silhouette of troops in fragmented columns heading toward us. Then I heard the rustle of soldiers emerging from the edge of broken, toppled trees and, farther down the line of troops, faint screaming. The men said nothing as they approached us in the cold night air. Their eyes were fixed on the ground or stared straight ahead with a hollowed-out, haunted look that hinted at untold horrors. I guessed they were German prisoners.

Then the first ones passed us, and I realized they were Americans. Some faces were barely recognizable from the blood and gashes. They must have been frozen, too. When they saw we were GIs, most showed little reaction. They shook their heads and warned, "Don't go in there." Some just babbled and spat blood.

I turned and looked behind me. Either Albers and I had slowed our pace, or the rest of the outfit had increased theirs, for they had closed the gap between us. I saw the men in my unit gaping at these bedraggled troops with the same incredulity I had felt looking at them. I did not want to form any opinions of these men walking past me; I had no way and no right to judge them. I knew nothing about them except what I saw. Still, suspicion simmered in my mind.

I saw Lud and a medic reach out to stop them.

I did the same, touching the arm of the man closest to me. "Hey," I asked, "what's going on?"

"Don't go in there," he said to me. "Don't go in there. Don't go in there!" His voice rose each time he said it, and then he continued his retreat down our line. "Don't go in there! *Don't go in there!*"

"Get back," another soldier told me. "They're going to kill you."

"Don't go in there," others echoed fiercely.

We tried not to let the evident horror of these retreating soldiers get to us, but these walking wounded gave the word *fear* new meaning. So deep was it, it felt invasive, and a few of our guys panicked.

"Whatever hit them was worse than anything *I've* ever seen," I heard one trooper say. "I know it already."

My own thoughts raced. We were seeing something really terrifying. Whatever had been thrown at them was as hot as lightning—a furious bolt that had come down and smashed these guys and everything in the place that these guys had just come from . . . the same place we were heading.

Fear gnawed at my stomach and sucked on my bones, quickening my pulse, leaving me broken—just as the men passing before us seemed completely shattered. Standing in the snow and fog of this unfamiliar battlefield, I could so easily have felt jinxed already, destined to one tragic fate. After all, we had not jumped properly into Bastogne; I had not hurled myself into a new battle; I'd not been provided with the basic gear I would need to fight and survive. I could so easily have said to myself, *I am stripped of the faith of my mother and bereft of her faith in a patron saint of warriors that have kept me safe until now.* I could have, but I did not. Instead I tried to harden myself for the fight.

I opened my field jacket and allowed the frigid air to shock me back to my senses. I marshaled within myself the esprit de corps that had attracted men to enlist in the airborne units, that had made us the target of envy in the barroom, that had prompted Winston Churchill to define paratroopers as the new, modern way to engage in warfare, that had kept me at John Simpson's side on the way to St. Lo, even when I thought I could escape.

Those ravaged, retreating GIs must not have had combat experience, I told myself. We're the mighty 101st, battle-hardened from Normandy and Holland. Nothing can get us down. We had pumped ourselves up with pride from the time we set out to break marching records from Camp Toccoa to Fort Benning more than two years before. If the Germans wanted another fight, we'd give them one they'd never forget!

I began to feel better, stronger. My mind flashed to the sandwich-billboard advertisement I had seen two years before outside the Orange, New Jersey, post office. It read: JUMP INTO THE FIGHT, reminiscent of the notes Pop had left for me before football games and similar to the Depression-era posters he had given me to hang in my bedroom. One urged: CHOOSE AN OBJECTIVE AND GO AFTER IT! Another read: KEEP PLUGGING! A third reminded: EFFORT IS THE DIFFERENCE BETWEEN WINNING AND LOSING!

Those exhortations had been the source of my shame when I saw my peers shipping out to fight Hitler while I was stuck at home, working in a factory. They had also motivated me to enlist in the service. Jump into the fight? Shit, I had *always* jumped! I brought to mind all the jumps I had made since training: over Normandy, from the prison train, over Holland to fight in Market Garden. I had jumped fourteen times from a plane before I had even landed in one.

Obviously the other guys in my unit saw the danger of falling victim to fear, for I could hear them yell to one another, "Be professional!" and "Get serious!" As the column of retreating men passed us, we called out for them to give us their ammunition, or we just dug into their pockets and picked out whatever matériel we could find.

I could have viewed this as opportunistic or predatory. These soldiers were in a hurry to distance themselves from the scene of battle, and there we were, slowing them, walking alongside them, asking: *Do you have rounds? Do you have any rounds left over? Do you have any fucking rounds left?*

I gathered enough rounds to share, and we were even able to salvage some of their antitank destroyers. I felt more at ease about my ammunition supply.

Seeing guys on our own side completely broken was not part of our deal—certainly not before entering battle ourselves. The sight had been a shock. It violated the conditioning that had become our way of life and united the 101st.

I steeled myself, summoning and meshing within my chest every source of strength and inspiration and conviction I had ever known, everything I needed for this coming battle. If the Germans were throwing everything they had left at us, then we would throw at them everything that we, the Screaming Eagles, had.

I was resolved—we all were resolved—that it would be more than enough.

CHAPTER 20

Our division, a part of Company I, was responsible for holding the line in a designated area between Bastogne and the small village of Foy. The Face Albers and I resumed our work as scouts, moving throughout the night. Lud Engelbrecht led the other men in our unit, keeping some distance between us and them.

The terrain in and around Bastogne was relatively flat. To the north, where we were headed, were a few scattered hills. We passed Bastogne's train station and a church used as a hospital and supply shelter. Then we arrived at the front.

We dug our pits to accommodate three or four guys and then settled in. I wanted to calm down and rest in the little time remaining before dawn. I managed to keep the visual memory of the broken men at bay as I sat in silence, grimly determined to stop the Germans' momentum.

Our position was close behind Company G's, and those men and a road were all that separated us from the Germans. If we wanted to take a peek at the enemy, we'd just have to cross the lane. I thought Company G's position was exposed and awfully vulnerable. I hoped I'd be proved wrong when, on the morning of December 19, the Germans launched heavy, constant fire, a seemingly nonstop *crash* and *boom*.

"Get in the ready position!" Lud shouted, and word went along the line, mixing with the roar of explosive detonations.

We broke out of our pits. I scrambled behind some trees, wanting to see what was going on ahead of us, but the snow, fog, and smoke masked everything save scattered movements and the bright flash of machine-gun fire.

"Don't move!" Lud ordered. "Watch for my signal to fire!"

"Hey! Above yous!" someone yelled.

I looked up to see huge, snow-laden limbs shaken from the ancient trees. They plunged down right on top of us.

Now a new sound thundered over the gunfire—the sound of German tankers blasting the area occupied by Company G.

"Retreat! Company G! Retreat!"

Not having revealed ourselves to the Germans, we remained hidden while creeping forward for a better view of the area Company G was abandoning. Those who survived the onslaught, those who could move under their own power, hobbled toward us. Very few men had lived through the attack, and their number offered proof of their vulnerability.

I watched transfixed as half a dozen Germans climbed down from their panzers and walked around the field, picking over the dead and dying Americans in the muddy, bloodred snow. The scavengers plucked watches and jewelry from the GIs, some of whom were horribly wounded, too feeble to resist the thieves. Long-coated Nazi officers stood in the distance, watching with seemingly little interest.

I tightened my grip on my weapon, more than ready for the Germans now. I turned and gave a quick thumbs-up to a new guy, Dicky Shin, who looked a little green around the gills. I figured the rookie replacement would develop into a good soldier once he had some experience—he'd already won a featherweight boxing title back home. But no matter how nimble and quick Dicky might be, Bastogne was a helluva place to see his first action, I thought. Like any other replacement, he would probably be timid with his rifle.

Six of us ran over the frozen ground to a large, loose haystack, clawed through it to the other side, and took aim. The Face managed to maneuver an old thirty-seven-millimeter cannon—a two-wheeled antitank weapon—through the snow.

Lud was waiting for the Nazi officers to become more visible. With supplies of ammunition so low, we needed every shot to hit its mark. Finally he was satisfied.

"Fire off one or two and make 'em count," he told the squad. "Then get your ass back here. If we all land shots, we'll have ten or twelve fewer Germans to worry about."

Lud went first. He picked off two or three Germans before the rest of us opened fire in a quick barrage. Then The Face unleashed the old 37 and struck the Tiger tank. A hard, fierce explosion rocked the land, and the tank became a fiery coffin. A second German tank swung its weapon parapet around to take aim at the haystack.

We took to our heels and raced for cover. With each step I expected to feel the burning bite of the panzer's weapons. The second German tank still did not fire, and I began to wonder if no one was inside it. We hustled to reload the 37 and fire off another shot. The second Tiger exploded in flames.

The German infantry moved in and shot at us. I fired at least five times, saving my dwindling supply of ammunition for when the Germans might be most susceptible.

Lud ran over to me and a few other men. "We've got orders for our company to move quickly into a new position." He cast a quick glance in the direction of the road. "Nothing I didn't expect."

I understood: The heavy casualties suffered by Company G changed the dynamics of this battle, so the strategy needed adjustment. I was eager to move out so I could get on with the job and destroy more tanks. Probably all of us had found our confidence while the Germans had lost theirs after that engagement. Surely they realized they were dealing with an infantry capable of stopping a tank attack.

Fog blanketed the trees, and snow fell over Bastogne as we moved to our new position, slightly farther north toward Foy. Almost immediately the enemy fired upon us. We shot back and for the next few days held our foxhole positions. The 506th regiment of the 101st Airborne, meanwhile, created and held a defensive line from our position near Foy southward to Bastogne proper.

To the west, the news was bad. The Germans had advanced, closing us in. The 101st Airborne, arranged in a ring around Bastogne, was now itself completely encircled by the enemy. The divisions of the 101st Airborne were surrounded many times in Bastogne; we got used to fighting that way. As one officer pointed out, "We're paratroopers. We're supposed to be surrounded."

For eight days we hid in our foxholes while German tanks with heavy .88 artillery closed in on us. On the rare occasion the snow and fog allowed any visibility, we darted from our trenches to shoot some rounds. Ammunition remained so low, we held off firing unless hitting our target was a sure thing.

The assaults we withstood were awful, but the enemy did not

break through our lines. After only a few minutes of exchanging rounds with the Germans, we would tend to our many wounded as best we could. Casualties were high in each attack. We lost at least one guy every time.

Our greatest concern was the shortage of medical supplies, especially morphine, up and down the line. We relied on trips back into Bastogne for reserves. The medics worked harder than I had ever seen, and even the lethargic Growdy moved faster to and from the makeshift hospital in the center of Bastogne than I would have believed possible.

The thick fog prevented supply drops from the base through the middle of the week before Christmas, so food at our location was scarce. With little sustenance, the wounded men had an especially tough time regaining their health and strength. In truth, none of the GIs was feeling well by this point. Spending so much time cooped up in the ground was not good for our health. Many, myself included, had only our field jackets for warmth. I was grateful to have boots; some guys did not and were paying dearly for it.

One night I was absolutely exhausted. An overnight rainstorm had soaked me to the marrow, and I was so cold, I could not control my shivering. Worse, I was on guard duty. As the hours passed, the temperature dropped, and I did the unthinkable: I abandoned my post and climbed into a foxhole for whatever warmth could be had. I closed my eyes and continued to shiver through the night. Fortunately the enemy did not try to violate the perimeter of our position—probably because the Germans were so terribly cold, too.

Most of the time they were not so cooperative. During intense combat in Bastogne, enemy tanks and machine-gun fire chased me and another GI—I did not know who was running alongside me— into a barn. After I had safely reached the shelter and examined myself for bullet wounds (I was unharmed), I took a moment to look at my companion. The Face was there with me, and I felt incredibly fortunate. We had worked together many times, and he was a fine soldier.

The Face and I estimated we were some hundred yards from our company's foxholes, which were north of Bastogne. We couldn't risk attracting the enemy's attention, and we knew our footsteps in the snow would make a crunch and squeak. He and I hid, unmoving and silent, for an entire day. Across from us inside the barn, three cows stood in a row, gazing at us serenely with long-lashed, brown eyes. My heart hammered every time the cows moved or made a noise. Would they cough? Would the Germans hear? Were they already coming for us?

By the late afternoon I decided our time in concealment had worked to our advantage. Soon darkness would fall, and then The Face and I could make our way toward our side of the line.

I was tempted to plan our departure for shortly after nightfall, but then decided we would be wiser to wait until the middle of the night. That strategy came with its own risks: No one knew he and I were okay. With the guys so tense, our guards would fire at anyone trying to approach them.

I was still weighing our options when, just after dusk, the enemy broke the long standoff. The Face and I must have heard the German tank fire on us, but before the roar of the cannon reached our consciousness, we both hit the dirt floor. The barn wall exploded just behind where we had been standing, and the wall opposite us collapsed in a maelstrom of smoke and wood chips. When the haze cleared, I saw that the cows had barely reacted to the attack. They were still standing. Their legs never buckled. But for some reason their serenity was gone. They looked defeated.

"Holy shit . . ." The Face whispered, and gaped at the animals.

Only then did I see that each cow had a giant hole ripped through its long torso.

He and I took off through the gap in the plank siding behind the cows. We wove through the debris of the hard-fought battle, leaping over fallen firs and circumventing craters created by the heavy artillery. The enemy's proximity lent our legs strength and agility, and the deepening darkness masked our movement. I reached for my mother's medallion around my neck. It wasn't there in substance but in spirit, and I felt better as Eddie and I neared our line.

We bent low, creating as small a target as possible for the Germans, who were firing at us now, and the Americans, who soon would be.

"Oh, shit," The Face groaned, panting as orange bursts in the twilight showed our guys had spotted us. They wouldn't be wasting their precious bullets, either. They'd be shooting to kill.

Then I realized every shot was well off the mark—much too high to be defensive. "They're covering us!" I was incredulous. "They recognize us!"

My heart thumping, my legs pumping, I closed the distance to our unit's entrenchment. My friend was at my heels. We were going to be all right.

Headquarters sent out no information about the progress—or lack thereof—of Germany's massive counteroffensive. Other than what we could discover with our own eyes, our only updates sprang from rumors that sped from foxhole to camp and ricocheted back again, utterly transformed in the retelling. These reports were all we received, so we hung on to every unreliable word.

One story that spread quickly was that the Germans had made huge strides to the west and southwest, and on December 22, a German courier waving a truce flag approached the American lines. He delivered a note from "The German Commander," which was to be handed up the ranks to "The American Commander."

The note suggested that the Germans' momentum was unstoppable, as evidenced by their recent advance to the west. The communiqué then demanded the Allies' immediate surrender of Bastogne. If the brass did not comply that very day, the Allies risked the pain of annihilation of "the USA troops in and near Bastogne."

General Taylor was in Washington at the time, and General McAuliffe had assumed leadership of our forces. His famous reply to the demand, which found its way back to the Germans, was a handwritten note that read, simply, "Nuts!"

Our officers told the story to us men in the foxholes, and we enjoyed a brief lifting of our spirits. It could not have come at a more opportune time. For the previous several nights at least ten German 88s had rumbled just beyond the hedgerow, and because of the thick fog, we could not pinpoint their position. The constant stress of the unknown had taken its toll on us all.

When the fog finally lifted, we quickly took advantage. On December 23 we got orders to move north, take the small town of Foy, and engage the enemy in that area.

We emerged from the woods and climbed onto an elevated road a few kilometers north. We let ourselves into a few of the many houses along the way, looked for signs of the Germans, and tried to find food. We could not find much, suggesting that the Germans had already been there.

As we walked along the road, a sergeant by the name of Geske looked as if a combination of the snow, the fog, and the Germans had pushed him to his breaking point. All color had drained from his face, leaving his skin pasty white and sweating. I decided to stay close and keep an eye on him.

After a few more miles, we found a battle raging along the road. We half slid down an embankment to the right, using the hill as a shield. I glanced at Geske during the touch-and-go combat. The Germans retreated, and we took off after them.

"You okay, pal?" I asked the sergeant as we jogged down the road after the enemy.

He stayed right next to me as we ran. "I'm going to get hit," he answered, his eyes unnaturally bright. "I know I'm going to get hit. Gonna get hit. Gonna get hit."

I took command of him and his outfit, and everyone seemed relieved when I started issuing the orders.

The sporadic fighting reminded me of being locked in the St. Lo prison camp during air raids so many months before. As captives we were helpless to protect ourselves. All we could do was remember to inhale deeply and try to stay calm. Even in those early days in Europe, I had accepted the stark reality that each breath could be my last. Death had become a way of life for me.

Now the sudden, sporatic combat brought back the St. Lo feeling of vulnerability and mortality. As we trekked along the road to Foy, I encouraged the other guys to take deep breaths and try to stay calm.

Ahead a monstrous wall of dense fog loomed, its façade seemingly as impenetrable as poured concrete. We continued forward, reluctantly allowing it to envelop us. Some distance down the road I detected vibrations in the ground, which alerted me to the close presence of armored tanks. A contingent of German soldiers was on our left, moving alongside us to Foy. Sometimes their armored tanks were perhaps only ten meters from us. Now we were more than grateful for the fog's protection. Otherwise the Germans could have easily turned their guns on us and wiped out our entire group.

As night approached and we neared Foy, we got into another skirmish with the Germans. I continued to issue orders for Geske and his men. Other Allied outfits to the south and east of us joined the battle. I was happy to see Captain Anderson among the officers.

The farther north we traveled, the hillier the terrain became, and I scanned the landscape for the best strategic position. The Germans were obviously doing the same; they and we competed to claim the same hill. It became a footrace. As the attackers, we were unencumbered by heavy armory and were the more mobile. We muscled our way to the hill first. Being the only outfit able to take advantage of the hill, we turned this small victory into some momentum for battle.

Below, the Germans protected their tanks—German 88 panzers—against which the 101st had been powerless, as if we were wielding butter knives against a gunfighter. These faceless, vicious juggernauts took center stage in Foy. The tanks' nightmarish power could lift us off the ground when they came close. The only way we had done damage to the armored vehicles was by sneaking up on them, and that opportunity was rare. With ammunition so low, we had to pick and choose our moment. In a few instances guys fired off thirty-eight-caliber pistols, wasting ammunition. The bullets spiked off the tanker like a piece of hail in a storm.

I watched one German 88, after being pelted with a 38, turn and aim at two American soldiers standing nearly alongside each other. They each held a handgun. A single shot from the Tiger tank cut both men in half. The smoke of that shot lingered on the hill long after we moved from it.

Our superior position on the hill could prove important—too important for the Germans to relinquish it without a fight. They attacked us continuously. After every assault we defended against, we were ordered to strike back. With almost every offensive, the enemy moved farther up the hill.

We dug ourselves new holes and took turns sitting in them and holding guard. We always tried to find our moment: Whenever the 88s' operators and sentries appeared to drop their guard, we sent a few guys to fire on them. The 101st threw whatever we could against the tanks, but for every one panzer our guys managed to hit, another ten seemed to take its place.

We were in terrible trouble, and everyone knew it. The battle had raged for several full days, leaving us exhausted and edgy. We had gone as far as we could go along the hedgerow and were hemmed in, with the enemy advancing. A lot of our men were badly wounded and in need of immediate medical attention.

We talked almost obsessively about ways to get out of the fix. Either the 88s' rumble kept us awake nights, or we made ourselves stay awake, looking for a way to get out of where we were stuck. We continued to hope for a German surrender, believing their morale had to be low, since we were holding on so long.

Just sitting and talking quietly with Engelbrecht and Albers sometimes helped me stay grounded. Hopeful we'd come upon a solution, we were willing to try anything and listen to any idea about how to end this thing in a hurry. No idea was too far-fetched. We *wanted* to try something different and imaginative—some maneuver not in the training manual or playbook. We were, after all, enlisted men—not West Point graduates—and we were younger than a lot of other guys, or at least that was how we thought of ourselves. The Germans' superiority in tanks, guns, and troop numbers forced us to use our imagination and ingenuity to devise ways to stand our ground.

Engelbrecht, Albers, and I had gathered in the middle of the night in Captain Anderson's foxhole to knock around ideas. I was glad he was on the hill with us. His field jacket was tattered, and he was just as tired as we were, but he kept moving forward and had even volunteered to be a scout at the bottom of the field.

"All we need is a turning point," Anderson said. His face was rough with dried blood and stubble. He was a shaver, but these days in Bastogne were too cold and too busy for him to use his knife on his face.

"The Heinies' morale has to be low, since we're holding on so long," Eddie said to no one in particular. "Does anyone think they might surrender?"

"They're on the ropes," Anderson replied. "We just need a quick jab to knock them down and get out."

"Jab and run," Al murmured. "We just need something to catch the Germans off balance." He rubbed his eyes with the heel of his hands. I could see he was concocting some plan.

The attack on and defense of Foy on this hill was like a great match. Momentum could shift with the lightest jab struck just when the other guy was off balance.

"What about the jeep?" Al said.

We had a jeep on the hilltop, and a sergeant named Sean Wall had started driving it down the hill and into Foy for supplies. Like a madman he sped around and past the Germans before they could react. We knew these runs were dangerous, but Sean was a thrill-seeker and claimed to enjoy the ride.

"We could run some stunt with the jeep that might help us end this thing," Al said. "We can use the fog to hide us."

"How about making a big run down the hill?" I asked. "We could speed the jeep down it, with Sean behind the wheel. I'm sure he'd do it."

"We can load up the guys who're hurting real bad, too," Anderson said.

"We can whoop and scream like Apaches on the warpath," Eddie said. "Or shriek like jungle animals as loud as our strength lets us."

"We'll run like hell down the hill and fire off what we have left to pick off as many Germans as we can," Al said.

We set the plan for the morning of December 23. Sean's toothy grin let us know how he felt about being behind the wheel of the jeep. Al, Eddie, Anderson, and I helped the medic Growdy carefully settle four wounded GIs into the backseat. Two more wedged themselves on the floor. Choosing the few passengers among the many wounded had been tough, but Growdy and a couple other medics worked it out pretty quickly. The GI's wounds could not be so awful that a wild ride would endanger his life, and yet he must desperately need a level of care the medics could not provide on the hilltop.

Once they were settled, Eddie settled into the shotgun seat next to Sean. "My frat brothers and I used to do pranks like this at Oklahoma State!" he said, gripping the windshield.

"Sure," Sean said. "And after we've dropped these guys off at the infirmary, maybe we can catch a show at the drive-in."

"Or go on a panty raid," one of the GIs said from the back.

Captain Anderson smacked the hood of the jeep. "Okay, men. Roll on out. I'll see you when you get back."

The German tanks were rumbling up the hill already, with a multitude of foot soldiers filling the gaps between the tanks, protecting the vehicles. In the thick fog they looked like zombies.

"Shitload of 'em," a wounded GI said quietly.

"Don't worry, buddy," Sean told him. "We'll have them wetting their pants in a minute."

"Scream like Indians, so they'll think we are more troops than we really are," I said from my place in the far back of the jeep.

Sean brought the engine to life, thrust the shift into gear, and roared down the hill. All nine of us screamed as loudly as we could, like frenzied Comanches on the warpath, charging into the cavalry.

"Whooop! Whoop-whoop-whoop-whoop-whoop!"

"Yip yip yip yip yip yip yip yip yip yip yip!"

The German foot soldiers stopped, uncertain what was coming at them. Then they turned and fled down the hill. Their now-unguarded tanks had no choice but to retreat, also.

Sean drove us safely through the enemy's line, and we didn't stop laughing until we were halfway to Foy.

Later that day the sun broke through the clouds, and the fog cleared for the first time in days. We heard the purr of C-47s and looked skyward to see more than one hundred planes dropping supplies south of us, around Bastogne's town center. Clear skies the next day, December 24, brought more planes to drop supplies, still to our south. Knowing that someone was aware of our dire situation and working to remedy it boosted our morale.

Still, we were a long way from being home for Christmas, and in our location around Foy, we would not see any immediate increase in our supplies or ammunition. In this season of giving, we had to be very stingy with what little inventory we had remaining. On this holiday that was all about love, we had to try not to get killed.

Much of our time we spent in silence, waiting for something to turn the tide of the battle. Those periods of stillness never frustrated or overwhelmed us. We had lots to do, mainly trying to keep everything orderly in our encampment. We could not move for periods, but we did not feel inert. Nothing could shield us from the conditions—the snowfall, the wind, the yelling and screaming between outfits that never seemed to end whenever it started.

We all had plenty to consider during these slow times. The war brought up huge issues that most kids just out of high school with an ordinary life don't think about—life and death, accomplishments and regrets. I wanted to plan some kind of future for when I got home, but I couldn't imagine anything beyond the reunion with my family. I thought about that again and again, being in the living room, my mom wiping away her tears as I talked about her family and village, my pop smiling with pride glowing in his eyes as he listened to my stories of adventure. I tried to concentrate on them and my sisters, hopeful they'd gotten the notification from the army that I'd been found alive in France, wanting them to believe I was still alive.

On Christmas morning I awoke in a foxhole, alongside Dicky Shin. We wandered downhill through heavy fog to a trench we had occupied before the enemy pushed us toward the top. He and I heard tanks rumbling, but in the thick haze we could not pinpoint their position. Then all became quiet.

"What should we do?" Dicky asked.

"Stay put, I guess," I replied. "When the fog clears, we'll be able to see where we are." We hunkered down.

When the fog finally lifted, I found myself staring down the barrel of two German 88s not twenty feet away.

"Dicky, get up!" I stood, poised to run, but Dicky's fear had paralyzed him.

A ferocious blast detonated, and the force of the explosion knocked me down and destroyed a tree behind us. The limbs blew off, and chunks of wood and clods of dirt pummeled us. I jumped up, but a barrage of German bullets knocked me on my butt.

I scrambled to my feet. "Jesus, Dicky! Let's get outta here!"

He and I looked at each other, and I detected something in his eyes, something strange. Suddenly he vaulted from the foxhole and fired at the German guards running alongside the tank. I fired at them, too, trying to hit them and cover Dicky at the same time. We managed to reach safety behind a stack of wood.

Dicky dropped his rifle and spoke to me. His eyes held a question I could not answer; I had not heard him. He kept asking me, so I read his lips: *Are you okay, Jimmy? Are you okay?*

I did not know what to say. I felt as if I were coming out of a dream . . . there but not there. I touched my face, and my fingers came away dripping blood. I got nervous. How badly was I wounded? Thoughts weighed the possibility I might die, and I pulled my mind away from them.

"Maybe it's not too serious," I told myself. I fired off some shots after being hit, and I couldn't have done that if I was in really bad shape.

Dicky looked at me closely and picked a few small pieces of shrapnel out of my face. His voice came to me faintly, down an echo chamber. "You are a lucky guy." He pointed to my helmet. "The big chunk hit your helmet, and the little ones got your face. It could have been much worse."

Lud suddenly appeared on the run. "Let's get out of here. We're all withdrawing."

"What happened?"

"German ambush, but we fought back."

Lud and Dicky helped me to my feet. "Merry friggin' Christmas from Adolf," Lud said.

After a few steps with them supporting me, I was able to walk without assistance. We attended to Chivas, a great soldier whose legs were badly wounded. Chivas was a big man, and I helped Lud, Dicky, and a few others pick him up. Some guys gave us a field of fire while Lud and I carried and dragged Chivas up the hill.

Bodies—American and German—surrounded us. The GIs roamed the field, looking for the American dead, and then picked them up and quickly carried them uphill. I had never witnessed a grimmer procession.

Between us and safety was a pigsty right out in the open. We started to haul Chivas through its deep muck, and when I looked back, I saw the mud was red with blood. Lud and I stopped in the sty, too exhausted to take another step, while Dicky jogged off to find a medic. I searched for Germans who might have been following us, but I could not see even one enemy soldier still standing.

Lud and I sank down in the sludge with Chivas and bandaged him as best we could with ripped cloth. Dicky came back with Growdy, who took a quick look at both of us. "I'll get Chivas to the hospital in Bastogne," he said, then looked pointedly at me.

"You're going, too, Jim," Lud told me. "Your face is covered in blood, but you'll be all right."

———

As I lay in the charred remains of the church-turned-hospital in Bastogne, I watched the sun move across the dome of the sky. The church roof was gone. From my cot I gazed through crumbling walls at the road, where speeding jeeps transported corpses. The stiff bodies were frozen in grotesque poses; each vehicle could carry only one or two at a time.

I was lucky. I had head and gut wounds and hepatitis B.

I was unconscious when I left Bastogne. I awoke on a hospital train as it passed Paris. I thought I saw fireworks. Or maybe that was all a dream.

The next time I opened my eyes, my brain was fully engaged. I was definitely in a hospital in England. A doctor stood beside my bed, gripping a clipboard. He held up three fingers. "How many do you see?"

"The hundred and first?" I asked him.

His eyebrows shot up, and he wrote something in my folder. Then he repeated the exercise, but with four fingers. "Well, young man? How many fingers?"

"The hundred and first," I repeated. "What happened to the 101st Airborne in Bastogne? Tell me about my unit, and then I'll play all the counting games you want."

I learned that on the afternoon of December 26, General Patton's Fourth Armored Division had broken the Germans' siege of Bastogne when its advancing tanks made contact with the 101st's lines to the southwest. A long convoy of trucks and ambulances immediately evacuated our wounded. That news could not have made me happier, unless it had been delivered to me by my family.

The Germans were not done fighting, though. The enemy continued to launch strong attacks for several weeks, but the 101st held its ground, giving the men of the U.S. Third Army time to fight their way up the Airborne's side. The tide turned on January 9, 1945. The 101st switched to the offensive and took the town of Noville, north of Bastogne. Just nine days later, the mayor of Bastogne presented his city's flag to the 101st commander, General Maxwell Taylor.

"Save Bastogne, at all costs" was the order given to General McAuliffe when the 101st had hurriedly entered the town. We learned the hard way the meaning of that command, and I am proud to say we honored it.

"Who's she?" Lud asked, his eyes following the shapely form of our most unyielding nurse as she walked briskly through the ward.

"Miss Kane. An unrelenting disciplinarian. Believe me, Lud, you want nothing to do with her."

"I'd be able to put up with a lot when a woman looks like that." He stood up from my bedside chair. "How bad can she be, for chrissakes?"

"Sit down, you horny bastard, and let me tell you. She insists on waking all fifty men in our ward promptly at six o'clock each morning."

"So?"

"So we were really pissed off because she wouldn't let us sleep, which we probably needed more than any medicine. We're all seriously injured. After she wakes us up so early, we've got nothing to do but lie here, miserable and in pain."

"It wouldn't be like you not to talk to her about it, Jimmy."

"We *pleaded* with her not to wake us up so early, but she wouldn't listen." I shrugged, resigned.

"Aren't we the men who figured out how to run a jeep past the Germans?"

I laughed at the memory of our sending the foot soldiers down the hill. "Yes . . ."

"So I'm sure we can plan a surprise for the rigid Miss Kane."

The idea occurred to me with amazing speed, and all the men in the ward agreed to cooperate. Before Lud left, he made certain every man had the necessary prop to pull off the plan.

The next morning, we were all awake and ready in advance of Miss Kane's appearance. Each man lay on his back, his legs flat on the mattress and slightly spread. Positioned between and parallel to his thighs was a carton of cigarettes—a full ten inches long from end to end. His hands gripped the end of the carton closer to his groin than his knees, and his bedsheet was pulled up under his chin.

We all tried not to laugh.

When we heard Miss Kane's footsteps coming down the hall, the plan went into action. We all closed our eyes and moaned. The ward's double doors swung open, and our nurse-tormentor stopped short in the doorway, apparently caught off guard by our anguished groans. At approximately the same time, we all raised the cigarette carton between our legs, until the end flap was pointing straight at the ceiling—fifty men, all looking as if they had the Allies' most formidable (and uncomfortable) erections.

Poor Miss Kane took one look at us, gasped, then turned on her heel and crashed through the double doors. She may have outrun the sound of our laughter—I don't know. But never again did she awaken us that early.

CHAPTER 21

Six hundred thousand American men fought three German armies in the Ardennes Forest of Belgium and Luxembourg and won the largest land battle ever fought by the United States Army. Eighty-one thousand American troops lost their lives or suffered wounds in the Battle of the Bulge in the Ardennes between December 16, 1944, and January 25, 1945. I was lucky. I lived to come home, to create a future for the man I had become in the 101st Airborne.

My family and friends needed to acquaint themselves with the more mature and confident James Sheeran. No longer was I the boy who had pleaded with my parents to sign the army's permission form. The adjustment was easier for some than others. My girlfriend, Lee, discouraged that I had not corresponded with her, had already accepted another man's marriage proposal. I was sad about losing her, but I understood her decision. The breakup left me without prewar obligations or commitments, and I welcomed having sovereignty over my own existence for the first time—ever. I felt briefly disoriented upon returning to West Orange, as I tried to fit my much-changed self into an environment with which I was intimately familiar.

No parents and child could have been happier to be reunited than my mom and pop and me, but we still had to figure out a new way of being around each other. My world had expanded to include scores of people my parents would never meet, places they would never visit, and experiences that were mine alone. I could share the stories or not; the decision was mine. Did I want to describe in detail all the terrible things I had witnessed? What purpose would that serve? None that I could think of, except to cause my parents grief. I knew I would protect my folks and focus on the more mild episodes.

From this perspective, I finally understood why Mom never told me and my sisters about her personal tragedies. She wanted to protect her young children from the horrors of war, not (as I had supposed) to withhold or distance herself from us. I had left France without learning what had ultimately befallen my grandparents and mother. Despite numerous opportunities, neither Madame Blondeau, my cousin Jean, nor Monsieur Faerbus at the fishing stream outside Domremy told the tale. I decided I needed to make peace with Mom's secrets and hoped that one day her sadness would lessen.

A couple of weeks after I came home, I awakened in the middle of the night, twisted in my sheets, my chest heaving with panic. A hand squeezed my shoulder, and I had no idea where I was until I heard her voice: "Jeemy. Eet eez joost a dream. *Tu es en sûrete. Tu es à la maison.*"

I struggled to sit up, and Mom perched on the side of my bed and clasped my hand. "Jesus, it seemed so real," I said, and combed my soaked hair off my forehead. "We were in the basement of an abandoned house and heard the Germans upstairs. This guy Walter went to find them and came back with his jaw blown off."

She nodded, understanding. *"Tu es ici et tu es là-bas en même temps."*

"Yeah." I blew out a long breath. "How long before I realize I'm not there anymore? That I'm here?"

My mother shrugged. *"Je ne sais pas.* Leetle theengs, you have forget already. Zee worst? You never forget, maybe."

"I heard about Albert and Eugene, Mom," I whispered.

"Ah." Her chin dropped to her chest.

"People thought I already knew about them. None of us meant to—"

"Quoi d'autre, Jeemy?"

I sank back on my pillows. "Your horse and the lieutenant. How your goose led people to your house when you had the flu. A little about Helen, not much."

"Quoi d'autre?"

"That you were a *terreur sainte.* Now I know where *I* got it." We laughed, and some of my tension faded. "But nothing about my grandparents." I took her hand now. "I would like to know, if you'll tell me. I think I could understand it now. I wouldn't have before . . ."

We sat in the darkness for a few moments, then she began, "I was living weeth Maman *et* Papa. Eugene and Albert were at the front, and Helen and our leetle sister lived een Paris. I went to the barn, like every day, to do my chores. A loud explosion so close knocked me off my feet. I did not know what happened.

"I ran to the house, so afraid! An artillery shell blew a huge hole een the roof, and German soldiers were everywhere. The house was on fire. Black smoke billowed from the roof and windows and door. I—" She shook her head and wept.

I didn't know what to do or say, so I just sat and waited. After a few moments, Mom continued. "Inside I found my mother at the cellar door. She was dead."

"I'm so sorry," I said softly.

"I know, Jeemy. *Merci.* Papa was gravely wounded. I tried to peeck them up, my mother and my father. I tried to carry them out to the yard. 'You'll be all right, I promise!' I told them. 'Just hold on!'" She took a ragged breath.

"Did the soldiers help you?"

"Non," she said angrily. "The Germans screamed at me, 'Leave them! Get out! They're dead, they're dead!' But I could not do that. Even if I died, too, I did not care."

She looked numb from the pain. She gathered herself again and told me how the German soldiers had left her holding her mother and father in each arm while watching their farmhouse burn.

Her father stayed alive for a few days. When he died, too, my mother's world was shattered.

"I remember nothing else from that day except terrible loneliness, even though I was rarely alone."

French soldiers taking a rest from the front line completed the most necessary repairs on the house. The rooms were often filled with soldiers and friends, keeping young Lucie Munier company in her mourning. Madame Blondeau moved in, and shortly thereafter, they traveled by rail to Paris, seated in the same car as my father.

One year later, he rolled off an army transport truck to land at my mother's feet. A few weeks later, he proposed, promising her a beautiful castle of dreams—love, family, and security in America. Mom said yes to his proposal but clearly stated her desire to remain in France.

"We went to a tributary of the Meuse. The stream runs in Domremy between the birthplace home of Joan of Arc and the Petite Eglise of Joan of Arc. We vowed to love each other." Her smile shone through her tears. "For centuries betrothed couples een France drink from the stream. They consider eet to be a blessing for their union."

My parents were married on May 19, 1919, in the small village church of Joan of Arc in Domremy-La-Pucelle.

"Did the tradition work for you and Pop?"

She patted my cheek. "Every life has some sadness, Jeemy, but I have been very blessed, *oui*, with your father and our children." She sighed. "When we received the telegram that you were missing in action, I tried to contact Cardinal Tisserant, in Rome—"

"Marie-Madeleine's uncle?"

"*Oui*. To see if he could find you. But I never doubted you were alive and would be coming home to us. You are blessed, too. Do you know that?"

"Yes. I felt it many times while I was over there. Was that wishful thinking?"

"*Non, mon cheri*. That was faith." She leaned to kiss me on the forehead, then went to the door. "You sleep, and I'll see you een the morning." She turned and gave me the Victory gesture, then left me alone with my thoughts about the terrible, long-lasting impact a war has upon innocent people all over the world, not just the Munier family in France. My mother suffered so much loss, she could not help but to bring her grief across the Atlantic with her.

What about me? What did I want to remember about the war? What would I choose to keep as a part of me for the rest of my life and use for the good of all involved? Lacking food, warm clothing, ammunition, and medical supplies, without replacements to relieve us, my unit had stood our ground. In the unrelenting snow, sleet, and fog of the bitter winter of 1944–45, we exacted a heavy toll from formidable opponents. Together and individually, we turned an apparent defeat into what British Prime Minister Winston Churchill called "an ever famous American victory."

I knew that for the rest of my life I would feel proud of our outfit. I would forever retain the lessons I learned in discipline, training, and fearlessness. I would treasure the friendships, and I would always feel my faith.

EPILOGUE

In March 1946, my hometown completed a three-week-long clothing drive as part of Project Patriotism, which permitted American escapees to send food and clothing to the people who had given them aid during the war. West Orange collected three tons of clothing for my friends in the French Underground who had sheltered and fed Burnie and me and helped us move across occupied France.

The clothing, packed in huge cartons and loaded onto U.S. Army transport planes for delivery in French villages, seemed to be a small gesture when compared to the terrible risk the Underground members willingly assumed for two lost GIs.

I knew I would visit France again and try to reconnect with the people who had been so hospitable and selfless. As the years fell away, my intentions came to fruition.

Also important was learning what had happened to my friends after D-Day. The last time I saw Johnny Simpson, the German surgeons amputated his hand. He ended up at a prisoner-of-war camp in Sweden and eventually was exchanged for a seriously wounded German POW. Because Sweden remained neutral during World War II, *Gripsholm* and her running mate *Drottningholm* were placed under the authority of the International Red Cross and used for the transport of more than twenty-five thousand civilian internees and prisoners of war between Europe and North America. Johnny was aboard the *Gripsholm*.

I wanted to find the family that helped Burnie and me after we fled from the forest following our time with the Resistance. I had never learned the family's surname; unbeknownst to me, the father was a member of the Resistance, and he protected his identity in adherence to that group's strict secrecy. I put out word that I was looking for "the little boy" who had saved Burnie and me. Locating the family required many attempts because no one, not even the now-grown boy's family, knew he had been the first to make contact with us and help us.

I also hoped to connect with the woodsman who guided Burnie and me from the Bergers' house. I never knew his name, but I recalled he looked to be of Spanish descent. When we met many years later, this gentleman introduced himself as Anastase Segovia and confirmed he was of Spanish origin.

At our first company reunion, I noticed a familiar-looking fellow, but I didn't place him until we stood face-to-face. It was Walter Lukasavage, who had been wounded during his emotion-driven attack on the unfriendly Sherman tank. We talked about that day, but Walter had no recollection of how he had been wounded or where it had happened. I was glad to fill in the blanks for him, although he had trouble understanding why he had behaved so irrationally.

I tried to explain it: The enemy had used an American Sherman tank in a deadly assault against us. The tactic infuriated everyone that night, Walter included. He had been the only one among us, how-ever, who was a professional athlete-turned-warrior. If anyone was going to attack a tank, all the guys would have voted Walter "Most Likely to Succeed."

As for Burnie Rainwater, he and I had forged a friendship that endured the passing decades, our divergent lifestyles, the demands of our families, and, most challenging, his ever-increasing preference for silence over conversation.

Not that I couldn't carry the conversation for both of us. My gift of gab came in handy during my two terms as mayor of West Orange, New Jersey. Governor Brendan Byrne made me a member of his cabinet, the state's insurance commissioner, in the 1970s.

Fifty years after the war, I returned to the deep, dark forest to attend a reunion with my Maquis friends, whom I lived with for four months. They handed me a gift-wrapped package.

Inside I found the lunch box I had left behind when Burnie and I fled the forest. These dangerous freedom fighters had cleaned it up, wrapped it in shiny paper, and returned it to me.

"Un souvenir," the presenter told me, grinning widely.

Acknowledgments

Since Jim is no longer with us, I will have to assume the duty of thanking so many who helped him with this project in so many different ways. Clearly, first and foremost, I know he would want to thank those who were mentioned in the preface, for without them the book could not have reached the public. They are Josette Sheeran, Chris Slevin, Laurie Rosin, and Scott Miller.

In that regard, we must also mention two other people who contributed in valuable ways to bring about this publication. First, Vince Travis, who further edited the draft following Chris Slevin's contribution. Second, Eric Poe, Jim's stepson, who researched the editorial field and wisely chose to recommend Laurie Rosin from among many professional book editors, thus setting the stage for Laurie's expert final editing of the book. Laurie's belief in the star quality of Jimmy's story allowed me to work diligently with her to finalize the presentation of this book to the distinguished agent Scott Miller, who within weeks acquired the book contract from Berkley.

I know Jim would also want to acknowledge his daughter Vicky Yokota, a recipient of the White House Picture of the Year Award from President

Ronald Regan, who spent many hours organizing the many pictures and expertly photographing the memorabilia that Jim so carefully collected throughout his lifetime.

Throughout the years, on the very top of the list of those whose faith in Jimmy propelled him forward in the pursuit of his book project is his lifetime best friend, Brendan Byrne, former governor of New Jersey. Governor Byrne was the president of Jim's West Orange High School class; the governor Jim supported and served as a cabinet member (in the position of commissioner of insurance) for two full terms. The governor's constant encouragement and his admiration of Jimmy's wartime accomplishments were most valuable in reinforcing Jim's determination to complete this book project.

Jim was forever thankful to everyone in the 101st Airborne Division who served with him during the war, and whose character gave the backbone to his story. In particular he wanted to recognize his comrade Burnie Rainwater for being the perfect partner to survive the escape with. Also he would want to give special thanks to his "top kick," Sergeant Al Engelbrecht (who later married his sister Frances), whose leadership allowed Jim and many others to mature into the brave soldiers they were.

Jim was most grateful to all of his rescuers from that part of France that we both came to regard as our second home. Their acts, which involved risking the security of themselves and of their families and homes in order to help Burnie and Jim survive their escape during the three months they were behind the lines in France, became the foundation for this book. We also want to thank them for later sharing all the information about Jimmy's escape with us when we returned to France in order to properly verify the events recorded in this book. Jim especially wanted to thank those who were members of the Maquis for their willingness to allow two American parachutists to participate in their Resistance activities during the war. He felt privileged to tell their story in a larger context to a larger audience.

Very special thanks are due to his French cousin Jean Gossot and his wife, Marie-Madeleine, and their family for hiding Jim and Burnie in their home for nearly a month before they were able to rejoin the Allied Army when it advanced into that part of France. I know Jim also wanted to thank his cousin Marguerite, sister of Marie-Madeleine, for arranging with me to take him back to France after forty-nine years, which began our rendez-vous with all of the French "saviors" mentioned here and in the book.

I know he would want to thank his family for enduring the long and arduous hours he spent recording and documenting his account of this very important period of his life. I know that he enjoyed telling the story to his children and grandchildren at the many family reunions we had.

Most important, I know Jim would want to acknowledge and indeed to dedicate this book to his parents. His father Jack, whose personality imparted to Jim the Tom Sawyer–like childhood attitude from which would later spring the resourcefulness and resilience needed to successfully negotiate the dangers he faced trying to escape behind the lines in France. His mother, Lucie Munier, gave him unbounded love and warmth and a carefree way to look at things even if it was the worst moment in his life.

I have been privileged to serve as Jim's alter ego in writing these acknowledgments. And I want to thank my daughter, Audrey, for provid-ing constant help and encouragement to me as I endeavored to support Jim in his pursuit of this book project.

Finally, to those who will now learn of Jim's experience through this book, we wish to thank you for your interest.

Lena Chang Sheeran

Index

INDEX

INDEX

INDEX

INDEX

INDEX

Sheeran, Lucie Munier (cont.)
Blondeau, Madame Adele, 84, 94, 163–171, 175, 286, 288
brother of best friend incident, 164–165
"cousin" in Maquis, 135, 138, 140–141
death of brothers, 181
death of parents, 169
Domremy-La-Pucelle and, 6, 23, 95, 112, 158–159, 162, 163–168
enlisting by Jimmy and, 35, 37–39
Eugene Munier (Lucie's brother), 167, 172, 180, 181, 287
farm, 95–96, 167–168, 173, 181, 287–288
"finished," 170
fishing with dynamite, 118–119, 135
goose as pet, 166, 287
Helen (Lucie's sister), 167, 181, 287
holiday specialties made by, 114
horse raised by, 171–174, 287
Jewish kid beaten by Jimmy, 53
Joan of Arc medallion given to Jimmy, 8, 9, 11, 39, 42, 86, 192, 271
Jules Munier (Lucie's father), 167, 171
larger-than-life woman, 117
loyalty to U.S. and France, 133
marriage to John, 149, 289
meeting John on a train, 23, 32, 83–84, 93–94, 202, 288
mirabelle plums, 96, 159, 160, 161, 162
model in Paris, 117
morale booster for Jimmy, 72
omelets prepared by, 100
pants pockets sewed up incident, 145
parents, truth about, 286, 287–288
personal tragedies, protecting family from, 286
reunion with Jimmy, 286
reunion with John, 202–203
swine flu, 165–166
wild streak of, 167, 170, 171, 172–173
Sherman tanks, 184, 187–189, 212, 233–235, 282, 292–293
Shin, Dicky, 267, 279–280, 281
shoes for POWs, 56, 57, 59–60
Simpson, Johnny "Philosopher." *See also* Sheeran, James J. "Jimmy" (paratrooper)
appearance of, 24
background of, 10, 24
fate unknown, 18, 29, 160–161, 190, 209
hand amputated, 28, 76, 160, 291
injuries of, 25–29
"King Corporal," 161
letter received from John (Jimmy's father), 161

prisoner of war (POW), 24–29, 41, 291–292
promotion of, 161
thrilled about battles, 10
VD incident, 28
Sinatra, Frank, 116
singing songs, 112, 115, 148
Sink, Robert (Colonel), 215, 233, 236, 237, 238, 239, 242, 248–249
Sixth Parachute Brigade (German), 4, 14
sixth sense of combat, 244
Smith, Betty, 24
"Smoky" (Maquis), 139, 140
sneezing incident, 97
snipers (German), 219, 224–228, 229, 230
Sorbonne (France), 171
spikes (anti-parachute), 11
spitting at POWs, 73, 75
SS troops (German), 75, 101
St. Come du Mont (France), 4, 212–213
St. Lo prison (France), 44, 45, 47–59, 69, 77, 192, 261, 273
Ste. Mere-Eglise (France), 4
Sterno disks (emergency heating units), 15
"stick" of paratroopers, 9, 222
still (alembic), 183, 186
strawberries shared by POWs, 48
streptomycin, 250
sulfanilamide powder, 26
supply camps, Maquis, 134
survival of the fittest, 67
surviving the war, chances of, 4
swastika warning, 98, 101, 104
Sweden, 292
Swindon (England), 209
swine flu, 165–166
Switzerland, 87, 93, 99, 107, 145, 153, 168
Syracuse (New York), 4

talking to enemies about simple things, 23
tams, 105
Taylor, Maxwell (General), 272, 283
Third Army (U.S.), 282–283
threat to kill 10 POWs for every escapee, 85, 88, 89, 101
Tisserant, Cardinal Eugene, 176, 289
torturing suspects by Germans, 101
training of paratroopers, 4, 7, 11, 36
train to permanent German POW camp, 76–90, 195
Tree Grows in Brooklyn, A (Smith), 24
trees, avoiding when landing, 11–12
trench warfare, 233, 235
Twain, Mark, 24

310